"A compelling portrait of a man once serenely confident, searching decades later for self-understanding . . . It offers insight into how Bundy, a man of surpassing skill and reputation, could have advised two presidents so badly. On the long shelf of Vietnam books, I know of nothing quite like it. The unfinished quality of Bundy's self-inquest only enhances its power, authenticity and, yes, poignancy. . . . Bundy emerges as the most interesting figure in the Vietnam tragedy—less for his unfortunate part in prosecuting the war than for his agonized search thirty years later to understand himself. . . . [Bundy's] astonishing, even touching, efforts to understand his own mistakes are far more persuasive than the shallow analysis McNamara offers in his own memoir. . . . An extraordinary cautionary tale for all Americans."

—RICHARD HOLBROOKE, *The New York Times Book Review*

"No American who has lived through the Iraq experience will doubt how important it is for us to understand why and how American presidents take our country to war. Key to understanding how John Kennedy and Lyndon Johnson took the nation into Vietnam is the story of McGeorge Bundy's service to both men as national security adviser. Thanks to his many long and penetrating talks with Bundy, his assiduous study of the written record, and his mastery of the interplay among personality, politics, and national security strategy, Gordon Goldstein has brought us a dispassionate, powerful, and brilliant assessment of McGeorge Bundy's performance during the years he was given his cardinal moment in history. Goldstein's book helps us comprehend how Americans were led, step by step, into the abyss of Vietnam. It also provides crucial lessons for future presidents, members of Congress, and citizens as we grapple with the problems of where, when, and how to apply American power around the world."

—MICHAEL BESCHLOSS, author of *Presidential Courage*

"Gordon Goldstein's *Lessons in Disaster* provides a close, careful look at Kennedy's mindset at the time of his assassination. . . . As the title suggests, this fast-paced, well-written book is organized around the abiding lessons of Vietnam. Barack Obama and his new foreign policy advisers should read it."

—*Concord Monitor*

"A compelling and personally sympathetic appraisal of Bundy as a brilliant statesman but also as a fallible human being. Despite his remarkable intellect, Bundy ultimately failed to grasp the fundamental novelty of the historical challenge posed by a communism fanatically driven by nationalistic and anti-colonialist passions. In that context, presidential decision making became increasingly focused on the imperatives of a local war and less on its damaging impact on America's world role."

—ZBIGNIEW BRZEZINSKI, former national security adviser
and author of *Second Chance*

"Obama must read this book. . . . It is fascinating for all kinds of reasons and a must read for the president."

—*The Daily Beast*

"Important, poignant and troubling . . . We have waited a dozen years since [Bundy's] death for Goldstein's book. It is worth the wait."

—JAMES BLIGHT, Truthdig.com

"[Goldstein] painstakingly recounts his subject's role as national security adviser and ponders the complexity of the elusive 'inner Bundy.' . . . Surprising revelations."

—*Publishers Weekly*

"Astute distillation of the essential lessons now-deceased national security adviser Bundy learned from Vietnam . . . An invaluable record of Bundy's thoughts and actions during the war, as well as unusually candid commentary on his admitted failures in 'perception, recommendation and execution' . . . A significant then-and-now reassessment."

—*Kirkus Reviews*

"Thanks to Gordon Goldstein's superb book, we have fresh evidence for judging between a facile mind and a wise one, and we can now assess more accurately the role of McGeorge Bundy in the Vietnam tragedy."

—A. J. LANGGUTH, author of *Our Vietnam*

"This meticulously researched book gives us remarkable insight into one of the most critical foreign policy decisions in U.S. history. Anyone aspiring to a leadership position in American politics or public policy should carefully examine this perceptive work and its many valuable lessons."

—WARREN B. RUDMAN, former U.S. Senator (R-NH) and
former chairman of the President's Foreign Intelligence Advisory Board

LESSONS IN
DISASTER

LESSONS IN DISASTER

McGEORGE BUNDY AND THE PATH TO WAR IN VIETNAM

GORDON M. GOLDSTEIN

A HOLT PAPERBACK

TIMES BOOKS / HENRY HOLT AND COMPANY

NEW YORK

Holt Paperbacks
Henry Holt and Company, LLC
Publishers since 1866
175 Fifth Avenue
New York, New York 10010
www.henryholt.com

Library of Congress Cataloging-in-Publication Data

Goldstein, Gordon M.
  Lessons in disaster : McGeorge Bundy and the path to war in Vietnam / Gordon M.
Goldstein.—1st ed.
      p.   cm.
  Includes bibliographical references and index.
  ISBN-13: 978-0-8050-9087-1
  ISBN-10: 0-8050-9087-8
  1. United States—Foreign relations—Vietnam.   2. Vietnam—Foreign relations—United States.
3. Vietnam War, 1961–1975—Causes.   4. Bundy, McGeorge.   5. Bundy, McGeorge—Political
and social views.   6. Political consultants—United States—Biography.   7. Presidents—United
States—Staff—Biography.   8. United States—Foreign relations—1961–1963—Decision making.
9. United States—Foreign relations—1963–1969—Decision making.   10. National Security
Council (U.S.)—History—20th century.   11. National security—United States—History—20th
century.   I. Title.
  E183.8.V5G64 2008
  327.730597—dc22   2008033291

Henry Holt books are available for special promotions and premiums.
For details contact: Director, Special Markets.

Originally published in hardcover in 2008 by Times Books
First Holt Paperbacks Edition 2009

Designed by Meryl Sussman Levavi

Printed in the United States of America
3   5   7   9   10   8   6   4   2

For Anne Ashby Gilbert,
whose support and solidarity made this book possible,
and for whom I have more gratitude than words can express

CONTENTS

THE KENNEDY AND JOHNSON ADMINISTRATIONS, 1961–65

THE WHITE HOUSE

John F. Kennedy, president of the United States (1961–63)

Lyndon B. Johnson, vice president of the United States (1961–63); president of the United States (1963–69)

McGeorge Bundy, national security adviser (1961–66)

Theodore Sorensen, special counsel and adviser to President Kennedy (1961–63)

Arthur M. Schlesinger Jr., assistant to President Kennedy (1961–63)

Bill Moyers, assistant and press secretary to President Johnson (1963–67)

Douglass Cater, special assistant to President Johnson (1964–68)

Walt W. Rostow, deputy national security adviser (1961)

Michael V. Forrestal, staff member, National Security Council (1962–64)

Chester L. Cooper, staff member, National Security Council (1964–66)

James C. Thomson Jr., staff member, National Security Council (1964–66)

DEPARTMENT OF STATE

Dean Rusk, secretary of state (1961–69)

George Ball, undersecretary of state (1961–66)

W. Averell Harriman, ambassador at large (1961); assistant secretary of state for Far Eastern affairs (1961–63); undersecretary of state for political affairs (1963–65)

Roger Hilsman, director, Bureau of Intelligence and Research (1961–63); assistant secretary of state for Far Eastern affairs (1963–64)

William Bundy, assistant secretary of state for Far Eastern affairs (1964–69)

U. Alexis Johnson, deputy undersecretary of state (1961–64, 1965–66)

Walt W. Rostow, chairman, Policy Planning Council (1961–66)

Thomas L. Hughes, director, Bureau of Intelligence and Research (1963–69)

Frederick Nolting, U.S. ambassador to South Vietnam (1961–63)

Henry Cabot Lodge, U.S. ambassador to South Vietnam (1963–64, 1965–67)

Maxwell Taylor, U.S. ambassador to South Vietnam (1964–65)

John Kenneth Galbraith, U.S. ambassador to India (1961–63)

DEPARTMENT OF DEFENSE

Robert S. McNamara, secretary of defense (1961–68)

Roswell L. Gilpatric, deputy secretary of defense (1961–64)

Cyrus Vance, deputy secretary of defense (1964–67)

William Bundy, assistant secretary of defense (1962–64)

John McNaughton, assistant secretary of defense (1964–67)

MILITARY OFFICERS

Lyman Lemnitzer, chairman, Joint Chiefs of Staff (1960–62)

Maxwell Taylor, military representative to the president (1961–62); chairman, Joint Chiefs of Staff (1962–64)

Earle G. Wheeler, chairman, Joint Chiefs of Staff (1964–70)

Arleigh Burke, chief of naval operations (1955–61)

Paul D. Harkins, commanding general, Military Assistance Command, Vietnam (1962–64)

William Westmoreland, commanding general, Military Assistance Command, Vietnam (1964–68)

CENTRAL INTELLIGENCE AGENCY

Allen Dulles, director of central intelligence (1953–61)

John McCone, director of central intelligence (1961–65)

Richard Bissell, deputy director, Central Intelligence Agency (1961–62)

Ray Cline, deputy director, Central Intelligence Agency (1962–66)

OTHER OFFICIALS

Robert F. Kennedy, attorney general (1961–64)

Mike Mansfield, U.S. senator from Montana; Senate majority leader

J. William Fulbright, U.S. senator from Arkansas; chairman, Senate Foreign Relations Committee

Richard Russell, U.S. senator from Georgia; chairman, Senate Armed Services Committee

LESSONS IN DISASTER

LEGEND OF
THE ESTABLISHMENT

The last time I saw McGeorge Bundy was on Wednesday, September 11, 1996. We met in midtown Manhattan for a working lunch in a private conference room of the Carnegie Corporation of New York, where Bundy was senior scholar in residence. "How are *you*?" he asked exuberantly as he entered the room, a stack of books and papers tucked under his arm. He seemed eager to begin our meeting.

I had been engaged in Bundy's professional life for several years during the completion of my studies for a PhD in international relations at Columbia University. My first assignment with him was as the staff director of an international commission of diplomats and arms-control experts for which he served as chairman, leading a study on the United Nations Security Council and the proliferation of weapons of mass destruction. My second project with Bundy was more historical in nature. It was also far more personal.

In the spring of 1995 Bundy asked me to collaborate with him on a retrospective analysis of the American presidency and the Vietnam War during his tenure as national security adviser to Presidents John F. Kennedy and Lyndon B. Johnson. We envisioned the book to be both a memoir of Bundy's experience with Kennedy and Johnson as well as a reconstruction of the pivotal presidential decisions about American strategy in Vietnam between 1961 and 1965. As our collaboration progressed and we produced a shared thematic, interpretive, and organizational model of the book, I accepted Bundy's proposal to be formally recognized as coauthor for a work to be published by Yale University Press.

In the year and a half we had worked in concert on the Vietnam project, Bundy and I had made significant substantive progress, encompassing all of the key historical inflection points and pivotal players in Vietnam policy during the Kennedy and Johnson years. Yet the actual text of the book was still inchoate, composed of scores of unique, individual passages of manuscript that Bundy had been drafting by hand. These so-called "fragments" were to be integrated with my research memoranda, outlines, and chronologies, as well as commentary extracted from the transcripts of my interviews with Bundy on a vast range of topics relating to the war. Individually these materials constituted the disassociated elements of an incomplete analytical history. Connected into a conceptual and chronological architecture, however, the fragments and research we were producing served as the foundation for what we hoped would be a meaningful contribution to the history of the Vietnam War.

As we met that afternoon, Bundy displayed an intensity that was different from what I had observed in countless hours of previous discussion. "I had quite an argument with my brother," he announced, referring to William Bundy, who had served as a senior State Department and Pentagon official during the Vietnam era. "Now I *know* I'm right," he added, with a smile of discernible but good-natured mischief. Bundy spoke with great energy and focus for more than five hours, discoursing on a wide range of themes late into the day. There was a dramatic difference between Kennedy and Johnson on the question of Vietnam, he once more insisted, recapitulating a perspective central to our study. "Kennedy didn't want to be dumb," he said. "Johnson didn't want to be a coward." Bundy was still struggling to understand the significance of the air-strike strategy he had advocated in the winter of 1965. What were its implications? Bundy asked aloud. Did it precipitate a chain of events that dramatically accelerated the Americanization of the war? He also revisited the failure of diplomacy in Vietnam, which he described as a delusion mistakenly embraced by opponents of the war. Why, Bundy now asked, didn't we settle the war at the negotiating table? He promptly answered his own question: After the American escalation of 1965, he declared, a diplomatic solution in Vietnam was simply not viable. On the question of Kennedy and Vietnam, Bundy instructed me to marshal the evidence once more and prepare an outline describing the choices Kennedy would have confronted in Vietnam had he lived to serve a second term. Clearly there was a great deal of work to be done to consolidate the rich but diffuse content of our collaboration.[1]

As the hours passed, I noted that Bundy's cheeks were unusually pink—perhaps from the strong late summer sun at his family's vacation home on the Massachusetts coast—or perhaps from sustained exertion. He interrupted our work session only once, to ask his devoted and attentive assistant, Georganne Brown, to schedule an appointment with his cardiologist. When the meeting ended Bundy dispatched me with a gracious but somewhat formal good-bye, shaking hands as he always did with his elbow locked in a sharp ninety-degree angle and head bowed forward ever so slightly. Five days later he died, following a massive heart attack.

A front-page obituary in the *New York Times* called Bundy "the very personification of what the journalist David Halberstam . . . labeled 'The Best and the Brightest': the well-born, confident intellectuals who led the nation into the quagmire of Vietnam." The *Times* noted that Bundy played a role in a range of foreign policy decisions serving two presidents, "but he is most remembered for his role in enlarging United States involvement in Vietnam."[2]

A similar verdict was rendered by *Time* magazine. "His laser-like intellect radiated from behind his clear-rimmed glasses with an intensity as hot as his smile was cold," wrote the magazine's managing editor, Walter Isaacson. "Had he been half as smart, he might have been a great man. Instead, McGeorge Bundy came to personify the hubris of an intellectual elite that marched America with a cool and confident brilliance into the quagmire of Vietnam." Isaacson argued that the early 1960s were "a moment when meritocracy and patrician elitism enjoyed a celebrated cohabitation, the rise and then fall of which Bundy came to symbolize." That era ended with Vietnam and men like Bundy, whom Isaacson called "the epitome of the well-intentioned arrogance" that would ultimately vitiate the Cold War foreign policy consensus. Isaacson recalled that Bundy told him once that there was no such thing as the foreign policy establishment. "If so," he then noted, "it was Bundy as much as anyone who brought about an end of an era in which foreign policy was entrusted to a noble club of gentlemen secure in their common outlook and bonds of trust."[3]

In *The Color of Truth*, his exhaustively researched and judicious biography of the Bundy brothers, the historian Kai Bird would criticize McGeorge Bundy's unwillingness to act on his growing reservations about the viability of America's intervention in Vietnam. "Why did presidential loyalty require Bundy to continue to defend the war long after he left government in 1966? And why, when in 1969–70 it was clear that Kissinger and Nixon were prolonging the war, did both brothers fail to come out forcefully against the war and the Vietnamization policies that were prolonging it? The Bundys never answered these hard questions."[4] Bird's sharpest criticism was directed not at Bundy's performance as national security adviser, but at his silence after leaving office: "Far from protesting the carnage, Mac quietly left the White House and continued to support the war in public. . . . This was [his] worst and most personal mistake, a failure of courage and imagination."[5]

There were, of course, countless other verdicts and views on Bundy's legacy as national security adviser in the Vietnam era. Bundy had delved deeply into the voluminous literature of the war but did not live long enough to address many of the histories that were part of his study, including works by David Barrett, Larry Berman, Lloyd Gardner, Leslie Gelb, Doris Kearns Goodwin, George Herring, Stanley Karnow, Neil Sheehan, Brian VanDeMark, and Marilyn Young.[6] With respect to the tough conclusions of a new generation of scholars, we will never know Bundy's response. Andrew Preston, the author of perhaps the single most comprehensive history of Bundy's role in Vietnam policy, dismissed the " 'Cold War context' myth" that the global anticommunist enterprise made intervention in Vietnam inevitable. Bundy, he argued, advocated Americanization of the war "in the face of tremendous internal opposition, external pressures, and a continually failing strategy. . . . Bundy was not a warmonger, but neither was he a tragic hero, unable to escape the curse of his tragic flaw. He should have known better and often did."[7]

Following his death, Bundy's loyalists tried to soften the blow, acknowledging but qualifying his identification with Vietnam. Francis Bator, a former White House colleague, praised Bundy's accomplishments at a memorial service at St. James Church in New York, noting that a number of good things had happened under his watch. "With the one very bad thing that happened," said Bator, "he had much less to do than the common version of the Vietnam story would have it."[8] James C. Thomson Jr., a former White House aide, argued in the *New York Times* that Bundy was not the unreflective hawk described by his critics. "He was a skilled adjudicator, not an advocate, especially on Vietnam," Thomson wrote. "He tolerated and even encouraged dissent from conventional wisdom, as long as it was expressed with brevity and evidence. He seemed to have no firm convictions on the inherited Vietnam mess. His loyalty was to the President and to our nation's security."[9]

Arthur M. Schlesinger Jr., a close friend and colleague of fifty years, concluded that Bundy represented "the last hurrah of the Northeast Establishment. . . . He was the final executor of the grand tradition of Henry Stimson, Dean Acheson, Averell Harriman, Robert Lovett, John J. McCloy—patricians who, combining commitment to international responsibility with instinct for command and relish in power, served the republic pretty well in the global crises of the twentieth century." About Bundy's role in the Vietnam War, Schlesinger observed: "A single tragic error prevented him from achieving his full promise as a statesman."[10]

᪐

McGeorge Bundy was born on March 30, 1919. His mother, the former Katherine Lawrence Putnam, was the niece of A. Lawrence Lowell, the president of Harvard University, and the poet Amy Lowell.[11] The family's Boston lineage dated back to 1639 and was characterized by a deep connection to Harvard University. Bundy's father, Harvey Hollister Bundy, was a native of Michigan who had migrated to New England for his education, first at Yale, where he was a member of the secret society Skull and Bones, and then at Harvard Law School and a clerkship for Supreme Court justice Oliver Wendell Holmes Jr.

Growing up in Boston, McGeorge Bundy, known as Mac, enjoyed a privileged childhood. He and his brothers attended the Dexter Lower School, a private elementary school founded by Harvey Bundy and several of his friends. Just ahead of Mac was another privileged boy from a prominent Boston family, John F. Kennedy. Summers were spent in Manchester, Massachusetts, where the Putnam family owned a seaside compound that included a nineteen-bedroom "cottage." A smaller house on the property was deeded to Katherine, which became the Bundy family retreat.[12]

Members of a verbally minded brood, Mac and his older brother, Bill, excelled in political debate, a ritualized feature of family life. "How well I remember our fights over the dining room table," recalled their sister Harriet. "Mother's sense of righteousness was very deep, and so's Mac's." She added, "For her, things were black and white. It's an outlook that descends directly from the Puritans and we all have it. But Mac has it more than the rest of us."[13]

In 1931 a young Mac Bundy joined his brothers, Bill and Harvey Jr., at Groton, a New England boarding school presided over by Dr. Endicott Peabody, an ordained Episcopal minister and passionate Anglophile who dreamed of replicating the elite British secondary school model in the United States. Peabody, who required compulsory cold showers before breakfast and daily chapel services, admonished his pupils that "obedience is one of the greatest of human virtues."

Groton was distinguished by an emphasis on public service. Its motto is *Cui servire est regnare*, "To serve is to rule." During Peabody's tenure, Groton graduates included one U.S. president, two secretaries of state, one national security adviser, one secretary of the treasury, one secretary of the army, one secretary of the navy, six generals, and three U.S. senators.[14] Dean Acheson, the future secretary of state, was nearly expelled for his nonconformity to Groton's rigid culture. Others, like Franklin Roosevelt, the future president, survived but left little imprint in the school's tight hierarchy of fewer than two hundred boys.[15] McGeorge Bundy, however, thrived at Groton.

The legend of McGeorge Bundy—first in his class, the editor in chief of the monthly *Grotonian*, president of the drama society, and captain of the debating team—begins at Groton. "The story is told," recounts David Halberstam, "that a group of outstanding students were asked to prepare papers on the Duke of Marlborough. The next day Bundy was called upon to read his paper in class. As he read his classmates began to giggle. The giggles continued all the way through the reading of his excellent paper."

The next day the teacher asked one of his students for an explanation. "'Didn't you know?' said the student. 'He was unprepared. He was reading from a blank piece of paper.'"[16]

There was only one college to which Bundy applied. "From Groton he went to Yale," writes Halberstam, "where the legend grew." As the new students arrived, the Yale dean of admissions explained that for the first time one of the 850 students in the freshman class had recorded three perfect scores on his college entrance exams. Bundy had achieved this distinction with an unorthodox strategy on the English test. Students were instructed to compose a paper on one of a few perfunctory topics in the vein of "How did you spend your summer vacation?" Bundy refused. Instead he wrote an essay attacking the questions for their banality and upbraiding the college board for choosing such insipid themes. At first penalizing Bundy for his stunt, the reviewers who graded the exam eventually decided to reward his impertinence with the highest possible score.[17]

Bundy majored in mathematics at Yale and was a member of Phi Beta Kappa, secretary of the political union and then leader of its Liberal Party, class orator, and a columnist for the *Yale Daily News*, which he would sometimes use as a platform for slyly inflammatory opinions, such as his proposal to abolish the football team. His classmates called him "Mahatma Bundy," as Bird notes, "partly because he was such a Boston Brahmin, and partly because he was constantly speaking out on the issues of the day."[18] In his senior year Bundy wrote an essay arguing for intervention against European fascism. It was published in an anthology entitled *Zero Hour: A Summons to the Free*. "Let me put my whole proposition in one sentence," Bundy wrote. "I believe in the dignity of the individual, in government by law, in respect for truth, and in a good God; those beliefs are worth my life and more; they are not shared by Adolf Hitler."[19]

Like his father before him Bundy was inducted into Skull and Bones, the Yale secret society whose members have included President William

Howard Taft, Secretary of State Henry L. Stimson, Governor Averell Harriman, Assistant Secretary of War Robert Lovett, Supreme Court justice Potter Stewart, President George H. W. Bush and his son, President George W. Bush (as well as his opponent for the presidency in 2004, Senator John F. Kerry). Bundy, who kept a ceramic skull and bones propped on the desk of his Manchester study, remained close to his fraternity of fellow Bonesmen for his entire life, receiving correspondence more than fifty years after his initiation addressed to "Odin," Bundy's collegiate persona, named for the Norse god of war, poetry, wisdom, and the dead.[20]

In 1941, a year after his graduation from Yale, Bundy made a brief and inauspicious foray into politics. Running as a Republican for what was considered a safe seat on the Boston City Council, Bundy was trounced, and he would never again seek elected office. He instead directed his energies to pursuing an academic career, accepting an appointment to a unique graduate program, Harvard's Society of Fellows. For those awarded a coveted spot in the Society of Fellows there were no classes to attend, no PhD exams to endure, no doctoral dissertation to grind out. For three years fellows had no requirements other than to pursue a scholarly project of personal interest.

World War II would interrupt Mac Bundy's fellowship, just as it would disrupt life for the other men of the Bundy family. Mac's brother Bill went to England, where he served as a cryptologist with a crack code-breaking team ensconced at a secret facility at Bletchley Park. Family patriarch Harvey Bundy Sr. was reunited with a former mentor, Henry Stimson, President Roosevelt's secretary of war. As Stimson's top deputy, the elder Bundy was one of a tightly contained circle of men involved in America's secret development of the atomic bomb.

Mac Bundy enlisted, circumventing the matter of his poor vision by memorizing the optometrist's chart, and received a posting in the Signal Corps. In 1943 he was appointed as an aide to Rear Admiral Alan G. Kirk, for whom he processed intercepted German air force attack plans and assisted in military preparations for Operation Overlord, the Allied invasion of France, which he observed from the flag bridge of the USS *Augusta* off the coast of Normandy.[21]

After the war, Mac Bundy returned to his Harvard fellowship and a new opportunity. Once again it involved a family relationship with Henry Stimson. In the autumn of 1945, Stimson suffered a massive heart attack, frustrating plans to compose his memoirs. Stimson would now need the assistance of an able and energetic collaborator. The choice was obvious. Harvey Bundy's twenty-seven-year-old son would be the ideal coauthor—trusted, discreet, prolific, and possessing a crisp and confident prose style. Moreover, Bundy's scholarly blank check from the Society of Fellows would allow him to pursue virtually any enterprise he wished. Their book, *On Active Service in Peace and War*, was published in 1948 and was greeted with generous reviews. The *New Republic* called it a "central document of our times," while *Foreign Affairs* praised it as "one of the most important biographical works of our generation."[22]

With the Stimson book and his Harvard fellowship completed, Mac Bundy deliberated over the next chapter of his career. A close family friend, Supreme Court justice Felix Frankfurter, tried to lure Bundy—a conspicuous nongraduate of the law school—with a clerkship. Bundy considered but declined the offer. The country's most influential newspaper columnist, Walter Lippmann, dangled the possibility of a book collaboration. Bundy toyed with the idea but ultimately passed.[23] Instead he jumped into the political game as a foreign policy adviser and speechwriter to the 1948 presidential campaign of New York governor Thomas E. Dewey, the heavily favored Republican nominee.

Nearly forty years later, Bundy recalled decamping from Cambridge to Manhattan. "We sat over there in the Roosevelt Hotel and received applications for embassies from affluent Republicans," he said. "We were too statesmen-like to get into vulgar politics." Bundy was responsible for drafting the candidate's speeches on foreign affairs. The job was not a taxing one. Most of Dewey's remarks, Bundy said, were lifted from a filing cabinet that cataloged the governor's previous statements.[24] Bundy's boss was Allen Dulles, the future director of central intelligence, a familiar figure from his time working with Secretary Stimson on Long Island. Dulles "was always looking for tennis partners," Bundy remembered.[25]

Harry S. Truman's stunning defeat of Dewey that November left Bundy without a ticket to Washington. So he signed on for a brief stint at the Council on Foreign Relations, directing a task force on Marshall Plan aid to Europe. The committee included Dulles and General Dwight Eisenhower, who was then the president of Columbia University. "He read a couple of papers of mine," Bundy recalled. "Marked them with a soft pencil and persuaded me that he was one of the best editors I ever worked for."[26] In 1949 Bundy returned to Harvard for a teaching position in the government department, the path smoothed by Justice Frankfurter.[27]

The Cambridge years were fruitful. Bundy's class on the history of U.S. foreign policy had a large campus following, with his lecture on the Munich appeasement of 1938 often performed to a standing-room-only audience. "My best lecture," remembered Bundy, "was actually the relief of General MacArthur" by President Truman in the midst of the Korean War. "It was the little guy from Missouri in the not very well-pressed grey suit taking care of the great fake! . . . Perfect hero. Perfect villain."[28] Bundy courted Mary Buckminster Lothrop, whose socially prominent family had accumulated a substantial fortune and was a fixture in Boston society.[29] The couple married and went on to have four sons. And after just two years lecturing at Harvard, Bundy was recommended for tenure by the government department. "Though Bundy was a good teacher, he was not in the classic sense a great expert in foreign affairs, since he had not come up through the discipline," Halberstam notes. "He was not particularly at ease with Ph.D. candidates, those men who might be more specialized in their knowledge than he." But because Bundy was the rising star of the government department, the consensus among his colleagues was to award him tenure. As Halberstam recounts, the case was presented to Harvard president James Bryant Conant, who had served as a distinguished member of the chemistry department before running the university. Was it in fact true, asked Conant, that Bundy had never taken a *single* undergraduate or graduate class in government?

"That's right," said the professor representing the government department.

Conant was puzzled. "Are you sure that's right?" he asked.

"I'm sure," the government professor replied.

"Well," said Conant with a sigh, "all I can say is that it couldn't have happened in chemistry."[30]

Bundy published a second book in late 1951, *The Pattern of Responsibility*, an edited anthology and commentary on the public speeches and statements of Secretary of State Dean Acheson, then under fire from Senator Joseph McCarthy for being soft on communism. Acheson was a family friend and the father-in-law of his brother Bill. "I have undertaken to prepare this book," Bundy wrote, "not because of this connection, but in spite of it. I have done so because I really do not believe that friendship, or indirect family connection, is a bar to fair and honest defense, especially when that defense takes the form of allowing a man to speak for himself."[31] The book, although based on Acheson's own public remarks, is peppered with vintage Bundyisms: "It is possible to persuade the reasonable student that there is alertness against Communism in the State Department; it is relatively easy to show that Senator McCarthy is a charlatan." The Acheson collaboration in 1951 also foreshadowed a seminal Bundy theme, integral to his presidential counsel in the years to come. "Very near the heart of all foreign affairs," he declared, "is the relationship between policy and military power."[32] How Bundy conceived of and explicitly defined that relationship in the crucible of Vietnam would, for better or worse, come to define his place in history.

In 1953, Bundy's swift Harvard ascent reached its apogee. Nathan Pusey, the university's newly appointed president, tapped Bundy to be dean of the faculty. He was just thirty-four years old. A Yale colleague circulated a playful limerick encapsulating the Bundy legend to date:

A proper young prig, McGeorge Bundy,
Graduated from Yale on a Monday
But he was shortly seen
As Establishment Dean
Up at Harvard the following Sunday.[33]

"Bundy was a magnificent dean," concludes Halberstam—a gifted tactician who, through his preternatural confidence and mastery of academic politics, "took the complex Harvard faculty—diverse, egomaniacal—and played with it, in the words of a critic, like a cat with mice."[34] Under Bundy's leadership the bureaucracy was tamed, decisions were made quickly, and dynamic new faculty members were recruited, including the social scientists Erik Erikson and David Riesman, the political scientist Stanley Hoffman, and even the playwright Lillian Hellman. The government department, in particular, was a remarkable incubator of talent in the 1950s, producing three future national security advisers: Bundy, Zbigniew Brzezinski, and Henry Kissinger, for whom Bundy helped secure tenure by coupling a pair of half-time appointments into a single permanent position. Nonetheless Bundy and Kissinger shared an uneasy relationship. "I thought him more sensitive and gentle than his occasionally brusque manner suggested," Kissinger said of Bundy. "He tended to treat me with the combination of politeness and subconscious condescension that upper-class Bostonians reserve for people of, by New England standards, exotic backgrounds and excessively intense personal style."[35] Riesman, the influential sociologist poached from the University of Chicago, called Bundy's management of the faculty a form of "aristocratic meritocracy."[36]

During his years as dean Bundy developed a relationship with John F. Kennedy, the junior senator from Massachusetts, who was also a member of the Harvard board of overseers. That connection was cultivated in part by two high-profile Harvard personalities: John Kenneth Galbraith, the economist who had been a college tutor to Kennedy in the late 1930s and remained an adviser and friend, and Arthur M. Schlesinger Jr., the historian who hosted a salon of sorts to introduce Kennedy to the brightest minds in Cambridge.

After Kennedy was elected president in 1960, he tapped Bundy to serve as his special assistant for national security affairs, a position that has come to be known as national security adviser. Bundy transformed what had been a post of marginal influence in the Eisenhower era into a dominant player in the management of American global strategy. The press coverage of his ascension invariably emphasized his access to power. "With his pink cheeks, sandy hair, springy step, and faintly quizzical expression behind plain glasses, Bundy could easily pass for a Washington junior civil servant," a *Newsweek* cover story reported. "Yet he is one of the most influential men in the U.S. Government."[37] According to the *New York Times*, the national security adviser was "one of the most influential custodians of the foreign policies of the United States, one of the very few Americans whose daily judgments directly affect the political history of the world."[38] As David Halberstam would later note, many who knew Bundy "thought of him as the best the country could offer, McGeorge Bundy of Boston, a legend in his time."[39]

Bundy would remain as national security adviser for five years, serving President Kennedy and his successor, Lyndon Johnson. The rapturous regard in which Bundy was held was captured by the columnist Joseph Kraft, who in 1965 said,

> Bundy is the leading candidate, perhaps the only candidate,
> for the statesman's mantle to emerge in the generation that is

coming to power—the generation which reached maturity in the war and postwar period. His capacity to read the riddle of multiple confusions, to consider a wide variety of possibilities, to develop lines of action, to articulate and execute public purposes, to impart quickened energies to men of the highest ability seems to me unmatched. To me anyhow he seems almost alone among contemporaries a figure of true consequence, a fit subject for Milton's words:

> A Pillar of State; deep on his
> > Front engraven
> Deliberation sat and publick care;
> > And Princely counsel in his face.[40]

Even Bundy's less than endearing qualities were exalted as proof of his superiority. In a cover story about Bundy in June 1965, *Time* magazine stated: "He is self-confident to the point of arrogance, intelligent to the point of intimidation."[41] Bundy was, in fact, willing to articulate convictions others could find impolitic or even pompous. "In the final analysis," he proclaimed in 1965, "the United States is the locomotive at the head of mankind, and the rest of the world the caboose."[42] Bundy's extraordinary stature made him the logical choice to present the Johnson administration's case for perseverance in Vietnam. "To the job of Ambassador to Academe, McGeorge Bundy brings solid-gold credentials," *Time* declared, describing Bundy's return to the Harvard campus to defend the administration's policies to more than one thousand students and professors who packed Lowell Lecture Hall, where Bundy used to teach his hugely popular class, "The U.S. in World Politics." Taking the lectern once more, he cautioned his audience that the collapse of South Vietnam would produce "a great weakening in the free societies in their ability to withstand communism."[43]

Bundy was determined to answer the administration's critics, and in doing so he espoused grand objectives for U.S. foreign policy. "We cannot limit ourselves to one objective at a time. We, like Caesar, have all things to do at once," Bundy professed in a May 1965 memorial speech at Franklin Roosevelt's grave site. "And this is hard. In Vietnam today we have to share in the fighting; we have to lead in the search for peace; and we have to respond, in all that we do, to the real needs and the real hopes of the people of Vietnam."[44]

In early 1966, after the essential decisions in Vietnam were made but before their true costs were apparent, Bundy left government service to become president of the Ford Foundation. Under Bundy's leadership the philanthropy initiated major advances in public broadcasting, energy conservation, public interest law, and the expansion of civil and voting rights.[45] Yet, despite his good works the question of Vietnam remained. His friend Kingman Brewster, who had been named the president of Yale University, remarked, "Mac is going to spend the rest of his life trying to justify his mistakes on Vietnam."[46]

Out of office, Bundy remained adamant in his refusal to criticize the Johnson administration and was completely intolerant of former government colleagues who did. He made his conviction clear in a debate held at Harvard in March 1968, when Bundy faced off against the political scientist Stanley Hoffman, whom he had recruited to the faculty the previous decade. "Particularly when you go to work as a staff assistant, you acquire an obligation of loyalty, which tends to increase through time," Bundy explained to a restive audience of students and faculty. "I have very little sympathy with those who write criticisms which appear over the heading 'former White House assistant.'" Bundy described such dissent as a form of political assassination aimed at the president. "When people do that they have taken a gun provided by someone else and aimed it at him, and I'm against it." In the audience that evening was James Thomson, an Asia expert who had worked for Bundy on the White

House staff and would soon publish a critical magazine article dissecting the anatomy of Vietnam decision making. Bundy was infuriated by Thomson's disclosures and would refuse to speak with his former colleague for years to follow. In his talk, Bundy cited his experience working with Henry Stimson, "a great cabinet officer who worked for seven presidents in different ways, and who made it his binding rule to engage in no criticism of any of the seven while that man was still in active public life. That is my position too."[47]

While Bundy was prepared to defend the decisions that enlarged the war, he declined to defend himself personally—or to allow anyone else to do so for him. When the *New York Times* published the *Pentagon Papers* in 1971, rumors circulated that there were other documents, still classified, that reflected Bundy's doubts about Vietnam. Francis Bator and Carl Kaysen, who had worked for Bundy in the White House, pushed him to disclose the information. "After Mac himself had brushed their inquiry off," recounts Kai Bird, "they went to Mary Bundy and told her, 'You've got to get Mac to publicize these memos.' Mary listened and asked her husband about it, but he would have nothing to do with any effort to defend his record."[48]

That same spring, Bundy delivered three highly anticipated lectures on the Vietnam War at the Council on Foreign Relations in New York.[49] Bundy said his purpose in giving the lectures was to "find instruction" from events in Vietnam "without engaging either in attack or defense."[50] Yet his lectures enraged many of the Council's members, who by that time, like the broader Establishment they represented, had turned forcefully against the war.

On the basic question of the war's justification, Bundy expressed his conviction that "it was necessary and right, in some form and by some means, to act to avoid a Communist victory by force of arms in Vietnam in 1965 and thereafter. I suppose this is not the majority view today, but it is mine, and I have to start, on these matters, from where I am."[51] Bundy acknowledged the criticism that "the Johnson administration campaigned against a wider war and then promptly started one," leading some to conclude, "this was sheer duplicity. It was not. The administration in 1964 did not know what 1965 would require in Vietnam and it preferred not to decide."[52]

When the turning point of 1965 finally arrived, Bundy stated, the American public should have been prepared: "Neither the possibility of bombing the North nor the prospect of a major commitment of ground combat forces to Vietnam—the two major decisions of 1965—was a secret to anyone before it happened. Both were extensively reported. If the Congress did not intrude itself in these deliberations—and it did not—it was by a clear and conscious choice."[53] Commenting on the 1964 Tonkin Gulf resolution, which authorized Johnson to use military force against North Vietnam, Bundy said, "The administration was almost forced to rely on the resolution and to make it carry a weight for which it was not designed." He called this "not a crime of intentional deception, but an error of democratic decision-making."[54] And in the end, Bundy offered only a terse expression of regret for the course of the war. "There has been very much more cost and pain," he said, "than most of us would have thought justified if we had perceived it as inevitable in 1965."[55]

In the years that followed, Bundy tended to avoid making public remarks about Vietnam. But questions about his role in the war persisted. In 1976 he accepted an invitation to address a meeting of Harvard's Nieman Fellows, a program administered by his former aide James Thomson, with whom Bundy had finally reconciled. After his talk, one of the fellows, a young journalist named Ron Javers, needled Bundy about Vietnam. "Your problem, young man," said Bundy, cutting off the exchange, "is not your intellect but your ideology." Javers would not be dismissed. He cornered the former national security adviser during a cocktail reception.

"What about Vietnam?" Javers asked.

"I don't understand your question," Bundy replied.

"Mac, what about you and Vietnam?"

"I still don't understand," said Bundy.

"But Mac, you screwed it up, didn't you?"

A glacial silence followed. Then Bundy suddenly smiled and replied, "Yes, I did. But I'm not going to waste the rest of my life feeling guilty about it." Later that evening, Bundy spoke with Thomson about the encounter. "I'll never be appointed Secretary of State," he said with a note of resignation, "or even a university president."[56]

After stepping down from the Ford Foundation in 1979, Bundy became a professor of history at New York University. Twenty-four of his future faculty colleagues protested his appointment, which was nonetheless approved. Many of those who objected would later find that he was a reliable ally in department votes on academic and administrative matters.

Bundy spent his years at NYU exploring the history of nuclear weapons and strategic doctrine, culminating in the publication in 1988 of his widely praised history, *Danger and Survival: Choices About the Bomb in the First Fifty Years*. As Bundy was writing the book, the journalist David Talbot asked him about Vietnam. "I did have reservations about that," Bundy replied, referring to his support for enlarging the war, "and it can be argued that I didn't press hard enough. But I didn't see any way of leaving Vietnam alone and simply getting out in 1965." He added, "Oh yes, I worry about that all the time, but I'm not prepared to sort it out yet. That's going to have to happen some years from now."[57]

☙

In 1995 McGeorge Bundy finally decided to revisit the question of Vietnam. The catalyst was the publication in April of that year of *In Retrospect:*

The Tragedy and Lessons of Vietnam, the historical memoir by his long-time friend and colleague, former secretary of defense Robert S. McNamara. In his book, McNamara conceded, "We were wrong, terribly wrong" about Vietnam; he also acknowledged that in 1967, while still in office, he concluded that the war could not be won but nonetheless remained silent, refusing to disclose his doubts.[58] That admission in particular stirred deep rage in some quarters and incited a national media firestorm.

The *New York Times* editorial page excoriated McNamara for his failure to "join the national debate over whether American troops should continue to die at the rate of hundreds per week in a war he knew to be futile." The *Times* concluded that McNamara deserved to be haunted by what he had done. "Surely he must in every quiet and prosperous moment hear the ceaseless whispers of those poor boys in the infantry, dying in the tall grass, platoon by platoon, for no purpose," the editors wrote. "What he took from them cannot be repaid by prime-time apology and stale tears, three decades late."[59]

Prominent veterans of the war also lashed out at the former secretary of defense. "It sure would have been helpful in May of 1967, when I volunteered for Vietnam, if he had said then that the war was unwinnable," said Max Cleland, who lost both legs and an arm in Vietnam and afterward served as head of the Veterans Administration. (He would be elected to the U.S. Senate in 1996.) "McNamara went to the World Bank, while a lot of other people went to their graves."[60]

McNamara's critics claimed that if he had voiced his dissent in 1967, he could have helped to end America's involvement in the war. "He was one of the highest ranking officials of the Johnson administration, he could have made a difference," argued Mary McGrory of the *Washington Post.* "That's what's unpardonable, not to have tried."[61] According to Townsend Hoopes, who served as undersecretary of the air force during the Vietnam War, "A McNamara resignation in 1967 or early 1968 would have changed history."[62]

Other commentators welcomed McNamara's admissions. "To condemn Robert McNamara for the arrogant lies of Vietnam is understandable," wrote Richard Cohen of the *Washington Post*. "But to condemn him also for finally telling the truth—no matter how late—makes no sense."[63] In *Newsweek*, Jonathan Alter agreed. "For a major public official to admit profound error is extraordinarily rare, perhaps unprecedented, in American history," he observed. "Anyone predicting in 1961 that Bob McNamara would one day cry publicly while admitting colossal error would have been laughed out of Washington."[64]

McNamara had asked Bundy to comment on early drafts of *In Retrospect*, and Bundy had responded with a balance of candid criticisms and warm encouragement. The first draft was not very good, Bundy wrote, but he could not explain precisely why. Perhaps, he suggested, McNamara had become preoccupied with Vietnam's vast paper trail of documents rather than the essential problems the United States was grappling with at each stage of the war's progression. Bundy counseled McNamara to exercise the patience required to produce the great book of which he was capable.[65] In another letter, Bundy acknowledged McNamara's choice not to criticize living colleagues with whom he differed, but he wondered whether McNamara might have gone too far in bestowing praise on those with whom he disagreed.[66] Bundy seemed to anticipate the intense public interest that would be sparked by McNamara's retrospective renunciation of the war; months before the book's publication, he offered his friend a list of potential press questions and illustrative answers, including queries about McNamara's reliance on quantitative data and the flaws in American military strategy.[67]

On April 17, 1995, Bundy appeared on *The MacNeil/Lehrer NewsHour*, on public television, as one of a panel of commentators invited to discuss the fierce national argument McNamara's book had generated. "I think Bob McNamara has tried very hard to tell it as he now understands it," Bundy said. "It's an honest contribution and it will be a very much valued one."

The anchor, Jim Lehrer, asked about McNamara's retrospective appraisal. " 'We were wrong, terribly wrong.' Would you accept that yourself?" he asked Bundy.

"Sure," Bundy replied, with a casual shrug. An awkward beat followed before he added: "I think it's very unlikely that we were right looking at the evidence as we now have it."

Another panelist, the *Los Angeles Times* columnist Robert Scheer, quickly seized on the significance of Bundy's admission. "You have a guest on your program, McGeorge Bundy, who was certainly as complicit as McNamara," he told Lehrer. "I don't know why McNamara should take all the heat."[68]

The camera cut away for a reaction shot. Scheer's attack appeared to rattle the seventy-six-year-old Bundy. His sharp blue eyes darted back and forth behind his thick glasses with the clear plastic frames, the same signature style he had worn in the Kennedy and Johnson years. When his gaze finally steadied, Bundy appeared to betray an emotion utterly inconsistent with his cool, confident Vietnam persona. It was not a look of fear, exactly, but something related to it: a thinly suppressed expression of sudden alarm. The fierce anger directed at McNamara had suddenly been focused on him, and for an instant, he appeared uncharacteristically vulnerable. Within days of his television appearance, however, I received a call from Bundy seeking my help in composing his own memoir and retrospective analysis of America's path to war in Vietnam. Despite the enormous clamor surrounding McNamara's book and the certainty that such residual animosity would be directed toward him, Bundy wanted to commence work as soon as possible.

Bundy's death made the completion of the original conception of the book an impossibility. There were simply too many narrative and historical gaps in the collected fragments to render a manuscript that would honestly reflect Bundy's intended design, which was a proposition still very much in formation when he passed away. Yet there was a critical mass of content from our collaboration more than sufficient to present a distillation of many of his essential recollections and retrospective judgments.

With the encouragement of Mary Bundy and the generous financial support of the Carnegie Corporation, in 1997 I commenced work on an extensive edited volume based principally on the materials drawn from our collaboration. That book melded a variety of historical sources relating to Bundy with the content produced during our work together and my detailed narrative charting the progression of American strategy in Vietnam from 1961 to 1965. A pair of advisers appointed by Mrs. Bundy periodically reviewed and commented on drafts of the book. Completed in late 2001 after various delays and amid other professional obligations, a complete draft of the edited volume was formally evaluated by its prospective publisher, Yale University Press, in 2002. An independent expert committee of historians and former senior policy makers read the manuscript and unanimously recommended it for publication. However, following an extended period of discussion with Mrs. Bundy about the creative control of the manuscript and various efforts to address her concerns, she decided that she no longer wished to proceed with a posthumously published work. In 2004 Mrs. Bundy donated her late husband's papers to the John F. Kennedy Library in Boston.

The book that follows is not the Yale University Press manuscript—it is neither an annotated volume of Bundy papers nor a comprehensive history of Vietnam policy making. It has been composed without any involvement whatsoever from the Bundy family or its advisers. This is an original work that is informed by my experience with Bundy but which draws conclusions that are my own. In the chapters to come, I have attempted to distill what I believe are the pivotal lessons of Bundy's performance as national security adviser with respect to the vital question of American strategy in Vietnam. Some of these lessons are consistent with the retrospective analysis Bundy and I were trying to complete. Other lessons are based on what I regard as the illuminating aspects of Bundy's conduct in office—particularly his failures—and offer conclusions he may not have supported. Throughout I have been careful to differentiate between Bundy's retrospective views and my own commentary and conclusions. Moreover, I have attempted to be neither Bundy's advocate nor his critic. My objective is different. I have sought to convey the essential insights of my collaboration with Bundy while also offering an independent analysis of his role in the highly complex narrative of America's entanglement in Vietnam. The reader should therefore understand that in no way is this a book *by* McGeorge Bundy but rather it is a book *about* him.

Why did Bundy commit himself to a retrospective study of Vietnam that would inevitably revive the passions of the war? In the last years of his life I believe he labored under the weight of a powerful perceived obligation to history. I feel certain that Bundy, had he lived to complete his final work, would have attempted to address his own shortcomings during his years at the center of Vietnam strategy. As Bundy observed in one of his draft fragments: "I had a part in a great failure. I made mistakes of perception, recommendation and execution. If I have learned anything I should share it."[69] In another fragment he wrote and underscored: "*You owe it to a lot of different people*. Because it hurt them or their families; because it matters what lessons are learned . . . there are a lot of errors in the path of understanding."[70]

Bundy explained that he had embarked on his account of the war in response to the "driving force" of a pair of questions that he had "deliberately put aside for decades": How did the "tragedy" of the Vietnam War come to pass? And what guidance can it provide for the future?[71]

Bundy acknowledged a dramatic shift of perspective about Vietnam.

"One can begin, as I do, with agreement that the war was, overall, a war we should not have fought and then try to sort out from one man's experience why it was that different judgments prevailed at the time." In sharp contrast to his fervent public arguments in 1965 in favor of Americanizing the war, Bundy admitted that at the time and in the years that followed, "the doves were right." He would therefore try to explain "the ways in which the executive branch continuously got that great choice wrong."[72] Finally, Bundy explained, his Vietnam inquiry would be constrained in scope and far less ambitious in historical breadth than his study of the nuclear danger because he was "too close to some of it, too far from the rest, and too old for the sheer hard work."[73]

Bundy credited his choice to write about Vietnam "largely . . . to the example" of his colleague and friend Robert McNamara. "His book *In Retrospect* is a remarkably straightforward account," Bundy wrote, "and I think its value for the long run will far outweigh its obvious cost in short-term anger from readers with their own strong feelings about Vietnam."[74] What he did not acknowledge—but must have known—was that like McNamara, Bundy would pay a price in public opprobrium for finally recanting his belief in a ruinous war he had in large part designed and had passionately promoted, but had not renounced for three decades.

Bundy's decision to speak out about the war was historically significant. The accounts of all of the other central protagonists in the Vietnam drama—from the beginning of U.S. military engagement to the painful conclusion of the war—had already been added to the historical record. That literature includes works by Lyndon Johnson, William Westmoreland, Maxwell Taylor, Henry Cabot Lodge, Dean Rusk, George Ball, Walt Rostow, Clark Clifford, Richard Nixon, Henry Kissinger, and, finally, McNamara.[75]

"I have tried to respect the sacrifice of those who died . . . and their families," Bundy wrote, noting that America "has learned hard lessons from their sacrifice" that helped to ensure victory in subsequent wars.[76] Vietnam, Bundy told me, was "a major and tragic event in American history and I have something to contribute to understanding it."[77]

"My wish now is that we had done less" in Vietnam, Bundy confided in another interview. "I wish that I had understood that more clearly. Why did I *not* understand it? . . . What can we learn from this episode that will help us do better in the world ahead?"[78]

COUNSELORS ADVISE BUT PRESIDENTS DECIDE

I n my meetings with McGeorge Bundy, time seemed to stop and reverse course, back to the years of the Kennedy and Johnson presidencies, as Bundy would recall the storied cast of characters with whom he had served three decades earlier—men like Robert McNamara, the Ford Motor Company president whom Kennedy tapped to run the Pentagon; Dean Rusk, the former Rhodes Scholar and famously reserved foundation president who served as secretary of state; and Richard Bissell, Bundy's old friend from the Yale economics department, who led the CIA's so-called Black Operations to overthrow foreign leaders in Central America, Africa, and Southeast Asia.

Bundy would ruminate out loud, reconstructing the power structure of the two different administrations and the proximity of the key players to the president. He revisited bureaucratic and policy turf battles, elucidating the tactics that won influence with the president or preempted rivals.

Bundy would test various historical propositions about the Cold War or American politics, circuitously weaving his observations back to the question of Vietnam. He would continually return to the theme of personality, which he treated as an intangible variable of the decision-making process. The real state of play, Bundy often reminded me, could not be discerned by the documentary record alone. He advised me to be wary of the "paper trail way of missing the political point."[1] Throughout all of these varied discussions, Bundy seemed content to follow a subject of interest until it yielded some insight of value or, perhaps, until it yielded nothing at all. No phones would ring. No interruptions would be allowed. Outside, the business of Manhattan bustled but the traffic below on Madison Avenue would glide by silently. Inside, free of distraction, the hours would pass, the two of us simply talking.

These initial meetings, although untethered to a formal agenda, were nonetheless instructive, producing a checklist of questions, themes, events, and personalities that Bundy would want to elaborate on in the course of our work together. But these first discussions had a deeper value as well. They captured something impalpable and difficult to distill—a sensibility specific to Bundy, a quality of perspective, a basic orientation of how he conceived of Vietnam as a subject of historical inquiry.

While the McGeorge Bundy who reigned as a legend of the Establishment was reputed to be brisk, quick, calculating, and overconfident, the retrospective Bundy of thirty years later was in many ways the opposite: patient, reflective, curious, and humble. In fact, on the question of Vietnam Bundy appeared tentative and unsure—maybe on some level even mystified. Although he never said so explicitly, he seemed to be as perplexed by the disaster of Vietnam as any of the historians who studied the decisions in which he had been a central participant. How did Bundy, the star of his generation and the preeminent mind of the Kennedy and Johnson presidencies, get Vietnam so terribly wrong? And how would he explain his failures of judgment three decades later?

It was clear from the beginning that Bundy was distinctly uninterested in the topics of Vietnamese nationalism and the origins of the communist insurgency. Early in our collaboration Bundy's friends and colleagues from Brown University, James Blight and Janet Lang, lobbied him strenuously to chair an American delegation with McNamara that would travel to Hanoi in 1997 for a historic meeting with the surviving members of the Vietnamese political and military leadership. The purpose of the exercise was to revisit the origins of the war from both American and Vietnamese perspectives and to fill the gaps in the historical record about the key inflection points that fueled the war's escalation in the mid-1960s. While McNamara was driven to seize the historical opportunity of an unprecedented dialogue with America's former enemy, Bundy had no enthusiasm for examining the Vietnamese calculus of interests that contributed to war with the United States. The decision to Americanize the Vietnam War in 1965, Bundy told me, was a decision made in Washington and not in Hanoi. It was inherently a *presidential* decision, he argued, and thus had to be studied through the prism of the two men he served who held ultimate authority for questions of war and peace—President Kennedy and President Johnson.

To understand his own role in shaping America's fate in Vietnam, Bundy would have to see it illuminated by the presidents he counseled. We would therefore begin at the point of exposition most logical to Bundy, with a systematic examination of how Kennedy encountered Vietnam in his first year in office, and of the decisions he made about the deployment of American power there in the course of his presidency.

Bundy had, of course, read innumerable histories of the Kennedy administration, but in the decades since he left government he had not read the gradually accumulating body of declassified government documents on Kennedy and Vietnam, many of which were compiled by the State Department and published in the bound crimson volumes known as *Foreign Relations of the United States*. This voluminous chronological compilation of documents about Vietnam policy—memoranda, meeting summaries, cables, correspondence, intelligence estimates, defense analyses, mission reports—was unexplored historical territory for Bundy. It was here, in the thousands of pages of government documents rather than in a conference room in Hanoi, where Bundy wanted to search for insights into the Vietnam War. For Bundy it was the right course. He learned that sometimes pivotal episodes in history can hide in plain sight.

As I compiled various outlines and research memoranda for Bundy about the history of Kennedy's first year in office, it became obvious that the prospect of intervention in Vietnam was among the major challenges he confronted. In fact, in the fall of 1961 Kennedy's most senior advisers almost unanimously warned him that the odds were sharply against avoiding a catastrophic defeat in Vietnam unless the president approved the first increment of a ground combat force deployment that might ultimately reach six divisions, or more than two hundred thousand men. Among the president's advisers to join that recommendation was McGeorge Bundy. "Remarkable," he told me when I brought the 1961 recommendation to his attention. "I have no memory of this whatsoever." But there it was in the documents for Bundy to see—the narrative of an emerging crisis in Saigon and Kennedy's struggle with his counselors, including his national security adviser, over how to respond.

Kennedy's management of Vietnam in 1961 became a central focus for Bundy and an inflection point in his retrospective conclusions about the history of the war. While he did not complete his history of Kennedy's decisions of that year he left no doubt about the importance he ascribed to them. "The policy I want to consider was in fact adopted by President Kennedy late in 1961, and sustained—though not explained—through his time as President," Bundy explained in a draft fragment. "It was maintained by Lyndon Johnson through the election year 1964, and abandoned as quietly as possible in 1965. It was the course of not engaging American ground combat troops in the war."[2]

※

"We would not have called ourselves cold warriors," Bundy observed of the new Kennedy administration. But Kennedy's men were united in their awareness that the Cold War was a global competition, and they shared a belief that the United States "should play our necessary part." Bundy described the New Frontier mindset as one in which foreign policy was to be guided by considerations of national interest and a calculus of "circumstances and capabilities," which might take the form of a formal alliance, foreign assistance, or—if appropriate—disengagement.[3] He added: "To understand the American war in Vietnam we must understand the prevalence of strong political sentiment that it was right to oppose the world-wide expansionist effort of the Soviet Communists and their allies."[4]

The rising tensions of the Cold War contributed to an anxious political atmosphere in the 1960 presidential race between Senator Kennedy and Vice President Nixon. The election turned out to be the closest of the century. Of more than sixty-four million votes cast, Kennedy's margin of victory was approximately one hundred thousand, about one-tenth of 1 percent. Pivotal to Kennedy's victory was his adept and opportunistic positioning on national security. Relentlessly attacking from the right— campaigning aggressively against President Eisenhower's foreign policy record and, in part, on a mythical "missile gap"—the Democratic challenger crafted a message of toughness. That same message of resolve would be infused in Kennedy's soaring inaugural address in January 1961, which promised the world, "We shall pay any price, bear any burden, meet any hardship, support any friend, oppose any foe, in order to assure the survival and success of liberty."

McGeorge Bundy, a lifelong Republican, had spurned Nixon in 1960 to support Kennedy. The candidate was pleased to have his endorsement, said Bundy, "although reinforcement in Massachusetts was hardly his most urgent need."[5] In the weeks following Kennedy's razor-thin victory, prospective senior administration recruits—a talent pool drawn primarily from the Establishment waters between Washington and Boston—waited expectantly for an overture from the president-elect. Bundy was no exception. Sargent Shriver, the president-elect's brother-in-law, queried Bundy about his interest in joining the new administration. "For an interesting job," Bundy told him, "I would indeed be interested." About a week later Kennedy and Bundy met in New York. Bundy was offered the chance to work with the new secretary of state, Dean Rusk, as the third-ranking official in the State Department, undersecretary for political affairs. Bundy had already expressed to Kennedy his high esteem for Rusk, noting that a Harvard dean who did not know the president of the Rockefeller Foundation "was not doing his job." Bundy called Rusk "bright, experienced, and straight—I said he would be a good boss." Bundy returned to Cambridge "full of hope" but soon heard from Kennedy that the job they had discussed in fact did not exist.[6]

The snafu was the result of a Kennedy staff error. It was assumed that the State Department hierarchy would remain the same as it was in the Eisenhower administration, in which the number-two slot, held by the financier C. Douglas Dillon, was responsible for economic affairs. Kennedy explained that his nominee to serve as the number-two official at the State Department, Chester Bowles, would claim the politics portfolio rather than economics, meaning that the number-three slot would be filled by the undersecretary for economic affairs. "Neither you nor I could get away with that," Kennedy said, but he closed the call by promising he would get back to Bundy at some later date.[7]

Bundy remembered an interminable period of waiting following that telephone call with Kennedy, although it may not have lasted more than a week. Throughout he was comforted by the attentive telephone operators assisting the president-elect, who continually asked where the Harvard dean could be reached on short notice. They finally tracked Bundy down at a Manhattan restaurant where he and his wife were having dinner with their friends Kingman and Mary Louise Brewster. The president-elect had a new proposal. Unfortunately, it was even less appealing: Kennedy now offered Bundy the fourth slot at the State Department, the inglorious post of deputy undersecretary for administration. Bundy recalled that it was a perfectly dreary position, "the guy who watches the promotions and tends to the foreign service and goes up on the Hill and explains how the department doesn't cost as much as the Hill thinks it does, and so forth—*terrible* job." He had to find a politic way to decline. He asked Kennedy for ten minutes to mull over the offer and rushed back to the table.

"What the hell do I say?" Bundy asked Brewster, his college classmate who was now the provost of Yale University.

"I take it you don't *want* the job?" queried Brewster.

"I don't," Bundy declared.

"I take it you're perfectly willing not to get any job rather than take that job?" continued Brewster.

"That's right," Bundy said. "But I've got to have a good reason. I can't just say, 'It's not important enough for me.' "

"I tell you what you say," advised Brewster. "You call him up and say, you've *had* it with administration" and have been doing it for years.

Bundy called Kennedy to deliver the news. "I *can't* do it," he told the president-elect. "I've just *had* it with administration."

"Well, I can sure understand that," replied Kennedy. "We'll see what else we've got."

The next call from Kennedy came two days later, with an offer to serve as special assistant to the president for national security affairs.[8] Although Bundy did not know it at the time, he was not Kennedy's first choice for that position. The president-elect had already offered it to Paul Nitze, a veteran government official who had been the architect of NSC-68, a government strategy document drafted in 1950 for President Truman that became the foundation of America's Cold War containment policy. Doubting the influence he would have as a White House staffer, Nitze declined that post and instead accepted a senior assignment in the Pentagon. Kennedy confided to John Kenneth Galbraith that he had also considered offering the position of national security adviser to Arthur M. Schlesinger Jr.[9] Looking back, Bundy said he was fortunate that the State Department job Kennedy originally offered him did not exist and that Nitze had declined the White House position. "Paul really honestly thought that the special assistant's was a paper-pushing job," Bundy said, "and that the line departments were where the serious business got done."[10] Bundy was ultimately shrewder in crafting a path to power. "I wanted to join the Kennedy administration and I got the best job in sight," he said.[11]

At the time, and perhaps in the years that followed, Bundy may have harbored an ambition to be secretary of state, the one other position he was said to covet. During the transition there was some discussion about nominating him to be America's premier diplomat, a scenario supported by Walter Lippmann, the influential columnist. Theodore Sorensen, one of Kennedy's closest advisers, reports that the president-elect openly mused about appointing Bundy, arguing that he was a more dynamic choice than the two other finalists under consideration, Senator J. William Fulbright and Dean Rusk.[12] Bundy dismissed as "particularly foolish" the notion that he was a serious candidate for the job, noting that "a forty-three year old President from Massachusetts would not need as his senior Cabinet officer a forty-one year old Academic/Republican/Bostonian with no visible experience of government." He offered a facetious aside that nonetheless betrayed the insularity of his prior experience: "My Yale years might suggest breadth to Cambridge but not to Washington or the country."[13]

Bundy, of course, had an ideal profile to become one of Kennedy's men. The president-elect was searching for counselors with whom he felt comfortable but who were "also acceptable to what was then called the Establishment," Bundy observed. (He added that his experience was of limited relevance to the generations that followed, for whom "there is no recognizable Establishment left." Aspiring foreign policy experts "are expected to have battle scars" from experience in government or politics, he said, "and I think it's better so.") Bundy surmised that Kennedy perceived it advantageous that his prospective national security adviser was not only a Harvard dean but also a Republican who had strong affiliations with Henry Stimson and Dean Acheson.[14]

While much of the coverage of Bundy's appointment was fawning, the conventional wisdom was accompanied by another, less flattering perspective on his arrival in the White House. "He was bright and he was quick but even this bothered people around him," David Halberstam wrote. "They seemed to sense a lack of reflection, a lack of depth, a tendency to look at things tactically, functionally and operationally rather than intellectually; they believed Bundy thought that there was always a straight line between two points."[15] David Riesman, the sociologist whom Bundy had recruited to the Harvard faculty and considered a friend, was among those who viewed his political ascent with a degree of trepidation. When Bundy left Cambridge, said Riesman, "I grieved for Harvard and grieved for the nation; for Harvard because he was the perfect dean, for the nation because I thought that very same arrogance and hubris might be very dangerous."[16]

ॐ

The first major foreign policy decision in which Bundy participated became the signature failure of the entire Kennedy administration.

The new administration inherited a covert plan to topple the Cuban leader Fidel Castro with an invasion force of 1,300 exiles being trained in Guatemala. It was a CIA plot actively incubated under the Eisenhower administration—which had recently broken off diplomatic relations with Cuba—and then presented to the new president for execution within the first months of his administration. The code name for the invasion was "Operation Zapata."

In February 1961, just weeks after the president's inauguration, Bundy presented Kennedy with two papers on the proposed invasion. The first was from CIA deputy director Richard Bissell, a Groton graduate and Yale economics professor whom Bundy had known and been friendly with for years. Bissell had been one of the principal architects of the overthrow in 1954 of Guatemala's president, Jacobo Arbenz Guzmán, in a coup that had been actively lobbied for by the United Fruit Company. As he developed his plans for the exile invasion at the Bay of Pigs, Bissell had reassembled members of his Guatemala team, including the future Watergate burglar E. Howard Hunt.[17]

The second memo Bundy presented to Kennedy was from Thomas C. Mann, the recent assistant secretary of state for inter-American affairs and the new administration's ambassador to Mexico. In a cover memo to the president, Bundy called Bissell and Mann the "real antagonists at the staff level" on the invasion debate. Bissell, who aspired to succeed Allen Dulles as the head of the CIA, was the intelligence community's champion of Operation Zapata and managed its planning. Mann, who was not part of the intelligence apparatus, was highly dubious of the overthrow plot. He questioned the causal logic of the regime change scenario, doubting that an invasion by the small expatriate force would actually become the catalyst for a vast popular uprising across Cuba.[18]

Bundy was inclined to accept Bissell's sanguine projections. "Defense and CIA now feel quite enthusiastic about the invasion," he reported to President Kennedy in early February. "At the worst, they think the invaders would get into the mountains, and at the best, they think they might get a full-fledged civil war in which we could then back the anti-Castro forces openly."[19] Washington's support for the exiles, however, was already widely known, and rumors about Zapata quickly mutated into noisy media stories. On January 10, 1961, the *New York Times* had run a front-page article with the not-so-covert headline "U.S. Helps Train an Anti-Castro Force at Secret Guatemalan Base." The New York *Daily News* was reporting "35,000 saboteurs ready to strike from within. 6000 Cuban patriots ready to storm ashore."[20]

Bundy received private expressions of caution about Operation Zapata from his own colleagues. The young presidential aide Richard Goodwin anticipated the United States would fall into an untenable trap. "Even if the landings are successful and a revolutionary government is set up," he told Bundy, "they'll have to ask for our help. And if we agree, it'll be a massacre. . . . We'll have to fight house-to-house in Havana." Arthur Schlesinger Jr., who had also come to Washington from Cambridge to serve as an assistant to the president, sent Bundy a pair of memos opposing the invasion. "I am against it," he bluntly declared.[21]

Despite these pointed internal critiques of Operation Zapata—Goodwin's heresies so annoyed the national security adviser that the young speechwriter was banished from White House meetings on Cuba—Bundy continued to support the CIA plot.[22] In mid-March he told President Kennedy the agency had done "a remarkable job of reframing the landing plan so as to make it unspectacular and quiet, and plausibly Cuban in its essentials. I have been a skeptic about Bissell's operation, but now I think we are on the edge of a good answer."[23] Central questions nonetheless remained unaddressed. How probable was it that the exiles could stimulate a wider national revolt? How large would an uprising need to be to overwhelm Castro's state security forces? If the invasion failed to stimulate a popular revolt, how long and how effectively could a force of 1,300 Cuban exile soldiers fight Castro's much larger army? Was there any real evidence to support Bissell's claim that the exile force could sustain itself indefinitely? What were the military risks and potential contingencies associated with the invasion, including the potential need for American air support? In light of the rumors and the media reports, had operational security already been fatally compromised? The documentary record does not reflect any effort by Bundy to evaluate and mitigate these concerns.

On April 7, 1961, Schlesinger made a final appeal to the national security adviser. "Dick Goodwin and I met for breakfast to see whether it would be worth making one more try to reverse the decision," Schlesinger wrote in his journal. "But Bundy and Rostow joined us and discouraged our efforts."[24] Walt Rostow, who had been appointed as Bundy's deputy, was another academic talent recruited to the Kennedy administration. A former Rhodes Scholar and a Yale PhD who had taught economic history at Cambridge, Oxford, Columbia, and most recently the Massachusetts Institute of Technology, Rostow had a reputation as a bellicose anticommunist.[25] "He is absolutely interminable," said Bundy of Rostow's relentless hawkishness. His "view of the world . . . is always complete, three-dimensional, graphic and wrong."[26]

On Monday morning, April 17, 1961, the 1,300 members of the Cuban exile brigade landed on the beaches of the Bay of Pigs on Cuba's southwestern coast. Fighting with its back to the ocean and already infiltrated by Castro's agents, the exile brigade was outnumbered and outmaneuvered. Within a day it was surrounded by 20,000 Cuban troops. There were no stirrings of a spontaneous popular revolt that would sweep across Cuba. And in a stunningly inept lapse in planning, the exile force soon realized that eighty miles of swamp blocked its escape route into the mountains.[27] A crushing defeat was imminent.

As the grim reports poured into the White House, Rostow drove to CIA headquarters to meet with Bissell, his former professor, who was haggard, unshaven, and panicked. As the journalist and historian David Talbot notes, President Kennedy had insisted throughout the planning for the invasion that he would not intervene militarily to salvage the operation, at one point sending a military aide to the exiles' Central American training camp to reiterate that the U.S. Marines would not come to their rescue.[28] As Rostow met with Bissell and his aides, however, he soon realized that the CIA planners did not believe Kennedy would continue to withhold American military support if the success of the operation was imperiled. Such an outcome, Rostow later wrote, "was inconceivable to them."[29]

Rostow urged Bissell to make one final appeal to the president. A meeting was convened for shortly before midnight. As Talbot recounts, President Kennedy, Vice President Johnson, Secretary of State Rusk, and Secretary of Defense McNamara were all returning from a formal reception in the East Room, dressed in white tie and tails. They were joined by General Lyman Lemnitzer, the chairman of the Joint Chiefs of Staff, and Admiral Arleigh Burke, the chief of naval operations. Bissell, "acutely aware of the desperation of those whose lives were on the line," as he later recalled, made a passionate case for intervention.

"Let me take two jets and shoot down the enemy aircraft," he implored the president.

Kennedy refused, reminding Bissell and Burke that he had consistently insisted that no American military forces would be deployed to salvage the invasion. A heated exchange ensued. Burke grew angry. He pressed the president for just one destroyer, which would be sufficient to "knock the hell out of Castro's tanks."

"What if Castro's forces return the fire and hit the destroyer?" Kennedy asked.

"Then we'll knock the hell out of them!" the admiral promised.

"Burke, I don't want the United States involved in this," admonished Kennedy.

"Hell, Mr. President," retorted Burke, "but we *are* involved!"[30]

Bundy presented President Kennedy with a dire recitation of the facts on the afternoon of Tuesday, April 18: "The Cuban armed forces are stronger, the popular response is weaker, and our tactical position is feebler than we had hoped. Tanks have done in one beachhead, and the position is precarious at the others. . . . The real question is whether to reopen the possibility of further intervention and support or to accept the high prob-ability that our people, at best, will go into the mountains in defeat."[31] Kennedy did not waver. He refused to authorize the "further intervention" raised in Bundy's memo. The operation was doomed. "The secret hope of the leaders of the CIA," Bundy later acknowledged, was to pressure the president into reversing his position, a fact Bissell conceded in his mem-oirs.[32] "It wasn't in Bissell's mind that he was tricking the president," Bundy told me. "It was that Bissell was the inheritor of legitimacy who thought he knew what the national interest would require and what *any* president would see when the issue was sharply presented."[33]

Kennedy had anticipated Bissell's attempted manipulation. "They were sure I'd give in to them and send the go-ahead order to the *Essex*," Kennedy told his confidant Dave Powers. "They couldn't believe that a new president like me wouldn't panic and try to save his own face. Well they had me figured all wrong."[34] In 2005 a government document sur-faced that confirmed the CIA expectation that the Bay of Pigs invasion would fail without direct American military support. The intelligence memorandum, dated November 15, 1960, concluded that an invasion would be "unachievable, except as joint Agency/DOD action"—in other words, a dual invasion conducted by both the CIA and the Depart-ment of Defense.[35] But this conclusion was never shared with the White House.

By the end of the week, 114 Cuban exile fighters had been killed and 1,189 had been captured. American responsibility for the operation was quickly exposed, humiliating the Kennedy administration and prompt-ing a wave of global condemnation.[36] The debacle ensured that Kennedy and his top military advisers would never have confidence in one another again. "Pulling out the rug," General Lemnitzer later remarked, was "unbelievable . . . absolutely reprehensible, almost criminal."

For his part, Kennedy was determined not to repeat his mistakes, as-suring Arthur Schlesinger Jr. that he would never again be "overawed by professional military advice." Speaking to his friend Red Fay, whom he had appointed assistant secretary of the navy, Kennedy insisted, "Nobody is going to force me to do anything I don't think is in the best interests of the country." The president added: "We're not going to plunge into an irresponsible action just because a fanatical fringe in this country puts so-called national pride above national reason."[37] Kennedy made a similar point to Schlesinger, dismissing the notion that American prestige would suffer if the cause of the Cuban rebels was not once more embraced. "What is prestige?" asked the president. "Is it the shadow of power or the substance of power? We are going to work on the substance of power. No doubt we will be kicked in the ass for the next couple of weeks, but that won't affect the main business."[38]

As the full scope of the Bay of Pigs disaster became clear, Bundy offered his resignation. "You know that I wish I had served you better in the Cuban episode, and I hope you know how I admire your own gallantry under fire in that case," he wrote to the president. "If my departure can assist you in any way, I hope you will send me off—and if you choose differently, you will still have this letter for use when you may need it."[39] Bundy was not fired. Instead Kennedy pulled him closer, installing Bundy in a basement office in the West Wing, where his proximity would provide greater access to the president and, presumably, greater influence. Kennedy also authorized the creation of the White House Situation Room, which would function as the central node of communications for the government's disparate national security agencies. For his part, Bundy pondered the lessons of the Bay of Pigs disaster. He summarized his insights in an April 24 memorandum whose pithy conclusion was rich in dispassionate self-criticism of the young administration's failures in Cuba and prescient in anticipating some of the same challenges for strategy in Vietnam. "The morals of those failures are readily drawn . . . ," Bundy advised. "The President's advisers must speak up in council. . . . The President and his advisers must second-guess even military plans. . . . We must estimate the enemy without hope or fear. . . . Those who are to offer serious advice on major issues must themselves do the necessary work. . . . The President's desires must be fully acted on, and he must know the full state of mind of friends whose lives his decisions affect. . . . Forced choices are seldom as necessary as they seem. . . . What is and is not implied in any specific partial decision must always be thought through."[40]

In the aftermath of the failed invasion, Kennedy transferred authority for covert paramilitary operations from the CIA to the Department of Defense and fired Dulles and Bissell.[41] Looking back on the Bay of Pigs disaster, Bundy wrote sympathetically about Bissell, suggesting that his "mistakes, large as they are, pale in comparison to his achievements," such as the implementation of the Marshall Plan and the creation of the CIA's U-2 aerial surveillance system.[42] Yet Bundy also admitted that "one of the reasons I was inefficient was that my favorite college teacher was in charge, Dickie Bissell."[43] Bundy's close relationship with Bissell may have compromised his judgment and thus his counsel to President Kennedy. "It never *occurred* to me," he explained, that Bissell "was so captured by his own goddamned invention of this invasion that he would accept adjustments and limitations, because *his* political judgment was when you really get down to it you need to be rescued or surrender. The president will *have* to act. So it was an entrapment."[44]

Bundy retrospectively focused on the military's responsibility for the failed invasion. "One could *imagine* the Brigade succeeding on its own," he wrote, "but should one really bet a brand-new Presidency on such a gamble?" In the aftermath of the failed invasion, Bundy observed, President Kennedy assigned particular blame to the Joint Chiefs of Staff, who possessed the greatest expertise for judging the operation's prospects for military success yet still appeared to endorse it. "What he neglected, and what I for one was too green to recognize and point out," was the perceived inhibition on the part of the Pentagon to challenge the CIA's plans. The chiefs "were bureaucratically cautious about dissecting another agency's most cherished enterprise."[45]

The Bay of Pigs was an "initial baptism of power," Bundy concluded, "because it's sitting there, right there, loaded, ready to go off, won't keep, has to be decided."[46] It also remained somewhat mystifying. "You know what we still don't know about the Bay of Pigs?" asked Bundy. "What did Eisenhower think *he* was going to do? He never told anybody."[47]

Despite its enormous political costs, Bundy believed the Bay of Pigs ultimately strengthened Kennedy. "This is a detached and self-contained human being who, as far as I perceive him, had enormous inner confidence," Bundy told the political scientist Richard Neustadt in 1964, speaking of the president. Bundy noted "the number of times he had accomplished things that people said could not be accomplished. So that 'no' was a word he was used to hearing and used to disproving. . . . The great blow of the Bay of Pigs was that it broke the picture of infallibility and its great service to him was that it did exactly that."[48]

At a moment just before that aura of infallibility was shattered, President Kennedy met at the White House with Bundy and four other advisers: Arthur Schlesinger Jr., Dean Rusk, Richard Bissell, and Adolf Berle, a Columbia Law School professor affiliated with the State Department. It was Saturday, April 15, according to Schlesinger, "as the pace of action began to mount in Cuba." The group, he recalled, was "discussing the next step with the president, when Mac brought down the house—and especially JFK—by saying . . . 'Mr. President, do you realize that you are surrounded by five ex-professors?' "[49] Bundy recalled telling Kennedy "in a cheerful way that this was bound to be all right" because of his advisers' academic stature, "and I've often hoped that he didn't remember that remark, because I remember it so well. But he did go through a process of saying there must never be another Cuba. I remember his remarking to me that in any other form of democratic government he would be out of office on the strength of the Bay of Pigs, and that no English Prime

Minister could have survived. . . . He used to say, 'Well, at least I've got three more years—nobody could take that away from me.' "[50]

There was at least one other lesson to be learned from the Bay of Pigs. Despite pressure from the CIA and the Joint Chiefs, Kennedy did not capitulate on the basic question of maintaining firm presidential authority over the deployment of military force. "Kennedy had refused that support and the lesson was burned into his mind: the Commander-in-Chief had better be careful to ensure his own control over the use of American combat forces. *He* is the one who will inevitably be held accountable for their success or failure." Bundy added that while counselors to the president may pursue agendas of their own which were "usually honorable and sometimes right," he cautioned such aides were "not necessarily thinking about the *President's* responsibility."[51]

୬୮

Just as Kennedy rejected his advisers' entreaties to salvage the hapless Bay of Pigs invasion, the new president would have to exercise similar resolve in deflecting proposals to intervene in Laos, an Asian country ten thousand miles away, sandwiched between Vietnam and Thailand.

A growing distress over the fate of Laos was evident even before Kennedy's inauguration. On his last full day in office, President Eisenhower provided Kennedy and several of his key advisers with an alarming national security presentation, focused, improbably, on the fate of Laos. Clark Clifford, a prominent Washington lawyer and fixture of the Democratic Party, attended the meeting as Kennedy's private counsel. "It may seem incredible in retrospect," he wrote, "but the outgoing President considered the fate of that tiny, landlocked Southeast Asian kingdom the most important problem facing the U.S." If Laos fell to the communists, Eisenhower warned, then South Vietnam, Cambodia, Thailand, and Burma would follow.[52] Eisenhower's fixation with Laos was consistent with a larger worldview. During his presidency, he had become a committed adherent to the "domino theory," which envisaged the successive collapse of teetering states into the orbit of communist power—like so many clattering dominos falling in a row.

As Kennedy assumed office, Laos was a nation in disarray and a presumptive target for insurrection. Three factions fought for control of the country: the communist movement Pathet Lao, which was committed to Prince Souphanouvong; a neutralist group loyal to Prince Souvanna Phouma; and government loyalists led by General Phoumi Nosavan. The third faction became the focus of U.S. policy. "There's a special niche in John Kennedy's picture of international statesmen," said Bundy, "in which the stubborn weak—who insist on things they can't do for themselves, and that it is not in the interest of the United States to do for them, are enthroned—and General Phoumi Nosavan is in that category." As a result, "you literally had no choice but to work for a neutralization in Laos" because ensuring Phoumi Nosavan's control of the country would have required "a wholly undesirable level of military investment."[53]

Disregarding Eisenhower's more hawkish advice, on March 23, 1961, President Kennedy affirmed his desire for a "neutral and independent Laos." Peace talks proceeded in Geneva, where the United States was represented by the industrialist and former New York governor Averell Harriman, who was known affectionately within the White House as "The Crocodile." ("He just lies up there on the riverbank, his eyes half closed, looking sleepy," Bundy explained. "Then, *whap*, he bites.")[54]

As Harriman proceeded along a diplomatic track, the Defense Department warned of the need for possible military action in Southeast Asia. On April 26, just days after the Bay of Pigs debacle, the Joint Chiefs of Staff issued a global advisory to major U.S. military bases around the world. It reported that in response to new advances by the communist Pathet Lao insurgency in Laos, the Pacific Command was instructed to prepare for potential air strikes against North Vietnam and perhaps southern China.[55]

In a turbid meeting of the National Security Council the following day, Admiral Burke sat in for the chairman of the Joint Chiefs of Staff. The navy chief recommended the deployment of a large force from member nations of the Southeast Asia Treaty Organization (SEATO) to defend the Laotian capital, Vientiane, from imminent collapse. According to notes of the meeting, Burke argued, "strongly and repeatedly" that without U.S. intervention, "all Southeast Asia will be lost."[56] Bundy recalled that Kennedy, who had served in the navy, "did not miss the irony that among his chief military advisers one energetic supporter of a large operation in Laos"—which is landlocked—"was the Chief of Naval operations, who had nothing to fear from the Laotian navy."[57]

Confusion mounted. "The participants in the meeting found it hard to make out what the Chiefs were trying to say," Schlesinger recounts. The military recommendations were so numerous and convoluted that Vice President Johnson asked that they be put in writing. "The President, it is said, later received seven different memoranda, from the four Chiefs of Staff and three service secretaries. It was about this time that a group of foreign students visited the White House and the President, introduced to a young lady from Laos, remarked 'Has anyone asked your advice yet?' "[58]

With disorder reigning among his advisers, on May 1 Kennedy convened another meeting of the National Security Council. The Bay of Pigs humiliation was very much on his mind. "That operation had been recommended principally by the same set of advisers who favored intervention in Laos," recalled Theodore Sorensen. "But now the President was far more skeptical of the experts, their reputations, their recommendations, their promises, premises and facts. He relied more on his White House staff and his own common sense; and he asked the Attorney General [his brother, Robert F. Kennedy] and me to attend all NSC meetings." The majority of Kennedy's advisers favored the deployment of combat troops to South Vietnam, Thailand, and government-controlled positions in the

Laotian panhandle. If that failed to produce a cease-fire, Kennedy was advised to use tactical nuclear weapons and air strikes against the Pathet Lao. If China or North Vietnam intervened, those countries should be bombed and, if necessary, attacked with nuclear weapons.

Confronted with his military advisers' apocalyptic scenarios, Kennedy commenced a fairly withering interrogation: If the United States used nuclear weapons where would it stop? What other communist powers would the United States have to attack? Without nuclear weapons would the United States have to retreat? Or would Washington be forced to surrender in the face of a massive Chinese intervention? Is this, Kennedy asked, the best bet for a U.S. confrontation with China—in the mountains and jungles of its landlocked neighbor? Would deployments to Laos weaken the reserves to defend Berlin? Would forces landing in Vietnam and Thailand assume the responsibility of defending those regimes, too?[59]

Keenly doubtful of his military guidance, Kennedy decided to use the *threat* of force and press for a diplomatic outcome to the crisis. He conspicuously put ten thousand marines stationed on Okinawa on high alert, after which the communist and noncommunist factions agreed to a cease-fire. "If it hadn't been for Cuba," Kennedy told Schlesinger on May 3, "we might be about to intervene in Laos." He dismissively brandished a pile of memos from General Lemnitzer, adding, "I might have taken this advice seriously."[60] That summer Harriman successfully brokered a neutralization agreement at the Geneva conference, and American military action in Laos was averted.

President Kennedy's first critical decision in Southeast Asia, Bundy concluded, was equivalent to "an operational rejection of the domino theory." He also noted that Eisenhower in office had resisted "the deeper commitment he now urged on his young successor, but Kennedy eagerly chose to follow his example and not his advice."[61] He added, "I've heard the President say—and I'm quite sure that he meant it—that it would have been very much harder for him to decide not to move further into Laos if it hadn't been for the Bay of Pigs." President Kennedy, recalled Bundy, "made a special effort to look coolly on this kind of problem, and the Laos decisions were different, I'm sure, because the Bay of Pigs happened."[62]

જે

The Cold War competition between the United States and the Soviet Union made partition a logical and common feature of the geopolitical order—Germany was divided in two, as was Berlin, Korea, and Vietnam. Thus to most of Kennedy's men the contest in Vietnam represented yet another game board in the larger conflict with international communism. The new reality of two Vietnams, however, obscured an instructive history. From its earliest origins, Vietnam fit the paradigm of a classic small power repeatedly challenged to fight fierce wars of resistance against larger invading and occupying forces.

Following approximately one thousand years of domination by China, the Vietnamese launched their first rebellion in AD 39, led by the Trung sisters, who to this day are celebrated as among the greatest heroes of Vietnamese civilization. Mounted on elephants, the sisters led a futile battle against far superior Chinese forces. When defeat was imminent they chose martyrdom rather than surrender, drowning themselves in a Hanoi lake. Two centuries later, another female warrior, Trieu Au, stood at the head of an anti-Chinese uprising, but she, too, was defeated. It was not until the tenth century that the Vietnamese finally won their independence. The decisive victory came when the rebels destroyed a Chinese fleet by luring it into a river where they had planted iron-tipped spikes. In the thirteenth century Vietnam repulsed three Mongol invasions, and in 1426 it beat back another attack from the Chinese. When the French arrived and imposed a colonial regime in the late nineteenth and early twentieth centuries, the Vietnamese gravitated toward a more ideological form of resistance. In 1930 the French put down a revolt by intellectuals in the northern cities while also suppressing communist-backed rebellions by workers and peasants in the central part of the country. But as World War II drew to a close in August and September 1945, the League for Vietnamese Independence, known as Vietminh, assumed power and declared the country's independence following a months-long campaign of harassment against the Japanese occupation.[63]

Ho Chi Minh, the leader of the Vietminh movement, sought diplomatic recognition from the United States but was summarily rebuffed. The Truman administration was eager for French partnership to counter the growing power of the Soviet Union and readily acquiesced in France's desire to reassert its colonial presence. The United States provided naval vessels, aircraft, and arms to the French forces in Indochina, and by 1952 it was underwriting more than 40 percent of the cost of the war. By 1953, U.S. aid to France had grown to $800 million.[64]

Despite robust American support, the French occupation was under siege from a methodical, disciplined, and intensely determined Vietminh military campaign. The endgame played out at Dien Bien Phu, an expansive valley area three hundred miles west of Hanoi, the Vietnamese capital. Protected by thousand-foot hills considered too difficult to mount with artillery, the roughly sixteen thousand elite French paratroopers stationed in Dien Bien Phu were thought to be invulnerable. Their commander, General Henri Navarre, was confident he could annihilate the poorly equipped Vietminh troops that were forced to attack from exposed positions. He promised victory over the insurgents by the end of 1955.

In the first days of 1954 three divisions of Vietminh troops quietly scaled the hills that encircled the French garrison, hauling artillery and rocket launchers behind them. Remarkably undetected, an army of fifty thousand Vietminh soldiers now surrounded the French. They were led by General Vo Nguyen Giap, the architect of a new strategic concept for guerilla warfare. General Giap's war-fighting doctrine emphasized sustained endurance and diversified avenues of attack. "Accumulate a thousand small victories to turn into one great success," he wrote.[65] Supplementing the seven principles of guerrilla war enunciated by the Chinese communist leader Mao Zedong, Giap articulated four of his own: "If the enemy advances, we retreat. If he halts, we harass. If he avoids battle, we attack. If he retreats, we follow."[66]

Back in Washington, President Eisenhower proclaimed his opposition to any deployment of U.S. combat troops to assist the French. At a meeting of the National Security Council on January 8, 1954, Eisenhower called U.S. intervention "simply beyond contemplation." He presciently insisted, "There was just no sense in even talking about United States forces replacing the French in Indochina. If we did so, the Vietnamese could be expected to transfer their hatred of the French to us." Eisenhower added (with "vehemence," according to the official notes), "I cannot tell you . . . how bitterly opposed I am to such a course of action. This war in Indochina would absorb our troops by divisions!"[67] The president also rejected the appeals made by some of his more hawkish advisers. "When we talk about Dien Bien Phu, maybe I need to tell you this," he later confided to the newspaper publisher Roy Howard, in a secretly taped conversation, "but I was the only one around here who was against American forces going in. I tell you, the boys were putting the heat on me."[68] On May 7, 1954, after repeated "human wave" assaults by Vietminh troops and fifty-five days of bombardment with an estimated 1,500 tons of ammunition, the French garrison was finally overwhelmed.[69]

France signed an armistice in July 1954, ending French colonialism in Southeast Asia and creating the separate states of Vietnam, Laos, and Cambodia. Vietnam was temporarily divided along the seventeenth parallel into two spheres of influence—the North controlled by the Vietminh alliance and the South by the Western powers. The agreement called for nationwide elections in 1956 and prohibited the introduction of foreign troops or the establishment of foreign military bases.

South Vietnam's new leader was Ngo Dinh Diem. A Catholic ruling a nation of Buddhists, Diem came to power by rigging a plebiscite and successfully claiming 99 percent of the vote, thus deposing Bao Dai, the French puppet emperor. Diem refused to hold the countrywide elections designed to precede national reunification. A political realist, Diem knew that he would be crushed in an electoral contest against Ho Chi Minh and his Vietminh followers.

The Eisenhower administration supported the decision to cancel elections. So did Senator John F. Kennedy, who was part of a growing constituency interested in South Vietnam's role in Asia's regional security framework.[70] "Vietnam represents the cornerstone of the Free World in Southeast Asia," he said, "the keystone to the arch, the finger in the dike."[71] But Kennedy was also strongly opposed to the United States replicating the French military commitment to the South Vietnamese government in Saigon. In 1952, when he was still in the House of Representatives, Kennedy had visited Vietnam and conferred with General Navarre's predecessor, General Jean de Lattre de Tassigny. "We have allied ourselves to the desperate effort of a French regime to hang onto the remnants of an empire," Kennedy said on the floor of the House upon his return. "I am frankly of the belief that no amount of American military assistance in Indochina can conquer an enemy which is everywhere and at the same time nowhere . . . The forces of nationalism are rewriting the geopolitical map of the world."[72]

The growing threat of Vietminh infiltration prompted Diem's security forces to become even more brutal. Vietminh suspects sometimes were beaten, had their legs broken, or were raped. In 1959 Diem passed a law restoring the guillotine, and mobile military courts in the countryside were authorized to behead convicted communists.[73] By 1961, as Kennedy assumed power in Washington, the situation in South Vietnam was characterized by an ascending nationalist and communist movement and an oppressive regime that was progressively losing control of the country and credibility with its people.

Among the first official reports the Kennedy administration received came from General Edward Lansdale, the deputy assistant to the secretary of defense for special operations. Lansdale, an air force officer, had an extensive background in advising Asian governments on counterinsurgency strategy.[74] In January 1961, Lansdale toured South Vietnam to assess the intensity of the communist guerrilla movement. "The U.S should recognize that Vietnam is in critical condition and should treat it as a combat area of the cold war, as an area requiring emergency treatment," he reported.[75] Lansdale's warning was repeated by an interagency task force in Saigon, known as the U.S. Country Team Staff Committee. It concluded that without extraordinary action the South Vietnamese regime could be overthrown in months.[76]

The president convened his top advisers on Saturday morning, January 28, 1961, for the first formal meeting on Vietnam. Kennedy introduced a tone of skepticism to the dialogue with his counselors that would come to define his approach to American strategy in the country. "The President remarked that if the situation in Vietnam was now so serious he wondered why the recruitment of troops and training of police, who could become effective only a year or two hence, would be of any use," report the minutes of the meeting. "He also wondered why, if there were only 10,000 guerrillas, an increase from 150 to 170,000 in the army was necessary."[77] The president asked if "this order of magnitude of increase in the armed forces of Viet-Nam would really permit a shift from the defense to the offense. He asked whether the situation was not basically one of politics and morale."[78] On February 6 Kennedy instructed General Lemnitzer to ensure that the South Vietnamese army was deployed more coherently. "I would think that the redistribution of available forces immediately would make them more effective," he stated.[79]

The central threat in Southeast Asia in 1961, Bundy would recall, was the possibility that communist forces would wrest control of the entire country of Vietnam. "The instruments of their advance were both political and military," he wrote, while Washington's response had been limited to different forms of economic and political support to South Vietnam, supplemented by a small military advisory mission. "The existing policy was not likely to prevent an eventual communist victory," Bundy observed. "What should the new administration do?"

Bundy recalled that from the beginning the president's interest in Vietnam was trained on the premise and potential for the United States to assist Saigon "at levels of conflict short of the engagement of U.S. combat troops." For Kennedy, "advice and support, especially on unconventional warfare, were attractive," and he remained "regularly on the side of a diversified and innovative effort" that would take the form of varied programs to enhance the capacity of South Vietnam to contain a growing insurgency. What followed was an increase in expenditures and manpower devoted to South Vietnam. Bundy remarked that "both of these expansions were large against what we had before, and small compared to what came later."[80]

In April, Kennedy appointed Deputy Secretary of Defense Roswell L. Gilpatric to head the Presidential Task Force on Vietnam. In a memo to the president, Robert McNamara promised that the Defense Department would develop a "program of action to prevent Communist domination of South Viet-Nam."[81] The first version of that action program was a rambling assemblage of proposals to counter "the Communist 'master plan' to take over all of Southeast Asia."[82] On April 27 a draft of the report with an attached annex was forwarded to the president. The annex recommended the deployment of a small contingent of U.S. combat troops as a symbol of American commitment to South Vietnam. In Bundy's formulation, the term "combat troops" conveyed a specific definition and function: "U.S. Army or Marine forces—infantry, artillery, armor, or airborne—in companies, battalions, regiments, or divisions. Such units are here distinguished from supply and service forces and also from air forces and still more sharply distinguished from personnel whose mission was to advise or assist or support South Vietnamese combat forces."[83]

The next day another version of the annex was circulated, this time proposing the deployment of 3,600 U.S. ground combat troops to train two new South Vietnamese divisions and an American Special Forces unit to accelerate counterinsurgency training.[84] Kennedy endorsed the proposals of the draft report but not the recommendations for combat troops contained in the report's annex.[85]

The rejection of the combat troop proposal would be the first iteration of a repeated pattern pitting Kennedy against his counselors. Time and again, senior military and national security officials would directly recommend to the president that he deploy ground combat troops to Vietnam. Kennedy, in turn, would divert, defer, or deny their recommendations. As the thrust and parry between the president and his men continued through 1961, the proposed scope of the American commitment to Vietnam would grow.

On May 8, Gilpatric queried the Joint Chiefs: "In preparation for the possible commitment of US forces to Vietnam, it is desired that you give further review and study of the military advisability of such action, as well as to the size and composition of such forces." The chiefs replied, "Assuming that the political decision is to hold Southeast Asia outside the Communist sphere, the Joint Chiefs of Staff are of the opinion that U.S. forces should be deployed immediately to South Vietnam."[86]

President Kennedy did not approve the combat troop commitment recommended by the Joint Chiefs. But at a National Security Council meeting on May 11, he allowed the question to be analyzed further.[87] On May 18, the chiefs restated their recommendation. Lieutenant General Lionel McGarr, head of the American Military Assistance Advisory Group in Saigon, proposed a force of sixteen thousand combat forces. If President Diem resisted, McGarr suggested a force of ten thousand soldiers with the mission of establishing Vietnamese military training centers. McGarr's recommendation was supported by General Lansdale.[88] As observed in the *Pentagon Papers*, the secret Defense Department history of

Vietnam policy, senior officials were "primarily interested in getting U.S. combat units into Vietnam, with the training mission as a possible device for getting Diem to accept them."[89]

The deployment of U.S. combat troops to South Vietnam—to serve variously as a deterrent, a symbol of determination, or a means to train Saigon's army—had now been proposed five times: twice through the Gilpatric report and three times through the Joint Chiefs and by McGarr and Lansdale. Soon the Joint Chiefs found a fourth rationale to deploy American combat forces to the region. In a July 12 memorandum to McNamara, the chiefs asked for a formal decision to withdraw from the Laos negotiations at the next breach of the cease-fire. They recommended military intervention—with or without SEATO allies—to bolster the American negotiating position.[90] Walt Rostow supported the chiefs' proposal, recommending to Dean Rusk that the United States take air and naval action against North Vietnam as a means to influence the settlement in Laos.[91]

General Maxwell Taylor also favored a more assertive military posture in Southeast Asia. Taylor was a legendary soldier who had served as superintendent of West Point, commander of Allied troops in Berlin, and army chief of staff under Eisenhower. Following the Bay of Pigs fiasco, Kennedy asked Taylor to chair a task force to investigate the failed invasion. After concluding his inquiry, Taylor was appointed by Kennedy to serve as military representative to the president—in essence, Kennedy's personal military adviser. On July 15 General Taylor instructed the chiefs "to produce an outline plan" for military action in Southeast Asia.[92]

Twelve days later, Taylor and Rostow submitted their own memorandum to Kennedy that proposed three alternative approaches to Vietnam. In the time-honored tradition of Washington bureaucrats, they offered two extreme options that the president would be compelled to summarily reject and a middle course leading Kennedy down a path they ostensibly wished him to follow. One option called for the United States to "disengage from the area as gracefully as possible," ensuring a disastrous strategic loss that Taylor and Rostow characterized as unacceptable. Another option proposed that Washington "find a convenient political pretext and attack . . . the regional source of aggression in Hanoi," thus risking an immediately enlarged conflict in Vietnam and a potential war with China. By comparison, the middle option they advocated was both less damaging to American strategic interests and less precipitous in the risks it posed. It called for the United States to "build as much indigenous military, political and economic strength as we can in the area, in order to contain the thrust from Hanoi while preparing to intervene with US military force if the Chinese Communists come in or the situation otherwise gets out of hand. We assume it is the policy of this administration to pursue the third strategy," Taylor and Rostow advised, helpfully adding, "but some discussion of the alternatives may be useful."[93]

Kennedy made little effort to conceal his leeriness. In Bundy's contemporaneous notes of a July 28 meeting, "Questions from the President showed that the detailed aspects of this military plan had not been developed . . . The President made clear his own deep concern with the need for realism and accuracy in . . . military planning." Kennedy underscored that the Pentagon's atrocious performance in the Laos episode had eroded his confidence. "He had observed in earlier military plans with respect to Laos that optimistic estimates were invariably proven false in the event . . . He emphasized the reluctance of the American people and of many distinguished military leaders to see any direct involvement of U.S. troops in that part of the world."

Kennedy's men pushed back, arguing, as Bundy recorded, "that with a proper plan, with outside support, and above all with a clear and open commitment, the results would be very different from anything that had happened before. The president was not persuaded, remarking that General de Gaulle, out of painful French experience, had spoken with feeling of the difficulty of fighting in this part of the world."[94] Vice President

Johnson called for a more explicit military commitment to the region, including Laos, and a presidential decision to intervene if necessary.[95] "The President in reply offered no decision," Bundy continued, "but he made it very plain that he himself at present is very reluctant to make a decision to go into Laos . . . that nothing would be worse than an unsuccessful intervention in this area, and that he did not yet have confidence in the military practicability of the proposal which had been put before him."[96]

Despite Kennedy's continuing resistance to the combat troop proposal, the president's advisers continued to churn out new deployment recommendations. Drawing on previous proposals from Rostow, Taylor, the Joint Chiefs, and the Southeast Asia Task Force, Deputy Undersecretary of State U. Alexis Johnson elaborated on a "Concept for Intervention in Vietnam" at an October 11 White House meeting. Johnson, firmly aligned with the growing consensus for ground forces, proposed the deployment of 11,000 combat troops to be drawn from a total SEATO force of 22,800. Kennedy once again did not approve any new deployments but agreed to allow further discussion. He also authorized a mission to the region by Taylor and Rostow.[97]

The possibility of a U.S. combat troop deployment to South Vietnam quickly leaked to the press. "One question receiving considerable attention here in light of the Taylor mission is the desirability of sending United States troops to South Vietnam," the *New York Times* reported from Saigon on October 13.[98] Furious with the unauthorized disclosure, Kennedy swiftly orchestrated a leak of his own. "Military leaders at the Pentagon, no less than General Taylor himself are understood to be reluctant to send organized U.S. combat units into Southeast Asia," the *Times* clarified on October 14. "Pentagon plans for this area stress the importance of countering Communist guerrillas with troops from the affected countries, perhaps trained and equipped by the U.S., but not supplanted by U.S. troops."[99]

On October 16 the U.S. ambassador in Saigon, Frederick Nolting, reported that President Diem had requested a bilateral security treaty with the United States "and secondly and perhaps alternatively for the dispatch of US combat forces."[100] By October 18, however, Diem had reversed himself, indicating that he would not seek U.S. combat troops after all.[101]

Nolting disregarded President Diem's change of heart. He cabled Washington on October 20 arguing that a severe flood in the Mekong Delta region offered an auspicious opportunity for a "fast public demonstration of unity of purpose and action." The flood, he suggested, could be used as a pretext for "introducing . . . US military units for humanitarian purposes, which might be kept if necessary."[102] Taylor applauded the proposal. "To relate the introduction of these troops to the needs of flood relief seems to me to offer considerable advantages," he explained in an October 25 cable from Saigon. Taylor recommended an initial deployment of between six thousand and eight thousand combat troops.[103]

Newspaper articles again pointed to the possibility of the first U.S. combat force deployments to South Vietnam. Using Bundy as his enforcer, Kennedy ordered General Taylor to plug the leaks. "The President requests that your conclusions on Vietnam, especially those relating to U.S. forces, not be discussed outside your own immediate party in terms which would indicate your own final judgment," Bundy wrote to Taylor on October 28. "He is most concerned that you and he should have firm common ground when decisions are taken, and rumors of your conclusions could obviously be damaging."[104]

An undaunted Taylor continued to press his recommendation. He reported on October 31 that ten days of discussions in South Vietnam reflected "a virtually unanimous desire" for American forces. His conclusion was "based on unsolicited remarks from cabinet ministers, National Assembly Deputies, university professors, students, shopkeepers, and oppositionists." There was similar support outside Saigon. In Hue, said Taylor, "opinion among intellectuals and government officials in that city is almost unanimously in favor of introduction of American combat troops."[105]

Senator Mike Mansfield, the Democratic majority leader, wrote to Kennedy to express his alarm at the press reports of a potential major shift in U.S. policy. The deployment of combat forces to defend South Vietnam, he cautioned, "could be a kind of quicksand for us. Where does an involvement of this kind end even if we can bring it to a successful conclusion?"[106]

The Taylor mission returned to Washington and submitted its report to Kennedy on November 3. It advised the president "to introduce into South Vietnam a military Task Force to operate under US control," which would, among other missions, "conduct such combat operations as are necessary for self-defense and for the security of the area in which they are stationed." The American troops would also constitute "an emergency reserve to back up the Armed Forces" of the South Vietnamese army "in the case of a heightened military crisis."[107] General Taylor again proposed the flood-relief mission as the cover story for the combat troop deployment.[108]

Secretary of Defense McNamara joined the emerging consensus in support of Taylor's recommendation. The time had come, he argued at a November 4 meeting, to "tell the world and the US what our commitment really is; the '8000 man' force does not convince anyone of our resolve." Raising the stakes enormously, McNamara now declared that six to eight divisions would be required to meet communist escalation in Southeast Asia.[109] With one swift game-changing maneuver, McNamara shifted the debate from a focus on a small initial American deployment to the potentially broader commitment of perhaps more than 200,000 combat troops.

With his secretary of defense and personal military counselor now privately lobbying for combat force deployments to South Vietnam, Kennedy again went on the offensive, leaking stories to discredit the proposal in the press. One article reported that the president "remains strongly opposed to the dispatch of American combat troops to South

Vietnam" and implied that General Taylor had not recommended such a commitment.[110]

Ignoring Kennedy's now unambiguous and increasingly public opposition, McNamara plowed ahead. In a November 5 memorandum he again argued that the United States might be forced to deploy at least six combat divisions to forestall South Vietnam from collapsing into the communist orbit.[111] "The chances are against, probably sharply against, preventing that fall by any measures short of the introduction of US forces on a substantial scale," McNamara warned.[112] The Joint Chiefs supported the defense secretary's grim prognosis, conceding that an initial deployment of eight thousand men should be considered only part of a potentially larger commitment of combat troops.[113] The limited combat troop deployment proposed by Taylor under the guise of assisting with flood relief had now mutated into a down payment on a vast American ground force commitment to defend South Vietnam from its communist insurgency. McNamara was in essence recommending the Americanization of the Vietnam War.

On November 7, President Kennedy's most senior advisers prepared a stark summary of their views. "The Secretary of State, the Secretary of Defense and the Joint Chiefs of Staff agree: The fall of South Vietnam to Communism would lead to the fairly rapid extension of Communist control, or complete accommodation to Communism, in the rest of mainland Southeast Asia and in Indonesia. The strategic implications worldwide, particularly in the Orient, would be extremely serious. . . . The chances are against, probably sharply against, preventing the fall of South Viet-Nam by any measures short of the introduction of U.S. forces on a substantial scale." The memorandum anticipated a prolonged struggle and the possibility of North Vietnamese or Chinese intervention, which would require the deployment of as many as six divisions totaling 205,000 men. Rusk, McNamara, and the Joint Chiefs now proposed a revolutionary transformation of U.S. national security strategy in Southeast Asia. It was time, they recommended, "to commit ourselves to the objective of preventing the fall of South Viet-Nam to Communism and the willingness to commit whatever United States combat forces may be necessary to achieve this objective."[114] The following day another draft of the memorandum was circulated, repeating their dire warning. McNamara, Rusk, and the chiefs proposed an initial deployment of U.S. combat forces along the border with North Vietnam.[115]

With the State and Defense departments as well as the Joint Chiefs now united in their support for a potentially vast combat troop commitment to South Vietnam, Kennedy turned to a trusted colleague for advice. John Kenneth Galbraith, the Harvard economist who had been an undergraduate tutor and friend since the president's college years, was now serving as the U.S. ambassador to India. On the evening of November 8, President and Mrs. Kennedy held a small dinner party for Galbraith and British ambassador David Ormsby-Gore. The timing of the event was propitious. Galbraith had been conducting a private correspondence with Kennedy about Vietnam for months, and he shared the president's deep reservations about a major U.S. military commitment there.[116] Rostow and Taylor "are advocating exceedingly half-baked intervention," Galbraith recorded in his diary. At dinner his differences with Bundy erupted in a "very frank and at times heated" argument.[117] Appreciating Kennedy's need for an independent analysis of the situation, Galbraith offered to stop over in Saigon on his way back to India. Kennedy immediately accepted his offer.[118] Galbraith would remain an influential back-channel adviser on the question of Vietnam throughout Kennedy's presidency.

Undersecretary of State George Ball was another of the small coterie of senior officials who dissented from the administration's new consensus for combat troop deployments to Vietnam. "I told him that I strongly opposed the recommendations," Ball recalled. "To commit American forces to South Vietnam would, in my view, be a tragic error. Once that process started, I said, there would be no end to it." Ball implored Kennedy to learn from France's disastrous encounter with the Vietnamese insurgency in the 1950s, which culminated in the dramatic defeat at Dien Bien Phu in May 1954. "Within five years we'll have three hundred thousand men in the paddies and jungles and never find them again. That was the French experience. . . . To my surprise, the President seemed quite unwilling to discuss the matter, responding with an overtone of asperity: 'George, you're just crazier than hell. That just isn't going to happen.' " [119]

Ball was perplexed by Kennedy's response. "His statement could be interpreted two ways: either he was convinced that events would so evolve as not to require escalation, or he was determined not to permit such escalation to occur."[120] McGeorge Bundy had no doubt about how to interpret the president's remarks. Bundy observed that Ball was perceived to be " 'crazier than hell' to Kennedy because *Kennedy* is not going to do that (and he *does not*)."[121]

On November 15, Bundy joined the combat troop debate with his own recommendation to the president. "So many people have offered their opinions on South Vietnam that more may not be helpful," he noted in a memo to Kennedy. "But the other day at the swimming pool you asked me what I thought and here it is. *We should now agree to send about one division when needed for military action inside Vietnam.* . . . I would not put in a division for morale purposes. I'd put in later, to fight if need be."

As he studied the document carefully for the first time more than three decades later, Bundy found his 1961 recommendation to Kennedy to be a revelation. He simply had no recollection of giving this advice to the president. "Laos was never really ours after 1954," Bundy explained to Kennedy at the time. "South Vietnam is and wants to be." If Kennedy supported combat troop deployments, predicted Bundy, "the odds are almost even that the commitment will not have to be carried out." Reminding Kennedy that "your Vice President, your Secretaries of State and Defense, and the two heads of your special mission" shared this "inner conviction,"

Bundy chided the president for his unwillingness to make the combat troop commitment to defend South Vietnam. "I am troubled by your most natural desire to act on other items now, without taking the troop decision," he scolded. "Whatever the reason," Bundy added, implicitly challenging Kennedy's fortitude, "this has now become a sort of touchstone of our will."[122]

Bundy's recommendation, along with the other combat troop proposals that preceded it, were all acutely unwelcome. "They want a force of American troops," the president confided to Arthur Schlesinger Jr. "They say it's necessary in order to restore confidence and maintain morale. But it will be just like Berlin. The troops will march in; the bands will play; the crowds will cheer; and in four days everyone will have forgotten. Then we will be told we have to send in more troops. It's like taking a drink. The effect wears off and you have to have another. . . . The war in Vietnam could be won only so long as it was *their* war. If it were ever converted into a white man's war, we would lose as the French had lost a decade earlier."[123]

With precious few exceptions Kennedy's war council was encircling him, indifferent to his conspicuous denunciations of proposals to transform the American military commitment to Vietnam. Kennedy's abundant doubts about the combat troop proposal, his repeated refusal to endorse it, his aggressive efforts to rebut and thwart it in the press—all had been ignored. McNamara, Rusk, Taylor, Rostow, the Joint Chiefs, various interagency task forces, and his national security adviser, McGeorge Bundy, had now all joined the same position: President Kennedy must be prepared to stand and fight the insurgency in South Vietnam, intervening on a possibly massive scale with ground combat forces.

Given the scope, stature, and seniority of the coalition in favor of combat troop deployments to South Vietnam, how would Kennedy avoid becoming captive to his own counselors?[124] The president's solution was to effectuate a potent form of bureaucratic decapitation, removing the most influential source of support for his advisers' recommendation. As the moment of decision approached, Secretary of Defense McNamara suddenly and inexplicably reversed his position, joining Rusk—who had previously expressed some reservations about the Pentagon proposal in a cable from Japan—in favor of a revised proposal that authorized increased military assistance but not the deployment of any combat troop units.[125] In his memoir, *In Retrospect*, McNamara claims he simply changed his mind after further reflection.[126] Other students of Vietnam policy infer that the secretary of defense was instructed to alter his proposal by President Kennedy himself.[127] After studying the documentary evidence, Bundy was also inclined to observe the hand of President Kennedy in McNamara's eleventh-hour conversion. "Who changes the Secretary of Defense's mind about what kind of formal recommendation he makes?" Bundy asked. "There are many possibilities, but the most obvious is the guy in the Oval Office."[128] Kennedy was not in the habit of receiving unwelcome advice, Bundy recalled. "If you were a friend of his, and you were working for him as an advisor," then certain expectations were implicit, Bundy explained in a 1964 oral history. "And you know how this works. The President thinks so much in terms of appearances and of someone who is going to be helpful that the notion that you might ask someone for his advice, and he would then give you advice you didn't want, wouldn't really occur to you if the man was one of your crowd."[129]

With the reversal on combat force deployments, the most consequential element of the proposed Vietnam strategy of 1961 had been excised. The last draft of the McNamara and Rusk memorandum still asserted, "The chances are against, probably sharply against, preventing the fall of South Viet-Nam by any measures short of the introduction of US forces on a substantial scale."[130] However, in the final version of the national security directive recording the president's decision, this formulation was eliminated, along with a formal commitment to defend South Vietnam from a communist takeover.

Walt Rostow made one last appeal for troops, recommending a five-thousand-man force to be stationed on the border with North Vietnam. "If we move without ambiguity—without the sickly pallor of our positions on Cuba and Laos—I believe we can unite the country and the Free World," he argued with typical rhetorical excess, "and there is a better than even chance that the Communists will back down and bide their time."[131]

Kennedy remained resolute. "Troops are a last resort," the president said at a hastily convened White House meeting on November 11, at which he brought the matter to a close. Attorney General Robert F. Kennedy stated the president's position more definitively: "We are not sending combat troops. [We are] not committing ourselves to combat troops."[132]

The National Security Council convened once more on November 15, 1961, when Kennedy eviscerated the argument for combat troops more forcefully than he ever had before.[133] He began by dismissing the frequently invoked comparisons with the Korean War. "The conflict in Vietnam is more obscure and less flagrant," said Kennedy, adding, "The United States needs even more the support of allies in such an endeavor as Vietnam in order to avoid sharp domestic partisan criticism as well as strong objections from other nations of the world." Kennedy told his advisers he could "make a rather strong case against intervening in an area 10,000 miles away against 16,000 guerrillas with a native army of 200,000, where millions have been spent for years with no success."[134]

The following day the president spoke at the University of Washington in Seattle, delivering a major foreign policy speech. Kennedy dramatically recast the rhetoric of global activism so apparent in his inaugural address, replacing it with a new realism no doubt influenced by lessons learned in his first year in power. "We must face the fact that the United States is neither omnipotent or omniscient," Kennedy declared, "that we are only six percent of the world's population, that we cannot impose our will upon the other 94 percent, that we cannot fight every wrong or reverse each adversity, and that therefore there cannot be an American solution to every world problem." Ted Sorensen retrospectively pointed to the Seattle speech, with its emphasis on pragmatic realism and a recognition of the limits of American power, as the quintessential expression of Kennedy's foreign policy beliefs.[135]

ℐℛ

Presidential management of the crisis in South Vietnam—this was Bundy's stated historical and analytical interest in the last two years of his life. By its nature, Bundy's focus on Kennedy and Johnson diluted the intensity of introspection he might have trained on his own role in the war. Of his vague recommendation in late 1961 to "send about one division when needed for military action inside South Vietnam," Bundy recorded the mildly self-deprecating observation that, looking back on it, he did not find his advice to be convincing. Bundy was silent, however, on other aspects of his guidance to the president. "Laos was never really ours after 1954," he had instructed Kennedy. "South Vietnam is and wants to be." Decades later, what did Bundy think when he read these words again? Did he wince with the recognition of his prior arrogance? Did the casual hubris of his assertion give him pause? If Bundy struggled with any of these feelings, he never revealed it.

One must wonder, too, if Kennedy was troubled by the grandiosity of Bundy's counsel. And if Kennedy was troubled by Bundy's advice, he would feel similarly about Secretary of Defense McNamara, Secretary of State Rusk, his special military adviser, General Taylor, as well as Walt Rostow, the Joint Chiefs of Staff, and the other national security bureaucrats who urged on him a commitment he refused to make. Although surrounded, Kennedy was not intimidated. And he was certainly not persuaded. Kennedy knew one lesson that the crises of 1961—the Bay of Pigs, Laos and Vietnam—vividly illustrated: Counselors advise but presidents decide. This became a lesson that McGeorge Bundy also took to heart in his retrospective analysis three decades later. On questions of war and peace the paramount authority of decision ultimately rests with one individual. As Bundy noted, "A decision to keep troops *out* of war can be made and enforced by the single-handed use of the unquestioned powers of the president as commander-in-chief. That power was consciously if quietly exercised by President Kennedy in 1961."[136]

As he weighed the significance of the 1961 decision, Bundy repeatedly argued that Kennedy's rejection of his advisers' recommendation to commit U.S. ground combat forces to South Vietnam was an expression of his clear limitation on the level of military support and assistance he would provide the Saigon regime. "Kennedy firmly and steadily refused to authorize the commitment of ground combat troops—in that quite decisive sense, he never made Vietnam an American war," Bundy wrote in a draft fragment.[137] In another fragment he concluded that "Kennedy's ruling was profoundly farsighted."[138]

Bundy ascribed Kennedy's clarity in enforcing a no-combat-troop policy to the president's inherent pessimism about the American capacity to fight and prevail in a Vietnamese war of counterinsurgency. "Kennedy decided sometime in 1961 that he was not going to send in combat troops to South Vietnam," Bundy told James Blight of Brown University. "He was not going to do it because it was not going to work."[139] That certitude, Bundy observed, flowed in part from a belief the president shared with some of his advisers that counterinsurgency could not be fought through conventional forms of intervention. "Kennedy did not see South Vietnam as a war, in the traditional sense," said Bundy. "JFK saw this as a new kind of communist insurgency that had to be dealt with as such. Kennedy never believed it could be turned into a war that we could win."[140] Yet Bundy also noted the pitfalls of Kennedy's effort not to arouse the administration's hawkish critics by declining to make his no-combat-troop policy a declaratory doctrine for his administration. "The policy that is not acknowledged," Bundy often noted in our discussions, "is easily reversed." Kennedy's unwillingness to make his prohibition on combat troops a formally public policy would invite later speculation about his intentions in South Vietnam. As Leslie Gelb and Richard Betts argue about Kennedy in 1961: "Since he did not yet know what would happen in Berlin, where nuclear war loomed as a real danger, and since he was planning to settle for half a loaf in Laos, Vietnam seemed like one good place to make a stand."[141] Bundy rejected that assertion, calling it "an inherited legend . . . that's not right."[142] Bundy was also aware that the advisory mission that Kennedy had approved regularly put American soldiers in the midst of hostile conditions along with troops from the South Vietnamese army.[143] He stressed, however, that the American advisory and combat missions were fundamentally different and that the casualties among the former were an infinitesimal fraction of the latter.

In the final analysis, what is perhaps most remarkable about Kennedy's November 1961 combat troop decision is that despite the overwhelming pressure imposed on him by his senior counselors, the president's determination never wavered. The clarity of Kennedy's decision, which Bundy repeatedly described as decisive and irreversible, prompted the former national security adviser to conclude thirty years later that America's role in the Vietnam War could have been averted. The no-combat-troop policy, Bundy argued, precluded Vietnam from becoming an American war fought—and lost—by large-scale deployments of U.S. ground forces: "We adopted that policy in 1961; we could have kept it in later years; we did not, to our great cost."[144]

NEVER TRUST THE BUREAUCRACY TO GET IT RIGHT

I t was a personal admission enfolded into one of the many, often du-plicative, fragments McGeorge Bundy was drafting, a fact disclosed in his writings but otherwise never discussed or explained. "As one who makes regular visits to the Vietnam Memorial in Washington," he wrote, "I think it a heavy obligation on all who had a role in the decisions of the Vietnam War to omit no action open to us that may help to salute the lasting contributions of the sacrifice of those men whose names are on that long wall."[1] The image was striking. Here was one of the architects of the war, one of the most articulately passionate advocates of the American bombing and combat troop commitment, pondering the tens of thousands of names of the dead inscribed in the monument's mournful facade of black marble. As he examined those endless rows of names etched in stone—and as he observed the daily ritual of family members and loved ones leaving flowers and letters for the dead—what did Bundy think? What did he feel as he looked back three decades later and weighed the enormous human cost of the Vietnam War?

The fragments Bundy left behind offer some clues pointing to a deeper retrospective remorse about the war than he had previously acknowledged publicly. As Bundy wrote about the responsibility he felt to revisit the lessons of the war, "You owe it to a lot of different people." But in conversation Bundy did not typically reveal this side of himself. To the contrary, he often exuded a buoyancy that seemed incongruent with the challenges of producing a probing account of his role in the decisions to Americanize the Vietnam War. "How are *you*?" Bundy would begin each meeting cheerfully. "What shall we discuss *today*?" His good humor was welcome. But it was also perplexing. For a man wrestling with the demons of his most consequential encounter with history, Bundy often seemed to be very much at peace. Was his personal detachment real? Was it the product of a well-developed rationalization fortified by enduring years of often vitriolic criticism? Or was his sense of responsibility more diffuse, with some aspects of the Vietnam decisions weighing more than others?

Despite the breadth of our dialogue on disparate aspects of the war, the inner Bundy would remain elusive. I could therefore draw conclusions based only on what I directly observed. By this measure, the most dramatic insight to which I was privy was also the most obvious. Despite his aura of emotional distance, the man I observed was still struggling to understand how Vietnam happened. Although he had been a protagonist at the center of American strategy deliberations, Bundy still did not fully grasp the specific role he played in the series of decisions that placed the United States on the path to war.

One of the questions that appeared to preoccupy Bundy was how the process of managing presidential decisions for Vietnam could have become as disordered as it did for both Kennedy and Johnson. Bundy had come to the White House with a reputation for brilliance as a bureaucratic manager, the young academic dean who had tamed the fierce politics and formidable egos of the Harvard faculty. The conventional wisdom was that Bundy was decisive, commanding, and terse, and that he would cut through all of the noise and marginal arguments to arrive at the right decision, coordinating Kennedy's global agenda to serve the president's needs, not those of any particular constituency within the government. That premise would be tested in the final months of the Kennedy presidency, when the bureaucracy responsible for the day-to-day implementation of the president's Vietnam policy reached a nadir of dysfunction.

In the autumn of 1963 the client government in Saigon, which the United States had been assiduously assisting with growing amounts of arms and military advisers, violently imploded. The implosion was, in fact, an exercise in regime change engineered by senior members of the national security bureaucracy that quickly spiraled out of control, beyond the grasp of Bundy in the White House, Rusk at the State Department, McNamara at the Pentagon, as well as President Kennedy himself. The plot to topple President Ngo Dinh Diem illustrates the power of an untamed bureaucracy to produce dramatically unintended consequences and thereby change the context for future policy choices, for better or worse.

☙

On January 3, 1962, President Kennedy gathered his senior advisers in Palm Beach, Florida, where he had been celebrating the Christmas and New Year's holidays. "In the discussion concerning South Vietnam the President reemphasized the importance of the U.S. not becoming further involved militarily in that area," reported Roswell Gilpatric, the deputy secretary of defense. "The President also emphasized the importance of playing down the number of U.S. military personnel involved in Vietnam and that the U.S. military role there was for advice, training and support of the Vietnamese armed forces and not combat."[2] In its essence, this was the Kennedy strategy for Vietnam: to support the Saigon regime in its conflict with the communist insurgency but only through means that decisively excluded an American combat commitment.

By the close of 1962 there were more than nine thousand U.S. military advisers and support personnel in South Vietnam, roughly three times the number of the previous year.[3] The total amount of military hardware more than doubled between 1961 and 1962, including new shipments of armored personnel carriers and more than three hundred military aircraft.[4]

Despite an increase in American military aid, the insurgents—also known as the Vietcong—were gathering strength. The intensity and resilience of the Vietcong were vividly illustrated in the battle of Ap Bac, waged in the first days of 1963. In a stunning reversal, 350 guerrillas humiliated a modern South Vietnamese army that was four times its size, equipped with armor and artillery, and supported by helicopters and bombers.[5] Despite thousands of rounds of gunfire from the ground and 8,400 rounds and 100 rockets from the air, only eighteen insurgents were killed. Saigon's army, in contrast, suffered eighty fatalities.[6]

On the political front, the government's control over the country was unraveling. President Diem and his brother, Ngo Dinh Nhu, were widely perceived to be corrupt and authoritarian rulers, exercising rigid control over the National Assembly, Special Forces, police, and the press. All public gatherings, even funerals, required official state approval. Diem also resisted American leadership of counterinsurgency operations. "All these soldiers," the South Vietnamese president complained to the French ambassador, "I never asked them to come here. They don't even have passports."[7]

For Bundy and for all who served in the Kennedy administration, the seminal foreign policy challenge of 1962 was not in Vietnam but rather in Cuba. The Cuban missile crisis, the most profound test of the nuclear era, began for Bundy with the untimely interruption of a dinner party he and his wife, Mary, were hosting at their home on Monday, October 15,

1962. The deputy CIA director, Ray Cline, called to inform Bundy that reconnaissance photographs now confirmed that Soviet medium-range nuclear missiles were being deployed in Cuba. Bundy's response, viewed from decades later, seems remarkable and almost inexplicable. He decided to return to his guests and continue with his dinner party. Bundy eschewed the notion of a "hastily summoned meeting," as he later explained to President Kennedy. "So I decided that a quiet evening and a night of sleep were the best preparation you could have in light of what would face you in the next days." Bundy informed the president of the Soviet missiles at eight o'clock the next morning, when he found Kennedy in his pajamas, sitting in bed and reading the morning papers.[8]

In the perilous days that followed, Kennedy repeatedly convened the ExComm, an executive committee of current and former senior government and military officials tasked with managing the crisis and formulating the strategic choices now confronting the United States. The ExComm developed two principal options: an air strike or invasion to destroy the missiles, or a naval quarantine to preclude their completed deployment.

In the first phase of the crisis Bundy favored a limited preemptive military attack to take out the missiles. On the evening of October 16 he argued that "the political advantages are very strong, it seems to me, of the small strike. . . . The punishment fits the crime in political terms. . . . We are doing only what we warned repeatedly and publicly we would have to do."[9] Former secretary of state Dean Acheson joined Bundy in favoring air strikes. Attorney General Robert F. Kennedy violently objected. Secretary of Defense McNamara warned the president that a surgical air strike to destroy the missiles was simply not possible and that bombing would likely trigger a full-scale American invasion.

By the third day of deliberations the ExComm was coalescing around the quarantine recommendation, which would disrupt the further shipment of missiles to Cuba and open the possibility of a negotiating track with the Soviet Union. Bundy, who as national security adviser was ostensibly the coordinating force behind the ExComm, said it was too early to lock into one option. That evening he joined his wife for a cocktail before returning to another White House ExComm session. "I hope you all will choose the least violent course you can," Mary said to him. Later that evening, "somewhat to everyone's surprise," as Ted Sorensen recalled, "Mac Bundy urged that we not overlook the justification of no action at all." Bundy had discarded his recommendation for a preemptive strike and was advising, in essence, to accept the Soviet missiles as an accomplished fact. The ExComm summarily rejected his suggestion. When a vote was finally taken later that evening, however, Bundy joined the majority, which favored a quarantine over an air strike by a margin of 11–6.[10]

The next morning, Friday, October 19, President Kennedy found arrayed in the Oval Office a phalanx of his top military advisers—the Joint Chiefs of Staff and their new chairman, General Maxwell Taylor—joined by Acheson and Bundy. The group had come to lobby Kennedy for the air strike option, seeking immediate approval for an attack with a total of eight hundred individual sorties. Although he had voted for the quarantine just the night before, Bundy now reverted back to supporting the bombing option. By this point, President Kennedy was "a bit disgusted" with his national security adviser, Sorensen reported.[11] When the ExComm reconvened, Bundy reiterated his support for air strikes, urging "decisive action" that would "surgically" remove the missiles—precisely the option that McNamara had previously debunked as militarily impossible to achieve. "An air-strike would be quick," Bundy assured the ExComm, "confronting the world with a fait accompli."[12]

Bundy subsequently claimed that he had kept the air strike option open with the president's blessing, after privately encouraging Kennedy to do so. "I didn't sleep a bit well that Thursday night," Bundy recorded in a memorandum he composed in March 1964, "and went up and saw [the president] while he was dressing Friday morning and told him that I really thought this was very dangerous and uncertain and I wasn't sure it would bring an answer. He said, 'Well, I'm having some of those same worries, and you know how my first reaction was the air strike. Have another look at that and keep it alive.' "[13] Bundy recalled Kennedy's frustration with him, but he argued that it served a constructive purpose. "He gets very impatient with me in the height of the Cuban missile crisis when I want further study of the military option," he said. "But then he relents when he discovered that's one way of showing that the military option doesn't work. There is the time for an extra 24 hours. We take the time. It's argued out." Because Kennedy's military advisers cannot assure him that a preemptive strike will destroy all of the Russian missile sites, the result is sealed. "End of air attack," said Bundy.[14]

Kennedy ultimately rejected military preemption in favor of the quarantine and a diplomatic back channel that facilitated a secret deal to extract the missiles in Cuba in exchange for the removal of American Jupiter missiles from Turkey. As a result of groundbreaking scholarship on the missile crisis, we now know that if Kennedy had accepted Bundy's advice it could have triggered a nuclear war. Soviet forces in fact possessed a total of 162 nuclear warheads in Cuba, including at least 90 tactical warheads to be used to repel a U.S. invasion or attack.[15]

With the resolution of the Cuban missile crisis, the most severe national security challenge of the Kennedy years had been confronted and contained. But the uncertainties surrounding the American position in South Vietnam persisted. Tensions exploded there in the spring of 1963 with the emergence of what would be known as the Buddhist crisis. In Hue, a center of religious scholarship in South Vietnam, protestors defied a government ban against flying the Buddhist flag at a large rally. Government troops in armored carriers opened fire, killing nine and wounding fourteen civilians.[16] Another wave of protests followed, including hunger strikes by Buddhist religious leaders. On June 11, 1963, an elderly monk named Thich Quang Duc sat down at the center of a busy intersection in Hue, drenched his body with gasoline with the help of three other monks, and then set himself on fire. The haunting image of the monk remaining serenely fixed in the lotus position as the flames engulfed him appeared on the front pages of newspapers around the world.[17] Diem's sister-in-law, the politically invasive Madame Nhu, ridiculed the public suicide as a "barbecue" and expressed her hope that others would emulate the monk's example. "Let them burn," she exclaimed, "and we shall clap our hands."[18] Over the course of the Buddhist crisis seven other monks immolated themselves.

As the crisis dragged on, Diem attempted to negotiate an agreement with the Buddhists, but his effort was scuttled by Madame Nhu. Mass protests swelled. Students were hauled off to jail. On August 21 Diem declared martial law as Special Forces under the command of his brother launched coordinated raids in several cities across the country, vandalizing pagodas and imprisoning 1,400 Buddhists.

"This has been an extraordinary episode," Bundy noted in a private memorandum, "in that it has been a period of critical division not only between us and the Diem family but within the government both here and in Saigon." Bundy acknowledged that an "underlying question— whether our objectives in Southeast Asia can be met while the Diem government survives—has been a part of the problem of South Vietnam for many years, going back before this administration." Prior to the outbreak of the Buddhist crisis in May, "the dominant view at the top of every agency in Washington and Saigon had been that we should go with Diem, applying such gentle arts of persuasion and pressure as might tend to improve his performance." As a result of the summer's turmoil, however, "the conviction that there must be a major change in the Diem government stirred upward through most of the agencies on this side of the river"—the State Department, the U.S. Information Agency, and the U.S. Agency for International Development. In early August, Bundy's Vietnam staff specialist, Michael Forrestal, began to express his view that "there was now a need for major change, and he reported that Hilsman and Harriman were now also coming to this view."[19]

The troika of Roger Hilsman, Averell Harriman, and Michael Forrestal nourished a deep antipathy for the Diem regime. Recently appointed as assistant secretary of state for Far Eastern affairs, Hilsman was a graduate of West Point and a Yale PhD in international relations who had served as a jungle guerrilla in Burma in World War II. He was an avid student of counterinsurgency doctrine. Averell Harriman, the scion of the vast Harriman family railroad fortune, was a former governor of New York and had been Hilsman's predecessor at State before becoming undersecretary for political affairs and chairman of the Special Group for Counterinsurgency. Forrestal, just thirty-six years old, was the Vietnam specialist on Bundy's National Security Council staff. His father, James Forrestal, had been secretary of the navy and the first secretary of defense under President Truman. When James Forrestal committed suicide in 1949, his son was essentially adopted by Harriman and his wife, Marie, both close family friends. When Forrestal joined the White House staff, Kennedy joked, "You will be my emissary to that special sovereignty, Averell Harriman."

Forrestal, a Harvard Law School graduate and Wall Street lawyer, would actually play a far more important role in the Kennedy White House. The president granted him unusual access to the Oval Office and encouraged him to share his unvarnished views on the real progress of the war in Vietnam. Working through Bundy to see the president, however, was an ordeal Forrestal compared to a sterilizing bath. "Bundy wanted to know precisely what Forrestal intended to say and then hectored him about it with variations of 'Have you thought that out?'" notes the historian A. J. Langguth. "Forrestal found Bundy the least creative thinker on the NSC, always two cautious steps to the rear of a discussion. He suspected that Kennedy felt the same and kept Bundy out of his political decisions."[20]

In the waning days of summer in 1963, Forrestal was one of the Kennedy administration insiders who helped to draft and clear a weekend cable that would change the course of the war. "The Executive Committee level of the government was scattered more than at any other moment that I can remember," Bundy wrote in his contemporaneous notes of the weekend of August 24–25, 1963. His memorandum noted that President Kennedy was in Hyannis, Massachusetts; Secretary of Defense McNamara was mountain climbing in the far west; Director McCone of the CIA was in the state of Washington; Secretary of State Rusk was out of town; and Bundy himself was at his vacation home in Manchester, Massachusetts. "Consulting only the President," Bundy wrote, and coordinating "with the Defense Department through General Krulak—a devoted officer but not a senior policy-maker—Michael and his friends determined on and sent out the famous cable of August 24."[21] This cable, drafted by Hilsman and authorized without the usual vetting and approvals, sent new instructions to the U.S. ambassador in Saigon, Henry Cabot Lodge. "U.S. Government cannot tolerate situation in which power lies in Nhu's hands," the cable stated. "Diem must be given chance to rid himself of Nhu and his coterie and replace them with best military and political personalities available. If in spite of all your efforts, Diem remains obdurate and refuses, then we must face the possibility that Diem himself cannot be preserved." Taking an extraordinary leap, the cable then instructed Lodge to begin planning for a potential coup d'état to overthrow Diem: "Ambassador and country team should urgently examine all possible alternative leadership and make detailed plans as to how we might bring about Diem's replacement if this should become necessary."[22]

The genesis and approval of the coup cable remains a subject of avid interest among historians of the war. How could such a consequential shift in U.S. policy be engineered over a summer weekend? Thirty years later, Bundy recalled that he was "safely insulated by the process of being in New England," adding, with an admission hard to reconcile with the nature of his responsibilities as national security adviser, "and I cut myself out when I go away for the weekend." Bundy recalled that "this particular subject" was discussed in a channel that ran through Forrestal "directly to the President." Forrestal, Bundy said, was a very bright, straightforward young man, "but he's working for the President with one hand and Averell Harriman with the other, and he's got the Vietnam account with me, but not when I'm out for the weekend." It was in this context that Forrestal, "inexperienced" but possessed of "a clear point of view," takes the initiative to gain approval for the August 24 cable. "And he clears it in ways that are still disputed," said Bundy, who asked, "How much did people sign on?"[23]

Bundy's notes from the autumn of 1963 reflect the mounting discord within the Kennedy administration triggered by the decision to support a coup in Saigon. In the immediate aftermath of the hastily dispatched Forrestal cable, officials in the Department of Defense reacted strongly in opposition, amplified in force, Bundy suspected, by the fact that Taylor and McNamara found themselves "wholly and harmoniously in agreement on a major issue against others." The intensity of their response "was probably also sharpened, not altogether fairly," he continued, by the Pentagon's lack of confidence in Roger Hilsman. Bundy further noted Averell Harriman's view that the State Department should manage such matters on its own "and that it was a great mistake" to allow essential policy issues to be "pawed over" by the CIA or the Defense Department. Commenting on the military's effort to portray the cable as not fairly representative of U.S. policy, Bundy was inclined to sympathize with Harriman's view that the critics of the cable "were engaged in deliberate undercutting of something which the President himself had approved." Compounding the dispute was the fact that neither McNamara nor Taylor had directly approved a cable that touched on their "deep interests." Bundy regarded the dispute generated by the cable as "an almost perfect example" of the type of bureaucratic imbroglio that "produces honest outrage on both sides." Senior officials excluded from the process of consultation will predictably "feel that a cryptic decision in which they have not participated is something less than the law of the Medes and the Persians." As a result, said Bundy, "escalating annoyance is hard to avoid."[24]

Ambassador Lodge welcomed the new guidance from Washington, immediately instructing the CIA station in Saigon to send emissaries to two disaffected senior officers, General Tran Thien Khiem and General Nguyen Khanh. Lodge's message to the generals was simple: Nhu and his wife must be removed from power, and Diem's ultimate fate would be left to the Vietnamese military to decide. Moreover, the coup plotters would receive no overt assistance from the United States. "We cannot be of any help during initial action of assuming power of the state," the CIA station in Saigon explained in a report to headquarters in Langley. "Entirely their own action, win or lose."[25]

Fueling momentum for a coup was a conviction within the Kennedy administration that the Diem family's exercise of power had become dangerously dysfunctional. The president's brother "exercises an overriding, immutable influence over Diem," wrote Thomas L. Hughes, the director of intelligence and research at the State Department. Nhu was also a problem, Hughes suggested, because he despised the United States: "He has frequently claimed that the American presence must be reduced because it threatens South Vietnam's independence. . . . Nhu has claimed privately that should United States aid be cut he would seek help elsewhere. Should that fail, Nhu asserts he would negotiate a settlement with Hanoi. Nhu has convinced both Vietnamese and foreign observers that such a prospect is likely. . . . His megalomania is manifest in his claim that only he can save Vietnam."[26]

Despite the growing alarm within the administration, President Kennedy favored a pragmatic approach. He instructed Lodge in a private cable on September 17, 1963, "to obtain . . . if possible, reforms and changes in personnel necessary to maintain support of Vietnamese and U.S. opinion in war against Viet Cong." Kennedy observed that there was "no good opportunity for action to remove present government in immediate future. Therefore . . . we must for the present apply such pressures as are available."[27]

Concerned that the Saigon regime was increasingly unstable, Kennedy dispatched McNamara, accompanied by Taylor, for a broad reappraisal of the war effort. "The events in South Vietnam since May," noted Kennedy, "have now raised serious questions about both the present prospects for success against the Viet Cong and still more about the effectiveness of this effort unless there can be important political improvement in the country."[28]

Although Secretary of State Rusk would have been the logical senior official to advise the president on the political turmoil in Saigon, Kennedy relied instead on McNamara. This was typical of Kennedy. "He knew that he could not get an answer if he called the Secretary of State, and he could get one if he called the Secretary of Defense," Bundy later recalled. "He didn't do anything about that—he simply called the Secretary of Defense."[29] In 1963 Bundy described drinking whiskey after hours with Rusk and George Ball, the third-highest-ranking official in the State Department. "It was the most informal and comfortable conversation that I have had with the Secretary," Bundy observed. When the talk turned to the Bay of Pigs debacle, Rusk repeated his frequent lament that "he finds it very hard to give his candid and full advice to the President when there is a large mob of other people in the room." Bundy confided in his private memorandum: "My own internal feeling is that the President does not find that he gets that much more from the Secretary when they are alone together—I fear that the Secretary is in truth a very inward man whether there are two or twenty in the room." Bundy added that he was nonetheless committed to finding ways to meet Rusk's concerns.[30]

Following a ten-day tour of South Vietnam, the McNamara delegation produced a draft report containing a striking recommendation. President Kennedy was advised to set the end of 1965 as a deadline to transfer essential responsibilities carried out by American military advisers to the

Vietnamese. "It should be possible to withdraw the bulk of U.S. personnel by that time," the report noted, further proposing an announcement "in the very near future . . . to withdraw 1000 U.S. military personnel by the end of 1963." The new policy should be disclosed quietly, "as an initial step in a long-term program to replace U.S. personnel with trained Vietnamese without impairment of the war effort."[31]

McNamara, Taylor, and the other members of the delegation returned from Saigon early on October 2. Later that morning they briefed President Kennedy. The president asked for their recommendations in the event the war did not go as well as the White House assumed. "First, we believe we can complete the military campaign in the first three corps in '64 and the fourth corps in '65," McNamara assured Kennedy. "But secondly, if it extends beyond that period we believe we can train the Vietnamese to take over the essential functions and withdraw the bulk of our forces."

"What's the point of doing it?" queried a skeptical Bundy.

"We need a way to get out of Vietnam," McNamara replied. "This is a way of doing it. And to leave forces there when they're not needed, I think, is wasteful and complicates both their problems and ours."

Discussion continued, focusing on the flow of soldiers and weapons from the communist North. Bundy returned to the unresolved matter of a White House announcement. "The question that occurs to me," he asked, "is whether we want to get publicly pinned to a date."

"Well," said General Taylor, "it's something we debated very strongly. I think it is a major question." Taylor explained to Kennedy that all of the American officers he consulted in South Vietnam believed that the mission could be concluded in all areas of the country with the exception of the Mekong Delta by the end of 1964.

"Well, let's say it anyway," Kennedy instructed, leaving open the possibility that the date for an American withdrawal could be revised if necessary."[32]

McNamara jumped in, determined to persuade Kennedy that a public withdrawal date was essential. "I think, Mr. President, we must have a means of disengaging from this area," he said firmly. "We must show our country that means . . ."

The discussion continued. Kennedy asked about the impact of American advisers in stiffening the resolve of South Vietnam forces. McNamara conceded it was an important but small role, with just 270 U.S. advisers dispersed among 17,000 South Vietnamese soldiers at the battalion level.

"The difficulty," noted CIA director John McCone, "is that this whole thing could be upset by a little greater effort by the North Vietnamese."

"I don't think so," Taylor stated.

"Not on the withdrawal of U.S. forces," insisted McNamara.

"You're really talking two different things," offered Bundy. ". . . you're saying that the U.S. advice and stiffening functions you may want to continue but that the large use of U.S. troops, who can be replaced by properly trained Vietnamese, can end. I wonder if it isn't worth separating those two."

Kennedy brushed off Bundy's suggestion. "Well, just say, 'While there may continue to be a requirement for special training forces, we believe that the major United States part of the task will be completed by 1965.' "[33] Kennedy had made his decision. The withdrawal statement—including the pullout of one thousand advisers and completion of the entire U.S. mission by the end of 1965—would become official administration policy and would be announced publicly.[34]

Bundy was uncertain what precisely motivated the president to stake out a position anticipating a 1965 withdrawal from Vietnam. "I do not myself know exactly what those directly engaged had in mind in their original discussion of the withdrawal of a thousand men," Bundy told the historian William C. Gibbons in 1992.[35] And in a 1991 interview with John Newman, another historian of the war, Bundy said, "I remember it as very much coming out of conversation that was closely held between

Kennedy and McNamara. And what they meant by it beyond what they said, which was not very much, I honestly don't know."[36]

McNamara was less tentative in interpreting Kennedy's choice. "I believed that we had done all the training we could. Whether the South Vietnamese were qualified or not to turn back the North Vietnamese, I was certain that if they weren't, it wasn't for lack of our training. More training wouldn't strengthen them; therefore we should get out. The President agreed."[37]

The White House announcement of the 1965 withdrawal date was accompanied later by a formal directive, National Security Action Memorandum 263, issued under Bundy's signature.[38] Bundy remarked at a White House meeting that he "was surprised that some people were taking as 'pollyanna-ish' the McNamara-Taylor statement that we could pull out of Vietnam in two years. . . . Two years was really a long time," he said, "considering that by then the war would have lasted four years—or longer than most wars in U.S. history."[39]

With the debate over of a public withdrawal date resolved, an attentive White House returned its focus to the plot to overthrow the Diem regime. Bundy cabled Ambassador Lodge to emphasize President Kennedy's expectation that "no initiative should now be taken to give any active covert encouragement to a coup," but that there should be "urgent covert effort with closest security . . . to identify and build contacts with possible alternative leadership as and when it appears." Bundy warned Lodge to keep American fingerprints off of the plot to overthrow President Diem: "Essential . . . effort be totally secure and fully deniable . . . We repeat . . . effort is not to be aimed at active promotion of coup but only at surveillance and readiness."[40]

"The problems of Saigon were lively this afternoon," Bundy noted on in a private memorandum dated October 24, 1963. In an apparent reference to Lodge, Hilsman, Harriman, and Forrestal, Bundy observed, "the hardliners were in an advanced state of concern." John McCone and

Maxwell Taylor, Bundy reported, had voiced their criticism of a drifting U.S. policy in Saigon. "There is no doubt that there has been a kind of imprecision about the performance there which is troubling," Bundy conceded, "but the level of reaction here by John and Max strikes me as excessive." Kennedy, he wrote, was growing impatient, eager to see some change in behavior from Diem that would permit the president to modify America's "posture of strict aloofness and limited cooperation"—but no accommodation from Diem seemed likely. Lodge was planning to speak with Diem on Sunday, October 27, and Kennedy was hoping to send one last instruction to his ambassador "to see if he can produce some movement somehow."[41]

The following morning the president's most senior counselors convened for a "rump session," in Bundy's words, to discuss the deteriorating situation in South Vietnam and to provide President Kennedy "a chance to talk frankly" with Robert McNamara, Robert Kennedy, and particularly John McCone, who had recently clashed with Lodge when the ambassador replaced the CIA's station chief in Saigon. Reading passages from the overnight cable traffic, McCone expressed grave concerns about a potential "provocation," strenuously arguing "that there was no remaining prospect of plausible denial" of American support for the coup plot. Despite his earlier frustrations with the weekend cable, McNamara argued against a change in the official U.S. position. Robert Kennedy worried, in Bundy's telling, that "something" would be attempted "in circumstances where it had only a poor chance of success, and that failure would be laid at our door, no matter how much or little we really had to do with it." In a conversation afterward, Bundy learned that the president "understood this dilemma extremely well, although he also thought it important to call the ambassador's attention to the consequences of a failed effort." The president was also preoccupied with McCone's dissent and the CIA chief's growing friction with Lodge in Saigon. "It is ironic," Bundy observed, that Kennedy was now compelled to devote so much of his attention to the task of "soothing ruffled feelings between two dyed-in-the-wool and hard-boiled Republicans like the Ambassador and the Director."[42]

The crisis surrounding Diem was becoming something of a trap for the United States, Bundy wrote in another of his private memoranda. "A regime like the junta in Santo Domingo or the Diem family in Saigon," when confronted with an American desire to dilute or abandon its authority, is unlikely to comply, "because if all else fails it can always take the way out, with a bundle of cash, in any event." For Washington to exert leverage, Bundy concluded, "unless our request is in some way supported or reinforced by local force and feeling, it is not likely to be effective. But we on the other hand have no corresponding way out. Because to get out of the country or give up our interest is in fact for us a defeat."[43]

Bundy cabled Lodge again on October 29 to reiterate the president's concerns. If the coup was not executed decisively, he cautioned, avoiding either "prolonged fighting or even defeat," the result might be "serious or even disastrous for U.S. interests." Bundy stressed that the "burden of proof must be on coup group to show a substantial possibility of quick success; otherwise, we should discourage them from proceeding since a miscalculation could result in jeopardizing [the] U.S. position in Southeast Asia."[44] At a White House meeting that afternoon, Robert Kennedy voiced his doubts about fomenting regime change in South Vietnam. "I mean, it's different from a coup in . . . Iraq or [a] South American country," he admonished. "We are so intimately involved in this. . . . To support a coup would be putting the future of Vietnam and in fact all of Southeast Asia in the hands of one man not now known to us."[45]

The plot to overthrow Diem was launched on the first day of November. Major General Tran Van Don, the commander of the Army of the Republic of Vietnam, telephoned Paul Harkins, America's top military official in Vietnam, explaining that his senior generals "were assembled with him . . . and were initiating a coup."[46] The CIA station chief, Lucien

Conein, reported that the coup leaders had imprisoned several military officers loyal to Diem and had stated their demands: "If the President will resign immediately, they will guarantee his safety and the safe departure of the President and Ngo Dinh Nhu. If the President refuses these terms, the palace will be attacked within the hour by Air Force and Armor."[47] At 3:00 p.m., as 103 truckloads of troops were reported to be entering Saigon, Diem's presidential guard was deployed around his palace.[48] At 4:00 p.m. the American embassy in Saigon informed Washington that a ground and air attack was under way.[49] Conein huddled with the coup plotters of the South Vietnamese Joint General Staff. He reported that Major General Duong Van "Big" Minh, the military adviser to President Diem, had made contact with the president's brother. The general warned that if Diem did not resign and surrender within five minutes, "the Palace will sustain a massive airborne bombardment. At this, Minh hung up."[50] Finally, at 4:30 p.m., Diem called Ambassador Lodge.

"Some units have made a rebellion and I want to know: what is the attitude of U.S.?" asked Diem.

"I do not feel well enough informed to be able to tell you," Lodge replied. "I have heard the shooting, but am not acquainted with all the facts. Also it is 4:30 a.m. in Washington and [the] U.S. Government cannot possibly have a view."

"But you must have some general ideas," insisted Diem. "After all, I am a Chief of State. I have tried to do my duty. . . ."

"You have certainly done your duty," Lodge allowed. "As I told you only this morning, I admire your courage and your great contributions to your country. No one can take away from you the credit for all you have done. Now I am worried about your physical safety. I have a report that those in charge of the current activity offer you and your brother safe conduct out of the country if you resign. Had you heard this?"

"No," Diem answered. After a pause he added: "You have my telephone number."

"Yes," replied Lodge. "If I can do anything for your physical safety, please call me."

"I am trying to re-establish order," said Diem, as their conversation concluded. His rule over South Vietnam and failed relationship with the United States had come to a decisive end.[51]

President Diem and his brother were bound and shot to death in the rear hold of a South Vietnamese army personnel carrier. General Minh reported to Conein that the brothers had killed themselves while hiding out in a Catholic church, but CIA photographs depicted their mangled, bloody bodies with their hands tied behind their backs. "This is not the preferred way to commit suicide," Bundy archly observed in the White House staff meeting on the morning of November 4.[52] According to notes of the meeting, "Bundy and others were impressed with the fact that the Saigonese people threw garlands of roses on the tanks and seemed genuinely pleased with the revolt." Contrasting that image to coups elsewhere, "Bundy remarked that Latin American generals would do well to plan for some such demonstration of support. He made the remark half jokingly, but he was serious in noting that such things were important."[53]

When he learned that Diem and Nhu had been murdered, "Kennedy leaped to his feet and rushed from the room with a look of shock and dismay on his face which I had never seen before," General Taylor recalled. The killings, said Forrestal, "troubled him deeply . . . bothered him as a moral and religious matter, shook his confidence in the kind of advice he was getting in Vietnam."[54]

"I was shocked by the death of Diem and Nhu," Kennedy said days after the coup, dictating his recollections into a tape recorder. "I'd met Diem with Justice Douglas many years ago. He was an extraordinary character. While he became increasingly difficult in the last months, nonetheless over a ten-year period he'd held his country together, maintained its independence under very adverse conditions. The way he was killed made it particularly abhorrent. The question now is whether the

Generals can stay together and build a stable government or whether Saigon will begin—whether public opinion in Saigon, the intellectuals, students, etc., will turn on this government as repressive and undemocratic in the not too distant future."[55]

Later in the day on November 4, 1963, Bundy dictated his own memorandum for the record describing the government's turmoil as the coup plot spun out of Washington's control. "In the last long discussion before the event, the President's advisers were as divided as ever in their approach to the country," he wrote. Rusk, Harriman, and Bundy put forward the argument that because "a change of government was necessary," the cell promoting the coup should not be discouraged, for it "was likely to be the most serious and sensible available." McNamara generally concurred, "although he was very much concerned," Bundy said, "by what seemed to be the casual and unprofessional nature of our contacts with and information on the work of the coup group."[56]

The main opposition to the coup, Bundy recounted, had come from the chairman of the Joint Chiefs of Staff. "Max Taylor, all the way through, felt that it would be better to discourage and even prevent a coup. He doubted that there was any practical alternative," and his discussions with the generals plotting the coup made him question the "seriousness and determination of these officers." The attorney general shared Taylor's skepticism. "Bobby was much influenced by the views of Max who is his very good friend," Bundy wrote, "and much influenced also by his conviction that in the event of an unsuccessful coup the impact on the Administration's position at home would be very serious indeed." The CIA director oscillated in his views: "John McCone went up and down, but had finally settled just before the event on the conviction that a change was necessary and practicable."[57]

As for President Kennedy, Bundy speculated that he tilted toward the pro-coup camp. "The President's own inner conviction, I believe, was very close to that of Dean Rusk and Bob McNamara, but he was determined not to be in the position of having pushed anyone into something which did not work."[58] But later that day Bundy amended this conclusion, citing a conversation that afternoon with Mike Forrestal—who once again appeared to be closer to the president on the question of Vietnam than his boss—that prompted the national security adviser to concede "that I may not have been right." Bundy explained that President Kennedy had asked Forrestal to review the origin of the August telegram and to explain why the Pentagon "seemed so urgent to give an instruction to Lodge that would seem to commit the United States Government to the support of a coup attempt." Bundy now understood that "as he looks back at it, the President is clearly uncertain that it was wise to place the weight of Washington's advice so sharply on one side, in a single weekend cable. My own belief is . . . the decision itself was probably basically correct."

As the coup unfolded, Bundy described a White House that "watched intently, without much power to influence events." Throughout the day Kennedy's "principal interest," said Bundy, "was in avoiding any evidence of direct US involvement—which was easy in the sense that there really was none, and very difficult in the sense that very few newspapermen chose to believe it."[59] While Kennedy remained "uncertain all the way that he really desired" the coup, "he was clearly eager to have it succeed." At 6:30 that evening the president was informed that Diem and Nhu had offered to surrender, providing Kennedy "his first moment of relaxation from intense and immediate concern."

"At that moment," Bundy continued, the operation appeared to have been executed "with extraordinary skill and alertness . . . But unfortunately it did not stay so neat." Later that evening the White House received a report that Diem and Nhu had committed suicide, but by the next day it had become obvious that the evidence for suicide "was not very persuasive." For President Kennedy, "this news [was] very troubling, both because of his immediate personal sense of regret that Diem should be assassinated," and because the assassination would undermine the perceived standing of the new regime that would assume power in Saigon."[60] With news of Diem's death Kennedy "personally insisted" on two messages to Lodge expressing his concern. The president also cancelled a trip to Chicago "as a mark of personal respect to the memory of Diem." Bundy described "my own one regret" related to Diem's murder: "that as a matter of staff work we did not foresee this risk more clearly and get a flash message to Lodge in the course of the day on Friday which might perhaps have had some impact on the way in which the matter was controlled by the generals."[61]

In his 1964 oral history with the political scientist Richard Neustadt, Bundy characterized Kennedy as being conflicted over the coup but ultimately in favor of it. The president, said Bundy, "didn't wish to be overthrowing Diem and Nhu against the advice of Taylor and McNamara and McCone, and neither did he wish to be leaving them in place. . . . Meanwhile the war was certainly beginning to go worse, although this is still fighting language in the Pentagon where the gospel is that the war didn't begin to go badly until we distanced ourselves from Diem and Nhu, but that's clearly not so, I would think." In the autumn of 1963, the issue of whether to support Diem and his brother had been "maturing for six weeks in the President's mind, and he was quite clear and, I think, quite right in his judgment that they would either have to change or we would have to put ourselves in the position to expect a new set of people to make a new try."[62]

In mid-November 1963 the president's Vietnam advisers convened for a conference in Honolulu, Hawaii. Predictably, there was an absence of consensus among the administration's senior ranks. A draft presidential directive prepared by Bundy on November 21 reiterated President Kennedy's determination to limit the American commitment to Saigon. "The objectives of the United States with respect to the withdrawal of U.S. military personnel remain as stated in the White House statement of October 2, 1963," wrote Bundy, referring to the public commitment to a full withdrawal by the end of 1965. The draft directive also included a presidential rebuke for the conspicuously muddled performance of the national security bureaucracy and its internecine squabbling surrounding the Diem coup. "It is of the highest importance," wrote Bundy, "that the United States Government avoid either the appearance or the reality of public recrimination from one part of it against another, and the President expects that all senior officers of the Government will take energetic steps to insure that they and their subordinates go out of their way to maintain and to defend the unity of the United States Government both here and in the field."[63]

On the morning of November 22, 1963, with the president en route to Dallas for a political event, Bundy chaired a White House staff meeting that began with a discussion of the Honolulu conference, held two days before. Bundy said his "overall impressions of the conference itself were diffuse, and that this was probably significant. . . . There is no country team in Vietnam at the present time in any real sense. It is clear that Harkins feels he does not have the Ambassador's confidence, and this is affecting US operations in the country. Lodge is clearly the dominant personality, but it is not at all evident that he can handle the job he is now faced with. . . . In short, the course the U.S. country team will chart in Vietnam is by no means decided upon. . . . Turning to the regime itself . . . it was too early to see what course it would follow, but it was clear that the coalition of generals might not last."[64]

Later that day President Kennedy was murdered. Eight days earlier, Bundy had recorded his final journal entry of the Kennedy presidency. His memorandum for the record makes reference to a Ted Sorensen paper submitted to Kennedy, an analysis of "Presidential responsibilities which he seemed to find too formal in tone," but which nonetheless prompted Kennedy to ruminate on the obligations of his office. "His mind turned to the famous passage from Henry V in which the King talks about how 'we must bear all,'" wrote Bundy. "Since this is one of the few bits of Shakespeare I know by heart, I was able to waste a certain amount of time quoting passages which were as appealing to him as they were unusable because of their monarchical and slightly medieval tone." Bundy observed that Kennedy thought often about "the fact that the responsibility for all kinds of things only remotely within his control necessarily comes back to him," and noted that "there is a wide stretch of country in which he walks a good deal, usually but not always alone."[65]

At the time of President Kennedy's death the American military command had recorded a total of 108 U.S. military personnel killed in Vietnam.[66] The final tally of U.S. fatalities would exceed 58,000.

༄

The events of November 1963 punctuate what is arguably the end of the first act of America's entanglement in Vietnam. An autocratic leader in Saigon had been overthrown by his own generals. A determined but strategically dispassionate U.S. president who had rejected Americanizing the war was abruptly murdered. The mission of the American military would now fall under the authority of a new commander in chief. And a national election to choose the next president loomed just one year away. In this sense, in the late autumn of 1963 the path ahead in Vietnam had not yet been defined. Several scenarios could still come to pass: an opportunistic American withdrawal under the best circumstances available; the doubling-down of the U.S. commitment with combat forces; or perhaps some outcome in between.

In his reappraisal of the war, Bundy did not ascribe great significance to the violent overthrow of Diem and Nhu, which preceded the Kennedy assassination by just three weeks. "In the end," Bundy wrote, "the death of Diem was the result of a Vietnamese conspiracy, and in the end the Americans had done no more than make it clear that they would not be opposed to such action."[67] Neither did Bundy seem to hold himself particularly responsible for the coordination and performance of the national security bureaucracy that initiated the coup. While conceding that the process of instigating the coup was "hasty and imprudent," Bundy believed there was "no point in a post-mortem—the misunderstanding had been between the president and Forrestal."[68] About the August 1963 authorization to green-light the plot, a glib Bundy was fond of observing that Forrestal's hurriedly approved cable to Saigon was evidence of Bundy's dictum, "Never do business on the weekend." He used this quip often, seemingly untroubled by the appearance of the former national security adviser shrugging off a pivotal breakdown in the bureaucracy that culminated in the murder of two leaders of an American proxy regime. President Kennedy and his brother were less forgiving. "This shit has got to stop!" the president told Forrestal. In the aftermath of the bungled weekend cable, when Kennedy learned that both McNamara and CIA director John McCone had strong reservations about initiating a coup, Forrestal had offered his resignation. "You're not worth firing," Kennedy told his aide. "You owe me something, so you stick around." Robert Kennedy placed some of the blame on the national security adviser. "Mac Bundy wasn't particularly helpful," he said, acting too much as a "gatekeeper" and not enough as an adviser.[69]

In other comments about the coup Bundy was more critical and reflective. "The weekend cable is inexcusable," he told me.[70] "You're damned if you do and damned if you don't," said Bundy about Diem's overthrow. "Can we do it with Diem? No, we can't. Should we be the ones who force a change? No we shouldn't. So do we sit still and just wait for pot-luck? JFK was not that kind of a patient man." Bundy remarked that the troika of Harriman, Forrestal, and Hilsman was similarly impatient. "And the rest of us who may have been a little more patient were a little less attentive. . . . What do you do if you honestly think that you can't get there from here?"[71] Bundy answered his own question by citing guidance that contrasted dramatically with his activist counsel on Cuba and Vietnam. "You can begin with the presumptive negative, that we ought not to *ever* be in a position where *we* are deciding, or undertaking to decide, or even trying to influence the internal political power structure," of another country, he said.[72] With this pronouncement disavowing a broad category of intervention, Bundy had clearly traveled a great distance in his thinking since his years as national security adviser.

Some historians have suggested that American culpability for Diem's overthrow further committed the United States to defend South Vietnam against the communist insurgency.[73] It was a view Bundy was inclined to support in his later years. "There isn't much doubt in my own mind," he said, "that the degree of our responsibility for the change of regime deepens our stake and our role and the imperative on us that we quote 'do enough.'"[74] Yet did Kennedy share Bundy's sense of such an enlarged obligation?

Examined more deeply, the claim that responsibility for the Diem coup would stimulate an enhanced American commitment to Vietnam is predicated on the expectation that U.S. policy would thereafter be driven by a sense of guilt. This is a questionable historical premise. Kennedy had rejected pleas from his advisers in 1961 to deploy combat troops to Vietnam at a time when he was told the odds were sharply against saving the country without a potentially major infusion of ground forces. Why would the confusion surrounding the Diem coup two years later change Kennedy's decidedly negative assessment of a military mission he had previously rejected? No credible evidence exists to suggest that Kennedy's judgment would have been so fundamentally transformed by the replacement of the Diem regime.

Moreover, just two weeks after Diem's murder an unsentimental Kennedy publicly reaffirmed his limitation on ground troop deployments. "Are we going to give up in South Vietnam?" Kennedy asked rhetorically at a news conference on November 14, 1963. "The most important program, of course, is our national security, but I don't want the United States to have to put troops there." When a reporter asked about the forthcoming military conference in Hawaii, President Kennedy explained, "The purpose of the meeting at Honolulu . . . is to attempt to assess the situation: what American policy should be, how we can intensify the struggle, how we can bring Americans out of there. Now that is our object, to bring Americans home, permit the South Vietnamese to maintain themselves as a free and independent country."[75]

If Diem was not wholly a creation of U.S. policy, he was certainly a client of American power, the leader of a fragile regime increasingly dependent on American aid and support for its very survival. And as the history of the Kennedy administration in 1963 illustrates, the great power that sponsored Diem's rule was deeply divided over how his fate should be decided. Not only was the national security bureaucracy split over the fundamental question of whether the United States should support the military in its coup effort, the bureaucracy itself was operating without clear control. Bundy, the coordinating force in the White House, failed to manage the president's advisers, a failure shared with Kennedy's other most senior aides. Perhaps more important, Kennedy in 1963 also allowed the bureaucracy to elude his firm command—a sharp contrast to the vigilant control he exercised in response to the effort by many of the same members of the bureaucracy in 1961 to install ground troops in Vietnam. Diem's violent demise demonstrated a sharp contrast to Kennedy's vigorous management of the missile crisis but a similarity to the maladroit performance of his national security team in the Bay of Pigs fiasco. In retrospect, the lesson of the Diem coup suggested by the experience of the national security adviser as well as the president was perhaps the same: Never trust the bureaucracy to get it right.

POLITICS IS THE ENEMY
OF STRATEGY

As McGeorge Bundy reflected on American strategy in Vietnam in 1964, he put the bureaucracy's mess of the Diem affair behind him. What is there to say? Bundy asked himself. His answer was succinct: "It never worked."[1] Diem's assassination was "a bungled affair; but also a loser anyway, and not as bad as it looked."[2] Instead, he identified and repeatedly discussed another variable that was far more consequential to Lyndon Johnson's first year in the White House—the forthcoming presidential election. For Bundy, the 1964 campaign loomed over the political landscape, its shadow blotting out any sense of urgency, initiative, or imagination in the evaluation of America's strategic options in Vietnam. The 1964 election, Bundy observed, was the imperative force driving Lyndon Johnson. "The preemptive concern: win, win, win the election, not the war."[3] From Johnson's first day as president, Bundy wrote, the new president was consumed with "the inescapable reality" that he would face an election in less than a year, compelling him "to run and win and win as big as possible." Johnson confided to Bundy in the winter of 1964 that he felt he had only inherited the presidency and was simply a "trustee" who would not command a real political mandate to determine major policy questions unless he prevailed in a national election in November. "And then you can make a decision," Johnson explained.[4] Meanwhile, Bundy would later observe, "Vietnam is sort of going to hell . . . while all the center of political energy of the Executive Branch is on the election."[5]

As Bundy came to depict it, the forthcoming 1964 presidential election was a powerful deterrent for Johnson to take any definitive action regarding the American commitment in Vietnam. "My own impression, then and through the early summer," he recalled, "was that he wanted firmness and steadiness in Vietnamese policy, but no large new decisions."[6] In his later years, Bundy portrayed Johnson as a former Senate majority leader and legislative tactician who conceived of Vietnam in 1964 not as a strategic challenge but as a political threat. "LBJ isn't deeply concerned about who governs Laos, or who governs South Vietnam—he's deeply concerned with what the average American voter is going to think about how he did in the ball game of the Cold War," he recounted. "The great Cold War championship gets played in the largest stadium in the United States and he, Lyndon Johnson, is the quarterback, and if he loses, how does he do in the next election? So don't lose. Now that's too simple, but it's where he is. He's living with his own political survival every time he looks at these questions."[7]

As he sketched notes about the transitional year between the assassination and the 1964 election, Bundy identified some of the key themes that would merit emphasis in his narrative: the assumption of power and the continuation in office of most of the Kennedy team; a public stance of both resolve and "readiness for peace"; a maintenance of Kennedy's policy of "no American boys" deployed to combat in South

Vietnam; and the "accidental opportunity" of the Gulf of Tonkin incident, which combined both immediate electoral interests and "long-range needs." About the Gulf of Tonkin attacks and the subsequent congressional resolution authorizing military action in Vietnam, Bundy advised that the episode should be described in a detailed fashion because it captured Johnson's essential attributes as a political actor: his cunning, opportunism, ambition, and perpetual search for tactical advantage.[8] The Gulf of Tonkin affair emerged repeatedly in my interviews and discussions with Bundy, who described it as typically "Johnsonian" and reflective of how the president sought to conflate his political interests with political opportunities—with both subordinated to the goal of winning the 1964 election.

∽

Despite the shock and upheaval associated with President Kennedy's assassination, there was never any real doubt that McGeorge Bundy, the quintessential Kennedy man, wanted to remain in the Johnson White House. Some of the more passionate Kennedy loyalists, encouraged either by principle or by circumstance, would resign. Bundy, however, wanted to stay in power. In fact, he perceived an obligation to continue to serve as one of the president's preeminent counselors. "There was no other choice but to stay on at least through the election of '64," Bundy explained in a 1972 oral history. "After that one could have made a break if one hadn't wanted to go on." Bundy acknowledged, however, that he did want to serve in the Johnson administration, separating himself from the most committed Kennedy loyalists. Among those who remained close to Robert Kennedy there was, said Bundy, a "sense of succession . . . from the fallen President to Bob Kennedy" and a view "that it was wrong to stay in the administration if you were going to give full allegiance to the new president. I saw no way to stay in the administration without doing that. And I think I had an argument with Bob on exactly that topic at one point."[9]

As one of the senior aides that Lyndon Johnson had inherited but not chosen, Bundy had a limited relationship with the former vice president. Bundy conceded—with considerable understatement—that "there were differences of a somewhat cultural sort" between the new president and his national security adviser. Johnson was a political animal and "a practical full-time Washington operator"—a "self-made man" from Texas who had risen to become "the second most powerful man" in the nation's capital as Senate majority leader during the Eisenhower era. Bundy was, by contrast, "a Bostonian great-grandchild of self-made men (themselves often with head-starts)," as well as "an academic manager" and "a political zero." It was appropriate, Bundy noted, that as a member of the White House staff, it was understood that he would not be required to testify on Capitol Hill.[10]

Before Kennedy's assassination, the lines of authority descending from the White House defined the relationship between Bundy and Johnson. In large meetings, Bundy said, Johnson was reserved and "careful, as Vice Presidents surely should be," not to take a position that would put him at odds with the president. Bundy concurred with Kennedy's judgment that in light of Johnson's considerable self-regard and passionate views on many policy issues, the vice president deserved "considerable credit as a team player." Bundy did not know what Johnson truly believed about such issues as Cuba, Berlin, or Vietnam. It would have been "inappropriate," he noted, for him to query the vice president on such matters, and he surmised that Johnson similarly deemed it "wrong to seem to lobby" the national security adviser. It was "a cordial relationship," Bundy concluded, "but careful on both sides."[11]

During Kennedy's presidency, Bundy would periodically engage with Vice President Johnson and his staff, assisting with the preparation for his trips abroad. Johnson and his wife would in turn invite the Bundys to an occasional event or reception, "and we always tried to go," Bundy recalled, at first simply to be polite, but over time because the parties offered an opportunity to be introduced to "wonderful and interesting people" that did not travel in Bundy's circle, such as Representative Jack Brooks of Texas, "who combined natural shrewdness with a strong sense of political comedy" in a way that reminded Bundy of Johnson himself.[12]

Over time, Bundy became more familiar with Lyndon Johnson's circle and its idiosyncratic social rituals, many of which occurred at the president's beloved ranch in Texas. Bundy vividly recalled one of Johnson's favorite activities there. Sitting behind the wheel of "a battered old Cadillac," the president would "drive you around at rates of speed that would be totally terrifying," across "open fields" with the Secret Service in hot pursuit, "going crazy as they tried to keep up with him." Bundy remembered the ranch as a place where the president felt completely at home and where he felt comfortable conducting business, even around his swimming pool. "This was the only swimming pool I ever encountered that had a telephone at every corner," he said.[13]

In the days following the assassination, the political world converged on Washington. Former President Eisenhower not only attended the state funeral but also advised Johnson on his sudden assumption of power. "Ike was trying to get the new President to abandon all the bad habits of his predecessor," Bundy reported, calling it "a fairly hard-boiled and untimely kind of business." Bundy speculated that Eisenhower was responding to a direct request for advice from the new president: How should he reorganize the White House in light of the swift transition from one president to another? It turned out that what Eisenhower was most interested in reorganizing was Bundy's national security bureaucracy. "He has a picture of chaos-among-the-children, I guess," Bundy said of Eisenhower.

The former president advised Johnson to solicit blanket resignations from all of his senior advisers—in essence to sweep the slate clean and handpick his own team. Before any such order could be given, however, Kennedy's close adviser Arthur Schlesinger Jr. decided on his own initiative to submit a letter to the new president indicating he would step down. Johnson quickly told Bundy to see Schlesinger and make sure he did not quit. The president wanted the entire White House staff to continue without change because "he needed the staff more than Kennedy did." When Johnson left the room, Eisenhower reiterated his view, as Bundy put it, that "the President would be making a great mistake not to have routine resignations submitted. I strongly agreed and urged him to make the point to the President." When Johnson returned, Eisenhower and Bundy made their case. "The President reluctantly accepted our counsel," Bundy noted, "and by the following Tuesday or Wednesday he was beginning to ask where everyone's resignation was." Bundy believed the episode captured "a general characteristic of the President's mind." Johnson's real concern was not with Schlesinger but rather to prevent a mass exodus of the White House staff, "which he greatly feared (with some reason)." It would not be the first time Bundy would observe how Johnson would seek to straddle both sides of a particular political equation. He wanted the loyalty and reflected credibility of Kennedy's team, but he also wanted the latitude to dismantle it and fashion an advisory apparatus that served his own needs and interests.

Bundy's journal entry describes the frayed emotions of the transition from Kennedy to Johnson. Moments of great sadness were triggered by disparate routines and images: riding the White House elevator; reading cable traffic President Kennedy would have cared about; working alone in his office and looking "in Ted Sorensen's face at every stage."

"Only three years," Sorensen told Bundy mournfully, adding that "the President was his life." The sadness was enveloping. "I found myself barely able to conduct a staff meeting—but I did, I guess," Bundy wrote. On Sunday, November 24, 1963, Bundy recalled getting a black vest for the president's funeral, planning for the arrival of various dignitaries, and processing papers and memos for a meeting that afternoon between Johnson and Ambassador Lodge, who had flown in from Saigon. "I did not know then what the President told me later, that he had always found

Lodge a headline-hunting 'phony,'" Bundy noted. "Nor was it as clear then as it became later that the President never liked the idea of a coup in the first place." After huddling briefly with McNamara and Rusk, the president "gave Lodge a good firm piece of his mind," demanding that the ambassador pull his country team together, end the "backbiting," and get on with the war. Johnson told Lodge that "he would hold him personally responsible for progress." Rusk and Bundy shared the view that "the President did as well in this interview as Lodge did badly."

The following morning, the day of Kennedy's funeral, began with staff work on foreign visitors and included "a fuss" with George Ball at the State Department over the president's agenda of meetings with foreign dignitaries. It was one of several "wrangles" between the two men, suggesting to Bundy that Ball harbored the hope that the change of administrations would somehow liberate him from "the wretched White House staff." Bundy regretted his "squabbles" with Ball, whom he considered "a very able and useful man" but also a "scatter-brained administrator" possessing "erratic" judgment. Bundy also noted "a bit of a flurry" over security arrangements for the French president, Charles de Gaulle. In response to concerns expressed by CIA director John McCone that the world leaders marching behind President Kennedy's coffin provided "an enormous number" of "tempting" targets (in Bundy's words), Bundy and the State Department's chief of protocol, Angier Biddle Duke, urged de Gaulle to ride in a limousine rather than walk in the funeral procession. "He replied 'Non' in his most distant and nasal tone," Bundy noted. "We bowed and withdrew. He was right."

After the ceremony at Arlington National Cemetery, Bundy and his colleagues sped back to the White House for four hours of receptions. Jacqueline Kennedy had offered to receive the heads of the many visiting delegations. "She received them all like a queen," Bundy observed. He also reported her advice to de Gaulle that if he ever needed assistance or to speak to the right Americans, he should contact Robert McNamara,

Robert Kennedy, or Bundy. "I believe the first two," Bundy noted drily. Back at the State Department, President Johnson received a series of foreign dignitaries, while thirty-five governors waited for him in the Executive Office Building. Johnson, Bundy reported, did "a really splendid job with all comers."[14]

Nine days after the funeral, on December 4, Bundy noted, "There is still much uncertainty and concern . . . but the first great shock has passed," and his colleagues were returning to their daily routines. The most comforting five minutes of that day, Bundy reported, had been spent in conversation with Kenneth O'Donnell, President Kennedy's political confidant from the beginning of his career. "I have hardly been able to trade a sentence with him in the last two weeks, so deep has been his pain," Bundy wrote, observing that as national security adviser his first priority was to address the new president's immediate needs and problems, "even on the first awful Friday afternoon."[15]

In addition to his encounter with O'Donnell, Bundy also described being summoned for "a quite comical interview in the pool" in which Johnson indicated his desire to shift his focus that day from labor and business issues to foreign policy. "I did not produce any very good proposal," Bundy recalled in another memorandum for the record, but the president produced "a first-rate one" by the following morning. Johnson decided to deliver a "pep talk" to the State Department coauthored by Bundy. The result was a "much needed shot in the arm" to the department, Bundy said, and an expression of Johnson's "confidence in Dean Rusk."[16]

A few days later Johnson met with another of Washington's wise men, Dean Acheson. In advance of the meeting Johnson was presented with "a 3-page memorandum of the purest Achesonian gospel," in which the former secretary of state advised Johnson against supporting Charles de Gaulle's quest for an independent French nuclear weapons capability, and also to avoid negotiations with the Soviet Union on the future of

Germany. In a cover memo to Johnson, Bundy wrote: "Re your lunch with Acheson: He is a determined believer in the 'hard line.' . . . Acheson believes in action even during an election year (he remembers what Truman accomplished in '48) and has little patience for less developed countries, the UN, Adlai Stevenson, George Kennan, etc."[17]

Bundy described Johnson as "extremely shrewd and sensitive" in his appraisal of the document, adding that the president "is plainly first-rate in his ability to pick and choose from the counsel he gets."[18] But what of Acheson's guidance to take bold action in the realm of foreign affairs despite the strictures of a presidential election? Would Johnson take that advice to heart? Would Bundy encourage Johnson to grapple with the difficult choices ahead in Vietnam even though the White House race hovered on the horizon? These unanswered questions would prove pivotal to the politics and policy of 1964.

From the first days of Johnson's presidency, the record shows his preoccupation with the problem of Vietnam. "The President has expressed his deep concern that our effort in Viet-Nam be stepped up to highest pitch," Rusk informed Lodge in early December, "and that each day we ask ourselves what more we can do to further the struggle."[19] John McCone detected a discernible shift between Kennedy and his successor, noting, "Johnson definitely feels that we place too much emphasis on social reforms; he has very little tolerance with our spending so much time being 'do-gooders'; and he has no tolerance whatsoever with bickering and quarreling of the type that has gone on in South Vietnam."[20] Social reforms aside, the metrics that gauged security did not instill confidence, either. Mike Forrestal explained to President Johnson that the strategic hamlet program—a key element in the counterinsurgency strategy, focusing on evicting the Vietcong from rural villages—was in disarray. In Long An Province south of Saigon, only 45 of the 219 hamlets said to be operational had actually been secured. The implication, suggested Forrestal, was that either prior South Vietnamese reports had been falsified or the enemy was making rapid progress.[21] How could the discrepancy be explained? Johnson insisted on an eyewitness analysis, instructing McNamara to extend an upcoming NATO trip with a visit to Saigon. "The President gave McNamara quite a lecture on South Vietnam," Dean Rusk reported, "and expressed concern that we as a government were not doing everything we should."[22]

Two weeks later, Bundy described "an extraordinarily interesting meeting" following Secretary McNamara's return from a mission to Saigon. McNamara's audience was "a tense and subdued group" gathered before the fireplace in the president's office. It included Major General Victor Krulak and Bill Bundy from the Pentagon; John McCone and William Colby, the director of the Far East Division, from the CIA; Dean Rusk, George Ball, Averell Harriman, Roger Hilsman, and William Sullivan from the State Department; and McGeorge Bundy from the White House. McNamara told the assembled officials that the situation in South Vietnam was "unsatisfactory" as concerned the Saigon government, "unsatisfactory" in terms of the performance of the American country team, and "unsatisfactory in the field," particularly in the provinces of the Mekong Delta.

There was "no directing force" in the Saigon regime, McNamara complained, arguing "that a committee of a dozen generals is no instrument of government, but rather a device for keeping qualified military men away from their real duties." McNamara had confidence in only one of the army's leaders: Major General Big Minh, the chairman of the executive committee of the Revolutionary Council and president of the provisional government. McNamara had strongly encouraged Minh to take firm control of the country himself, but "he doubted if in fact there was the necessary will to power there."[23]

According to Bundy's account, McNamara described an "absence of central direction and leadership" from the American team in Saigon as well as a "complete absence of serious communications" between

Ambassador Lodge and General Harkins. The status of the counterinsurgency effort was also insufficient. The obvious and compelling question, Bundy noted, was how long the situation in Vietnam had been so dismal and why that finding had been rejected for as long as it had and so ardently by the Defense Department (up to and including McNamara himself). The dispiriting scenario that McNamara's report suggested was that the American advisers in Saigon had been manipulated by "the propaganda of Diem's provincial officers for quite a while." Bundy also observed that Johnson "listened quietly" to McNamara's report, not committing to any particular response.[24]

After the briefing, Bundy sat in a small meeting with McNamara, McCone, and the president. The CIA director and the defense secretary reported that Ambassador Lodge was unwilling to leave his position and would contemplate resigning only if he could justify it by some difference over policy or if he could return "on the wings of some visible success." Johnson castigated Lodge for "playing politics" when he should be focused on his responsibilities as ambassador. McNamara and Johnson both bemoaned Lodge's practice of "leaking to the press."[25]

"The situation is very disturbing," McNamara concluded in his official report to the president. "Current trends, unless reversed in the next 2–3 months, will lead to neutralization at best and more likely to a Communist-controlled state. The new government is the greatest source of concern. It is indecisive and drifting." The more favorable assessments of previous months were now questionable. "Viet Cong progress has been great during the period since the coup, with my best guess being that the situation has in fact been deteriorating in the countryside since July to a far greater extent than we realized because of our undue dependence on distorted Vietnamese reporting."[26] McCone concurred that the South Vietnamese reports of progress from the front were basically fraudulent.[27]

The Joint Chiefs lobbied for a more aggressive American strategy.

They argued in a memorandum of January 22, 1964, that Washington should renounce "self-imposed restrictions" and authorize "aerial bombing of critical targets in North Vietnam" and the deployment of "U.S. forces, as necessary, in direct actions against North Vietnam."[28] Exactly two months after Kennedy's death, the chiefs were proposing air strikes against Hanoi and the deployment of U.S. troops, not just in an advisory role but in offensive operations against the North. The Joint Chiefs of Staff were proposing, in essence, the initial steps to Americanize the Vietnam War.

One week after the chiefs issued their recommendation, the cabal of generals who had removed President Diem from power were themselves overthrown by a clique of younger military men led by General Nguyen Khanh.[29] David Nes, the new deputy chief of the U.S. mission, had been in South Vietnam for only two months before issuing a startlingly bleak assessment of the options confronting the United States. In a memorandum to Ambassador Lodge on February 17, Nes warned, "My reading of developments . . . lead[s] me to fear that General de Gaulle may be right in his belief that we are faced with the choice between accepting the possible collapse of our counter-insurgency efforts here or the escalation of the conflict toward a direct military confrontation of [North Vietnam] and China by the U.S."[30]

Responding to a request from McNamara for military recommendations, the Joint Chiefs proposed on March 2 that U.S. "air and naval elements" directly participate in attacks on military and industrial targets in North Vietnam, in addition to the mining of North Vietnamese harbors, imposition of a naval blockade, and in the event that China intervened, the possible use of nuclear weapons.[31] President Johnson met with the chiefs to discuss their politically incendiary proposals. He then phoned Bundy. "I just spent a lot of time with the Joint Chiefs," Johnson said. "The net of it . . . is—they say get in or get out. And I told them, 'Let's try to find an amendment that will—we haven't got any Congress that will go with us, and we haven't got any mothers that will go with us in a war.' And [for] nine months I'm just an inherited—I'm a trustee. I've got to win an election. Or Nixon or somebody else has. And then you can make a decision."[32] The president's phone call appears to foreshadow his legislative strategy to bring Congress along with the administration before the election, a strategy that would take concrete form in the Tonkin Gulf resolution.

As Johnson desperately tried to buy time until November, support grew for the neutralization of South Vietnam. From Paris, Charles de Gaulle insisted that the U.S. mission was doomed and that negotiations constituted the only realistic alternative course. Walter Lippmann, the influential Washington columnist, endorsed the French position. "The official American view is to say unreservedly that the war will be won and refuse to think about what we shall do if it cannot be won," Lippmann wrote. "A competent statesman, like any competent military strategist, never locks himself into a commitment where there is no other position on which he can fall back. In Southeast Asia we have bolted the doors and do not have that indispensable part of any strategy, a fall-back position." Lippmann argued that the French leader was correct to observe that a fundamental absence of realist analysis was pushing Washington to the precipice of a "disaster which will leave us an intolerable choice between a humiliating withdrawal and engaging in a much larger war, at least as large as the Korean War."[33] Two influential Democratic senators, Mike Mansfield and Richard Russell, had already urged Johnson to seek French support in achieving a settlement, even if such a course provided "only a faint glimmer of hope."[34]

Sentiment in favor of a negotiated neutralization was even bubbling up in Saigon, alarming the country's military rulers. The CIA speculated that some in the regime opposed to neutralization might be prompted to intervene. "It is possible," the CIA reported about General Khanh, "that he feels this alleged tendency . . . is becoming so pronounced that that he and his like-minded military associates must act to prevent a neutral solution."

Bundy was scornful of the arguments for neutralization, warning Johnson in a January 6 memo that if a diplomatic settlement were allowed to prompt an American withdrawal from South Vietnam, it would result in a cascade of dire geopolitical consequences: "A rapid collapse of anti-communist forces in South Vietnam, and a reunification of the whole country on Communist terms . . . Neutrality in Thailand, and increased influence for Hanoi and Peking . . . Collapse of the anti-Communist position in Laos . . . Heavy pressure on . . . Malaysia . . . A shift toward neutrality in Japan and the Philippines . . . Blows to U.S. prestige in South Korea and Taiwan which would require compensating increases in American commitments there—or else further retreat." Bundy further cautioned the president that neutrality for South Vietnam would be viewed by "all anti-communist Vietnamese" as a "betrayal," thus alienating a constituency with sufficient size and influence "to lose us an election." Here was Bundy brandishing the ultimate threat—not the loss of South Vietnam but the loss of a presidential election. And here was Bundy conflating the domino theory as it applied to Southeast Asia and the soft underbelly of Johnson's bid for victory in November—in a way that would be especially threatening to a president with Johnson's insecurities. Bundy elaborated on the risks of appearing soft in response to the communist threat in a second memo to Johnson. Reminding the president that he was an "ex-historian," Bundy invoked the legacy of Harry Truman, driven from Washington in disrepute and blamed by many Americans for not doing enough to avert China's fall to communism or to win the Korean War. "That is exactly what would happen now if we seem to be the first to quit in Saigon. . . . *When* we are stronger, *then* we can negotiate."[35]

Bundy's disdain for those urging an exploration of the neutrality option was illustrative of a larger dynamic. The national security adviser was often contemptuous of the administration's critics, whom he tended to dismiss as weak. That was his response in February 1964 to the rising skepticism of the *New York Times*. "The Times editorial page is a soft page, Mr. President," Bundy declared. ". . . They don't have a lot of judgment. You've got to show them you're a man of peace without letting them call the tune, I think, and you're damned good at that."[36]

As part of an effort to derail the momentum for neutralization, Johnson and his advisers sought to press President de Gaulle to publicly reverse his position. Meeting for lunch on March 24, 1964, Johnson, Bundy, McNamara, and Rusk agreed on the elements of a cable to Charles Bohlen, the U.S. ambassador to France, seeking a statement from de Gaulle in which he would clarify "that the idea of 'neutralization' does not apply to the attitudes or policies of the Government of Vietnam or its friends in the face of the current communist aggression." De Gaulle refused the American request, telling Bohlen that the United States had become embroiled in a conflict in Vietnam that was essentially the same as the French had encountered there at the end of World War II. De Gaulle argued that the neutralization of South Vietnam—perhaps through a Geneva conference including China—was the best course available to the United States.[37]

Bundy was rankled by the French position. He was also annoyed with the continued support it received from Walter Lippmann. When Lippmann visited Bundy at the White House on May 19, the national security adviser asked snippily, "Well, what's the French plan? I can't seem to find out, and you presumably know what it is, so tell me." The columnist, a friend of Bundy's, said that he did not reply to questions asked in such a tone. Bundy apologized but pushed ahead, belittling de Gaulle's neutralization proposal as simply a vehicle for communist hegemony. "Mac, please don't speak in such clichés," said Lippmann. It would be awful, Bundy replied prophetically, if American lives were lost in Vietnam only to have the country end up under communist control.[38]

The next morning Lippmann composed a column that appeared to take aim at Bundy—both for his reflexive rejection of the neutralization option and for his passivity in coordinating a realistic White House strategy for Vietnam. "We are missing the main point and we are stultifying our influence when we dismiss the French policies as not really serious, as expressions of personal pique ... as inspired by 'anti-Americanism' and a wish to embarrass the U.S.," wrote Lippmann. While the French plan for neutralization might be sketchy, the Johnson administration had "no credible policy for winning the war or for ending it." That absence of analytical rigor had produced only one implausible option, "the unconditional surrender of the enemy. . . . We are supporting and promoting a cruel and nasty war that has no visible end. There is no light at the end of the tunnel."[39]

Despite Bundy's dismissal of neutrality for South Vietnam, President Johnson appeared to harbor some of the same pessimism and doubt that characterized Lippmann's scorching columns. On May 27 he confided his concerns about Vietnam to Richard Russell, the chairman of the Senate Armed Services Committee and the president's political mentor. "Well, they'd impeach a President though that would run out, wouldn't they?" Johnson asked. ". . . And I don't know how in the hell you're gonna get out unless they tell you to get out."

"If we had a man running the government over there that told us to get out, we could sure get out," Russell replied.

"That's right," said Johnson, "but you can't do that. . . . Wouldn't that pretty well fix us in the eyes of the world though and make it look mighty bad?"

"I don't know," Russell chuckled. "We don't look too good right now. You'd look pretty good, I guess, going in there with all the troops and sending them all in there, but I tell you it'll be the most expensive venture this country ever went into."[40]

The president called Bundy moments after hanging up with Russell. "I'll tell you," said Johnson, "the more that I stayed awake last night thinking of this thing . . . I don't know what in the hell—it looks to me like we're getting into another Korea. It just worries the hell out of me. I don't see what we can ever hope to get out of there with, once we're committed. I believe that the Chinese Communists are coming into it. I don't think that we can fight them ten thousand miles away from home. . . . I don't think it's worth fighting for and I don't think that we can get out. It's just the biggest damn mess that I ever saw."

"It is," Bundy replied. "It's an awful mess."

"What does Bill think we ought to do?" asked President Johnson, referring to Bundy's brother, who had replaced Roger Hilsman as the assistant secretary of state for Far Eastern affairs. "He's in favor of touching things up," replied Bundy vaguely, "but you ought to talk to him about it." Bundy noted that Forrestal, his own Vietnam expert, "thinks we ought to be ready to move a little bit. . . . He believes really that that's the best way of galvanizing the South, that if they feel that we are prepared to take a little action against the center of this infection, that that's the best way."

Bundy appeared to be recommending direct military action against the insurgency by U.S. forces. But what strategy was connoted by "touching things up" and "take a little action"? Johnson tried to puncture his national security adviser's euphemistic imprecision. "What action do we take though?" the president asked.[41]

Johnson was obviously asking for a substantive statement of his military options in South Vietnam. Just two days earlier Bundy had submitted an emphatic but sketchy proposal to the president recommending a major military escalation "backed by resolute and extensive deployment" of an undefined number of combat forces. Bundy had warned the president that "in making this decision . . . we must accept two risks . . . the risk of escalation toward major land war or the use of nuclear weapons" and "the risk of a reply in South Vietnam itself which would lose that country to neutralism and so eventually to Communism." Bundy proposed a conference in Honolulu "which might occur early next week" to consult with Ambassador Lodge and others. "At the same time, or just after, we would communicate our basic determination and our opening strategy to the governments of Thailand, Laos and South Vietnam." Bundy further anticipated an approach to the United Nations, the purpose of which "is to clarify again that we have tried the UN and that it is not our fault that there has been an inadequate response." Following consultation with SEATO allies, Washington would implement the first deployment of an undefined number of U.S. and allied combat forces. "It is our recommendation that these deployments be on a very large scale, from the beginning, so as to maximize their deterrent impact and their menace. We repeat our view that a pound of threat is worth an ounce of action—as long as we are not bluffing." The final element of Bundy's plan was an unspecified "initial strike against the north" that would be "carefully designed to have more deterrent than destructive impact, as far as possible." The American attack would be quickly followed by an "active diplomatic offensive in the Security Council, or in a Geneva Conference, or both, aimed at restoring the peace throughout the area. This peacekeeping theme," Bundy assured the president, "will have been at the center of the whole enterprise from the beginning." In a cover note to Johnson, Bundy explained that his paper also represented Rusk and McNamara's current views. He conceded, however, that there were "several holes in this discussion, most notably on action in South Vietnam and on the precise U.S. objectives, but there is more thinking on these topics than this particular paper shows."[42]

Not surprisingly, in his conversation with President Johnson on May 27, Bundy was unprepared to explain what precise form of military action he was suggesting. He therefore dodged the question. "We really need to do you some target folder work, Mr. President," he replied nonchalantly, "that shows precisely what we do and don't mean here. The main object is to kill as few people as possible while creating an environment in which the incentive to react is as low as possible. But I can't say to you this is a small matter."

Having disclosed nothing specific about the president's military options, Bundy swiftly shifted gear, turning the discussion to the military draft and White House communications strategy. "There's one other thing that . . . I've just thought about overnight," he told the president. ". . . I'd like to know what would happen if we really dramatized this as 'Americans Against Terror' and 'Americans Keeping Their Commitment' and 'Americans Who Have Only Peace as Their Object.' " While Bundy had only hinted indistinctly at the elements of an American military plan for Vietnam, he had much more developed suggestions on how to market a deeper investment of resources there.[43]

Bundy and Johnson returned to the question of neutralization. Johnson proposed that Walter Lippmann visit the White House later that day, May 27, for further discussion. That afternoon Lippmann was ushered into the Oval Office for a meeting with the president, who was joined by Bundy, McNamara, and Ball. Johnson's line of attack parroted Bundy's arguments. The president challenged the columnist to explain how neutralization could prevent the communists from taking power in South Vietnam. Lippmann conceded that there was no guarantee that the communists would be held in check. But neither was there a realistic alternative. Relying on a military solution to resolve the crisis in Vietnam, he explained, would fail for the United States just as it had failed for France. Unperturbed and unconvinced, Johnson shoved a stack of top-secret documents across his desk which, he claimed, illustrated that the war was turning against the communists. Lippmann countered that the sources he consulted reported the opposite. "It is not easy for any country to repair its mistakes," Lippmann observed in his column the next day. But the United States must do so because even "if the prospects of a conference are not brilliant, the military outlook in South Vietnam is dismal beyond words." Despite ceaseless assurances from the White House, Lippmann noted, "there has never been a time when a military victory, or anything like a military victory, has been possible."[44]

In the months before the election, the plausibility of a military victory in Vietnam was not a subject that Johnson was inclined to address publicly. Generic invocations of American resolve in the fight against global communism were suitable; so were abstract encomiums about the U.S. commitment to support the government of South Vietnam. But anything more specific could require an exposition from Johnson on the ends and means of an American military strategy for Vietnam that his advisers had not developed and that Johnson had not decided. Yet by early June, as the insurgency continued to grow in potency and the Saigon regime showed no capacity to dilute its strength, there was a sense within the administration that sometime prior to the election Johnson would have to ensure the authority to operate with more military latitude in Vietnam.

On June 10 Bundy circulated a memorandum anticipating the need for congressional approval to enlarge the use of force against North Vietnam. "It is agreed that the U.S. will wish to make its position on Southeast Asia as clear and as strong as possible in the next five months," Bundy argued, sketching the timeline in advance of the November election. "The immediate watershed decision is whether or not the Administration should seek a Congressional resolution giving general authority for action which the President may judge necessary to defend the peace and security of the area. It is agreed that if such a resolution is sought, it should be general in tone. It is also agreed that the best available time for such a move is immediately after the civil rights bill clears the Senate floor. Finally it is agreed that no such resolution should be sought unless careful Congressional soundings indicate rapid passage by a very substantial majority." The proposed legislation, Bundy argued, would not reflect the "intent to usurp the powers of the Congress, but rather a need for the confirmation of the powers of the President as Commander in Chief in an election year."[45] As Bundy's memorandum was circulated in mid-June, it was clear that Johnson, for now, was disinclined to act on it.[46]

Johnson also did not act on another proposal Bundy floated in early June regarding the appointment of Ambassador Lodge's successor in Saigon. The national security adviser proposed six candidates—none of whom would eventually get the job—including Bundy himself. "I am no judge of my own skills and it is certainly true that I have never run an embassy or a war," Bundy wrote. "On the other hand, I think I do understand the issues. I know I care about them. I speak French, and I have a heavy dose of the ways of thinking of all branches of the U.S. team in South Vietnam."[47]

Another politically sensitive question Johnson would have to address in the summer prior to the election was the political fate of Robert F. Kennedy, whose ambition to be named as the president's running mate was among the worst-kept secrets in Washington. When his brother had been president, Robert Kennedy made little effort to cloak his distaste for Johnson. In the midst of the Kennedy-Johnson transition, the tension between the two men would spill out into the open.

In his diary entries in the immediate aftermath of Kennedy's assassination, Bundy describes his first decision on behalf of the new president. It was, he acknowledged, a mistake. Johnson asked where the best place for him to work would be, and Bundy advised him to move immediately into the Oval Office. "We did not stop to think how the family would feel—we were thinking, I believe, of how *we* felt and how much we needed a visible President. We were wrong."

The evening of the assassination Robert Kennedy called Bundy. After a pause when nothing was said, Kennedy came to the point. He and Jacqueline Kennedy were deeply concerned about the late president's White House papers. The national security adviser reassured him that the papers would be secured. Bundy then called Evelyn Lincoln, President Kennedy's personal secretary, and tasked her with the assignment. At eight o'clock the next morning, a Saturday, Bundy found Lincoln hard at work clearing out the late president's papers and personal belongings.

He left Lincoln and conveyed instructions for President Johnson not to come to the West Wing until her work was completed. But Johnson went straight to the Oval Office anyway. "This was too bad," Bundy recalled. "Because he walked into the office and naturally Mrs. Lincoln was upset. Bobby was there, as bad luck would have it, and it wasn't until I heard from the President on the phone that I was able to get upstairs and straighten things out. I explained how clear it now was that the Kennedys would prefer to put off the time of use of the President's office, and he quite rightly said I should have called him direct."[48] It was not until many years later that Bundy learned Robert Kennedy was probably in the Oval Office to remove the secret listening devices installed by President Kennedy. "I've only in later years figured out what was *bothering* Bobby so much," Bundy told me. "He was dismantling the tapes."[49]

Bundy ushered Johnson to the White House basement, where he fortuitously found John McCone, "and we put it out" that the president had come for a national security briefing. Bundy accepted blame for Robert Kennedy's awkward encounter with Johnson, explaining to the late president's brother that it was a "misunderstanding." Kennedy accepted Bundy's apology and the two men agreed to forget about the incident. "And publicly we all did. Privately it was less harmless. The air on the Kennedy side was already blue with tangled stories of asserted insensitivity on the way back from Dallas. I have never tried to understand either side of this fuss, and I think the short of it is simply that there was too much shock and too many wounded spirits and not enough space on that terrible flight. But this mistake of mine added one stick to the kindling." That afternoon the cabinet convened for a short, "drab little meeting" in which "Bobby was late and perhaps would not have attended if I had not told him he must." The attorney general's condition for participating was that there should be no photographers, "which I now know was as hard for the President as a ban against smoking for a 30-year addict—though he accepted it readily in the interests of harmony."[50]

As the Democratic National Convention neared, Johnson still with-held his choice for a running mate, refusing to clarify his intentions. This was primarily a ploy to inject a shred of anticipation into an exercise oth-erwise devoid of suspense. But Johnson's silence also reflected the fact that he had not yet solved what could be called his Bobby Kennedy prob-lem.[51] While Kennedy desperately wanted to be tapped for the ticket, the conventional wisdom in Washington was that such a political marriage was highly dubious.

"He wanted to run and I wanted him to," recalled Bundy of Robert Kennedy. "He was my preferred candidate." Through the winter of 1964 Bundy spoke with President Johnson "a good deal" about making Robert Kennedy his running mate and "a number of times urged" the president to do so "on the general grounds of reconciliation and overall ticket strength."[52] Bundy remembered discussing the question with Johnson re-peatedly, in the Cabinet Room, the Oval Office, the White House resi-dence, and even in the swimming pool.[53] "Well, there was no sale there," he noted. "We now know very clearly the President just wasn't going to do that."[54]

In the end, Bundy had to acknowledge that the president's thinly veiled loathing for Robert Kennedy made his selection as running mate impossible.[55] "I knew that President Johnson was going to tell the Attor-ney General he wasn't going to have him on the ticket," said Bundy, al-though Kennedy had not yet been informed of President Johnson's decision. "And I had a very difficult evening up here in New York with Bob Kennedy and Mrs. John Kennedy in which . . . they wanted me . . . to tell them more than I was free to tell them about President Johnson's views." Bundy had become a compromised intermediary in one of the most troubled relationships in American politics, knowing things "about the family that I never told the President and things I knew about the President that I never told the family because . . . in that complicated sit-uation that was what those obligations dictated."[56]

In June President Johnson had privately asked Robert McNamara to be his running mate. The defense secretary, still a registered Republican, declined. "I lacked political skills and I knew it," he later said.[57] And despite clamoring among some in the party to put Kennedy on the ticket, Johnson knew it would be politically perilous to do so. According to a Louis Harris survey, 33 percent of Southern Democrats said they would abandon the 1964 ticket if it included Robert Kennedy.[58]

In search of the right political optics to quash the Kennedy scenario, the president instructed the Democratic "wise man" Clark Clifford to draft talking points to be used in a meeting with Kennedy and subsequently inserted into the public record. The president pulled Kennedy into a White House meeting on July 28 to deliver his decision. "I have concluded . . . that it would be inadvisable for you to be the Democratic candidate for Vice President in next year's election," Johnson informed Kennedy, ostentatiously reading from Clifford's talking points. As the attorney general absorbed Johnson's staged remarks, he observed that the president's speakerphone was recording their meeting. When the exchange ended a disappointed Kennedy offered only muted parting words: "I could have helped you, Mr. President."[59] Johnson would eventually choose Senator Hubert Humphrey of Minnesota to join him on the ticket.

With Johnson's decision made, Bundy promptly abandoned Robert Kennedy's cause and urged him to remove himself from consideration as vice president, agreeing to act as an enforcer of sorts for Lyndon Johnson to contain the ambitions of the Kennedy wing of the Democratic Party. Bundy recounted that once Johnson had informed Kennedy he would not be named to the ticket, the president "asked me to suggest to him the advantages for all concerned of Bob's withdrawing from the race on his own steam." Bundy acknowledged that he was foolish to take the bait. "Now that may have been a very naive thing for me to think was a good idea, but I did think it was a good idea," he said. Pointing to Johnson's definitive but still private decision, Bundy urged Robert Kennedy to with-draw. Kennedy was indignant. "It struck him as an outrageous suggestion that would involve him in blatant disloyalty to a lot of people and he was going to pin that rose on Lyndon Johnson," Bundy recalled. "Well I thought that was not right and still think so. What I thought was still more surprising was that he got personally angry over it because there really was a darn good case for doing that."[60]

The president had finally cut the knot with Robert Kennedy. In the process he prompted one of the most prominent Kennedy appointees in his administration to turn against the family and definitively align his political fortunes with Lyndon Johnson. It was an elegant double play that would, of course, leak to the press. As Bundy's role became known, one member of the Kennedy camp told *Newsweek* that the national security adviser was "a Machiavellian turncoat."[61]

Far away from the fervid political atmosphere of Washington, on July 30, 1964, four high-speed South Vietnamese patrol boats attacked two North Vietnamese islands, Hon Me and Hon Ngu, that were suspected of supporting infiltration missions into the south. The attacks were part of a covert CIA mission known as Plan 34-A, conducted in concert with the Saigon regime. That program fell under the jurisdiction of the 303 Com-mittee, the global covert operations oversight group chaired by McGeorge Bundy. Frequently characterized as ineffectual by its critics, Plan 34-A op-erations generally resulted in South Vietnamese agents being captured or killed, while "the seaborne attacks," as Robert McNamara noted, "amounted to little more than pinpricks." Plan 34-A covert operations nonetheless persisted because, as McNamara explained, "the South Vietnamese gov-ernment saw them as a relatively low-cost means of harassing North Viet-nam in retaliation for Hanoi's support of the Vietcong."[62]

On the afternoon of Sunday, August 2, just three days after the covert 34-A attacks, the naval destroyer USS *Maddox* traversed the Gulf of Tonkin. The *Maddox* was engaged in a so-called DESOTO patrol, a routine military mission conducted in international waters to intercept radio and radar signals from shore-based stations in North Vietnam. At 3:40 p.m. Saigon time the *Maddox* encountered a cluster of enemy boats exhibiting an "apparent intention of torpedo attack."[63] Twenty-seven minutes later the *Maddox* reported it was under fire from three North Vietnamese patrol craft and had retaliated. "In the ensuing engagement," the State Department history reports, "the Maddox and aircraft from the U.S.S. Ticonderoga damaged two of the patrol craft which retreated to the North, and left one dead in the water. Reports on the incident reached Washington shortly after 4 a.m."[64] There were no U.S. casualties, and the *Maddox* suffered no damage. Yet, there was physical evidence of the hostilities in the form of a North Vietnamese shell fragment later examined by the Pentagon.[65]

Senior government officials in Washington first learned about the attack in the predawn hours of Sunday morning. At 5:00 a.m., a meeting was convened at Dean Rusk's home, where the secretary of state conferred with Deputy Secretary of Defense Cyrus Vance, Undersecretary of State George Ball, Thomas Hughes of the Bureau of Intelligence and Research, and General Earle G. Wheeler, the new chairman of the Joint Chiefs of Staff. As they gathered to puzzle through the significance of the attack, Rusk and the others pondered a map of Southeast Asia. Where was the Gulf of Tonkin? How many miles was it from shore? And what about the 34-A covert operations just recently conducted in the area? Following hours of inconclusive discussion, they went to the White House at 9:00 a.m. to brief President Johnson. Rather than a counsel of war, notes Hughes, their meeting "was a session full of levity."[66]

"Where are my *Bundys*?" Johnson thundered as his advisers assembled, notably missing the brothers Mac and Bill, who had fled Washington that August weekend for more inviting summer retreats. "I know where they are," the president continued. "They're up there at that female island of theirs, *Martha's Vineyard*. That's where you'll find them, playing tennis at the *female* island." Johnson was half-right. While Mac was at the Bundy vacation home in Manchester, Bill had just started an ill-timed family vacation on the Vineyard. Having dispensed his derisive opening salvo, Johnson turned to business. "What's the big emergency?" he asked.

"Well, Mr. President, one of our destroyers has been attacked," Johnson was told.

"One of our destroyers has been attacked?" Johnson shot back. "How do you know that?

Johnson was informed about the sketchy details of a torpedo attack by North Vietnamese patrol boats. The president paused. "We weren't up to any *mischief* out here, were we?" he inquired.

"Well, you remember, Mr. President," Ball explained, "that you signed off on those 34-A operations last December, that were left as recommendations from the previous administration."

"Oh yes, I remember," said Johnson. "Would it have happened that any of those 34-A operations might have occurred sometime in the vicinity of the attack?"

"Well, we're not sure if we keep exact traffic of Bundy's numbers," one of the president's men ventured. "But it could well be that something happened a couple of nights ago, attacking some of the islands."

"I see," said Johnson, "and that's all we know about it?" Yes, Johnson was told, that was all that was known. "Well," said Johnson, "it reminds me of the movies in Texas. You're sitting next to a pretty girl and you have your hand on her ankle and nothing happens. And you move it up to her knee and nothing happens. You move it up further and you're thinking about moving a bit more and all of a sudden you get slapped. I think we got slapped."

Hughes scribbled a note to Rusk: "Now that we know what happens in the movies in Texas, do you wish to continue to call this an unprovoked attack?" The secretary of state was not amused. "We'll ask Cy Vance, who's our lawyer," said Rusk.

"This was an unprovoked attack, was it not, Cy?" queried Hughes. Vance, "rising to the occasion with a wonderful non-sequitur," as Hughes recalled, offered his legal verdict: "Of course," said Vance. "It happened in international waters."

"Well, it seems a bit murky and we won't have any retaliation," declared Johnson. "But we will warn them against doing anything further. Now, let's get on to something serious." The president then stunned his advisers by shifting the subject of discussion from the hostilities in the Gulf of Tonkin to a somewhat less urgent legislative matter. Johnson asked General Wheeler to comment on the prospects of the U.S. Postal Pay Bill.

"Now, General, you're my chief strategist," explained the president, apparently without a trace of irony, "and this Postal Pay Bill is coming down Pennsylvania Avenue—it's already at 9th Street, going on 10th Street—and I'm going to be damned if I sign it, and damned if I veto it. You're my *strategist*. You tell me how to get out of this!" A flummoxed General Wheeler struggled to answer the president's question. Johnson grew increasingly impatient. "General, you're wasting time," admonished Johnson. "The bill is already at 12th Street!" As the meeting came to a close and the advisers shuffled off, a perplexed General Wheeler asked his colleagues, "Is it always like this?"[67]

Mac Bundy and Bill Bundy, reached in Manchester and Martha's Vineyard, were told to return to Washington. Before their arrival President Johnson met with several of his advisers at an 11:30 a.m. White House meeting.[68] General Maxwell Taylor, who had just replaced Lodge as the new U.S. ambassador to South Vietnam, recommended an immediate reprisal attack. Johnson overruled him, deciding only to send a note of protest to Hanoi and to dispatch another destroyer to conduct patrols with the *Maddox*.[69] Johnson's note was released to the press and broadcast on the Voice of America. The president warned North Vietnam to be "under no misapprehension as to the grave consequences which would inevitably result from any further unprovoked offensive military action against United States forces."[70]

Despite Johnson's posturing, it was well known within the administration that the CIA-sponsored commando raids in the Gulf of Tonkin had probably been the trigger for the attack against the *Maddox*. As McGeorge Bundy was informed by his aide, Mike Forrestal, "It seems likely that the North Vietnamese and perhaps the Chicoms [Chinese Communists] have assumed that the destroyer was part of this operation. . . . It is also possible that Hanoi deliberately ordered the attacks in retaliation for the harassment of the islands."[71] John McCone made the same point directly to President Johnson. "The North Vietnamese are reacting defensively to our attacks on their off-shore islands," he explained.[72]

The *Maddox* returned to the Gulf of Tonkin on Tuesday evening, August 4, accompanied by another American destroyer, the USS *C. Turner Joy*. At 7:40 p.m.—7:40 a.m. in Washington—the *Maddox* reported that unidentified vessels appeared to be preparing for an imminent attack. American fighter aircraft in the area were launched to provide protection. More than ninety minutes later no attack had been initiated, but the *Maddox* remained on alert, looking for signs of enemy action on a moonless night of low hanging clouds and thunderstorms.[73]

On that Tuesday morning, McGeorge Bundy was ensconced in his White House basement office intently monitoring the flow of cable traffic. The summer torpor of Washington had been replaced by a heightened sense of expectation. No attack had been reported, but what would happen next? It was a political moment that Bundy had prepared for and to some degree predicted, but he was nonetheless surprised by an unannounced visit from the president.

It was time to take the draft resolution to Congress, Johnson explained. "I know the firmness and strength of the President's decision because I was one of the first to question it," Bundy wrote years later of his encounter with Johnson in the White House basement that morning.[74] The day had started for the president with a congressional leadership breakfast at 8:45 a.m. to discuss his legislative program.[75] Johnson then descended to the national security adviser's office in the White House basement, which was itself "most unusual," Bundy remembered.[76]

"Get the resolution your brother drafted," Johnson instructed Bundy.

"Mr. President, we ought to think about this," Bundy replied.

"I didn't say that. I didn't ask you what you *thought*," said Johnson. "I told you what to *do*."[77]

Bundy now grasped Johnson's determination to proceed with the resolution. When the national security adviser briefed his staff later that morning, Douglass Cater, a special assistant to the president, asked essentially the same question Bundy had posed to Johnson.

"I would like to think about this proposal," Cater ventured.

"Don't," instructed Bundy. He later said he was not trying to cut off debate but rather to preempt Cater from engaging in resistance that would prove futile.[78]

President Johnson returned to the Oval Office and spoke by phone with the secretary of defense. Although an attack had not yet been reported, Johnson instructed McNamara to identify North Vietnamese targets, "one of their bridges or something," for potential reprisal action. "I wish we could have something that we've already picked out and just hit about three of them damn quick and go right after them," the president explained.

"We will have that," McNamara replied. "And I talked to Mac Bundy a moment ago and told him . . . we should . . . be prepared to recommend to you a response—a retaliation move against North Vietnam—in the event this attack takes place within the next six to nine hours."[79] At about 11:00 a.m. Washington time, more than an hour after McNamara's conversation with Johnson, a North Vietnamese attack was reported. McNamara later informed the National Security Council that nine or ten torpedoes were launched at the American vessels, which returned fire and reportedly sunk two North Vietnamese ships.[80]

At the time, the details of this second attack were hazy and the sequence of events jumbled. As Bundy noted in a chronology he prepared for President Johnson and other senior officials, a cable sent from the *Maddox* within hours of the presumptive torpedo attack "makes many reported contacts and torpedoes 'appear doubtful.' 'Freak weather effects' on radar, and 'over-eager' sonar-men may have accounted for many reports. 'No visual sightings' have been reported by the Maddox, and the Commander suggests that a 'complete evaluation' be undertaken before further action."[81]

At a 6:15 p.m. meeting of the National Security Council, McNamara reviewed the evidence supporting the occurrence of a second attack. He recommended a reprisal raid, a proposal that enjoyed unanimous support among the president's advisers. Johnson ordered naval aircraft to launch sixty-four sorties of air strikes directed against North Vietnamese patrol boat bases and a supporting oil complex.[82]

The debate over what happened that night in the Gulf of Tonkin has persisted for decades. The North Vietnamese, while acknowledging that an order was issued for the first attack on the *Maddox*, have consistently contested the facts about an alleged second attack.[83] The former North Vietnamese defense minister Vo Nguyen Giap told Robert McNamara in 1995 that the second attack did not occur, an assertion reaffirmed by General Nguyen Dinh Uoc, the director of Hanoi's Institute of Military History, at a June 1997 conference of American and Vietnamese scholars and former government officials. In late 2005 the National Security Agency leaked an internal review concluding there were multiple intelligence errors in 1964 contributing to the determination that a second attack occurred. The documentary record of those errors had been deliberately altered and kept secret for more than forty years.[84]

President Johnson, Bundy recalled, "clearly felt that Bob McNamara had told him he could count on there having been an attack. In terms of the real situation, this is all in a sense show business anyway. The real question of whether you wanted to stay and fight in Vietnam is much wider and deeper than what happens in the Gulf of Tonkin."[85]

At a 6:45 p.m. meeting with congressional leaders, the president formally set in motion the legislative strategy he had been preparing all summer. Flanked by McNamara, Rusk, and General Wheeler, Johnson explained that he would submit a resolution seeking congressional authority for U.S. combat operations in Southeast Asia if such escalation proved necessary.[86] "In my time with Lyndon Johnson, I do not remember a large decision more quickly reached," recalled Bundy. Johnson had concluded that the Gulf of Tonkin incident was the ideal pretext for the swift passage of legislation "long proposed and debated" in the State Department—a resolution that would deliver "clear cut" authorization from Congress "for a Presidential decision to conduct warfare in Southeast Asia."[87]

On August 7, 1964, after eight hours of debate, the Senate passed the resolution 88–2, with the ten absent senators publicly endorsing the measure. The vote in the House was 416–0.[88]

Twenty-four days after the successful passage of the Tonkin Gulf resolution and about two months before the election, Bundy recommended to President Johnson that he consider a dramatically enlarged U.S. military commitment to South Vietnam. "Our only really serious international problem is South Vietnam, but that could hardly be more serious," Bundy advised Johnson on August 31. "The immediate situation is that we just do not know whether Khanh still has it in him to resume full control. . . . The larger question is whether there is any course of action that can improve the chances in this weakening situation." Bundy noted the preparation of "contingency plans for limited escalation" in three areas, "naval harassments, air interdiction in the Laos panhandle, and possible U.S. fleet movements resuming a presence on the high seas in the Gulf of Tonkin." Yet there was a fourth option Bundy wanted the president to consider, "the use of substantial U.S. armed forces in operations against the Viet Cong." The scenario the national security adviser sketched represented a fundamental transformation of the American mission. "I myself believe that before we let this country go we should have a hard look at this grim alternative," he told the president, "and I do not think at all that it is a repetition of Korea. It seems to me at least possible that a couple of brigade-size units put in to do specific jobs about six weeks from now might be good medicine everywhere."[89] While Bundy's proposal for an initial combat troop deployment to South Vietnam was in itself momentous—the brigades would have arrived two weeks before the election—his memorandum was silent on the broader strategic concept for how the United States would prevail in a counterinsurgency ground war.

As Johnson campaigned across the country, he reiterated his opposition to deploying combat troops to South Vietnam. "We don't want our American boys to do the fighting for Asian boys," he declared on September 25 in Oklahoma. "We don't want to get involved in a nation with 700 million people and get tied down in a land war in Asia."[90] Speaking in New Hampshire a few days later, Johnson pointedly assured voters that he would recognize a limitation on the American commitment, promising the Vietnamese "only to continue to try to get them to save their own freedom with their own men, with our leadership, and our officer direction, and such equipment as we can furnish them. We think that losing 190 lives in the period that we have been out there is bad. But it is not like 190,000 that we might lose the first month if we escalated that war."[91]

Back in Washington Bundy advised the president against making such categorical statements on the campaign trail. "I think you may wish to give a hint of firmness," he advised Johnson. "It is a better than even chance that we will be undertaking some aid and land action in the Laotian corridor and even in North Vietnam within the next two months, and we do not want the record to suggest even remotely that we campaigned on peace in order to start a war in November."[92] As Bundy later recalled, "I remember having that hassle with him, that you didn't want to say something that you'd be sorry about if you did decide to do these things, and I think the language gets very marginally modified as a consequence of those arguments, but not enough. There's not much doubt that he was responding to the claims of the campaign hour and the difference between himself and [Barry] Goldwater, as he did in many other speeches on many other subjects."[93]

Sensing an impending Johnson victory, George Ball, the administration's prescient and articulate advocate of caution, now clearly envisioned the debacle that could ensue. The administration was fast approaching a decision point on Vietnam, with only a handful of options. Dictating the elements of his analysis into a tape recorder while working from home on evenings and weekends, Ball churned out a sixty-seven-page single-spaced memorandum titled "How Valid Are the Assumptions Underlying Our Viet-Nam Policy?" The paper outlined four possible American strategies:

1. Continue the present policy of providing advice and training.
2. Mount an air offensive against North Vietnam.
3. Assume responsibility for the war and take over its management from the South Vietnamese.
4. Pursue a negotiated political settlement.[94]

Ball's analysis projected that the continued reliance on an American advisory role would not arrest the downward spiral of Saigon's military weakness and political instability. Bombing, he argued, would not break North Vietnam's will or capacity to support the insurgency. Assuming responsibility for the war, he predicted, would produce a heavy loss of American lives with no promise of victory in a guerrilla conflict fought in the jungles and rice paddies of Southeast Asia. Thus, according to Ball's analysis, the first three strategies would each fail.

The logic of Ball's analysis suggested that a negotiated political settlement, however arduous it would be to achieve and however tenuous it would be to maintain, was the only viable course for the United States. Emphasizing that his memorandum was presented "not as a definitive document but as a challenge to the assumptions of our current Vietnam policy," Ball hoped his analysis would stimulate a substantive debate among the president's three principal architects of Vietnam policy: Bundy, McNamara, and Rusk.[95] But in a meeting on November 7, Ball was immediately put on the defensive. Bundy, McNamara, and Rusk were not prepared to examine the limitations of the advisory mission, the inherent shortcomings of an airpower strategy, or the enormous costs and risks of Americanizing the war. Instead, Ball was forced to defend the plausibility of achieving an enforceable political solution with North Vietnam. In this task he failed. Ball's fourth option—pursuit of a political exit strategy—served as the only real focus of debate and was promptly eviscerated and rendered obsolete.[96]

A more important development for America's involvement in Vietnam had occurred just four days before Ball's memorandum was debated and denounced by Bundy and his colleagues: Lyndon Johnson won a massive victory over Senator Barry Goldwater in the 1964 election, consolidating his power and confirming his primacy independent of his predecessor, John F. Kennedy. Johnson won forty-four states and 61 percent of the vote. His plurality was the largest in history. The Democratic Party dominated both houses of Congress, with a 68 to 32 margin over the Republicans in the Senate and 297 to 140 in the House of Representatives.[97]

Ironically, in a coda emblematic of the compromising influence politics exerted on strategy in 1964, an analysis that cogently anticipated and deconstructed the false military options the administration would ultimately embrace was buried under the weight of the election. But Bundy insisted that he did not withhold Ball's analysis from the president's attention. Correcting the "persistent myth" that he had suppressed Ball's memo, Bundy remembered passing it along to Johnson who, in the final month of the campaign, left it unread. "I didn't get any reaction from sending it to the president," said Bundy.[98] By the time it was finally reviewed by President Johnson weeks later, Bundy, Rusk, and McNamara had already dismissed it, focusing not on the futile military options they would soon pursue but on discrediting the diplomatic track they would always abjure.

∂∕∂

As Bundy retrospectively reflected on the Vietnam decisions of 1964, he invariably returned to the litany of nondecisions produced in that year—the decision *not* to withdraw, *not* to escalate, *not* to neutralize, *not* to debate the domino theory, and, fatefully, *not* to examine the military limitations and implications of a massive deployment of U.S. ground combat forces to South Vietnam. The cause of the disparate nondecisions of 1964 that emerges from Bundy's varied reflections and fragments is Lyndon Johnson's preoccupation with the domestic politics of an election year. In Bundy's appraisal it was politics—specifically *Johnsonian* politics—that created multiple disincentives to challenge the status quo and analyze rigorously the limited options and difficult choices in Vietnam.

Politics became the enemy of strategy in 1964. Because winning the presidential election was Johnson's overarching goal, he could not permit the situation in Vietnam to deteriorate to a deeper level of crisis. The impending election further constrained Johnson from either escalating the American commitment or embarking on a strategic withdrawal.

Bundy recalled that Johnson had muted his own disagreement when three of Kennedy's men—including Bundy's top expert on Vietnam—had engineered their weekend maneuver in August 1963 to stimulate a coup in Saigon. Now Johnson had to live with its consequences, a pattern of dysfunction in the South Vietnamese government that suggested, in Bundy's words, "that the only durable result of the coup against Diem was durable political instability in Saigon."[99] What Bundy observed in Johnson was a pressure, perceived by the president and redirected to his advisers, to deliver results without substantially enlarging American involvement in the war. "I think you'll find that even in 1964," Bundy recalled, "there are lots of meetings in which he has the brethren in and saying, 'Look, you know I can do practically anything but be a good commander-in-chief, and I'm not getting results out of this, and you're letting me down!' Hammer! Hammer! Hammer! Hammer!" The meetings, said Bundy, occurred "within a framework in which he wasn't authorizing that much action, nor was there that much fertility of imagination as to what additional kinds of action were needed, just more and better of the same."[100] Johnson was nonetheless explicit in demanding that the United States maintain the status quo, admonishing the Joint Chiefs of Staff on March 4 that Vietnam must not be lost before the November election, nor could it become a full-scale war.[101]

As Johnson had told Bundy in March, without a congressional vote affirming his authority in Vietnam and without an election victory of his own, he was merely a "trustee," a political actor without real political power. By late summer, with the presidential contest on the horizon, the Gulf of Tonkin affair presented itself as the perfect vehicle for Johnson to ride from August through election day. There was sufficient "hostile action" in the Gulf of Tonkin to justify supporting Johnson's resolution "as a kind of solemn warning," Bundy concluded thirty years later. Although two separate attacks had been reported, "after an intense but short review only one of them was certain."[102]

As demonstrated by his swift deployment of the draft legislation even before the facts of a second attack had been established, Johnson was exploiting an unusual political opening.[103] Bundy argued that what was essential for Lyndon Johnson about the Gulf of Tonkin affair was its inherent connection to the "election politics" of 1964. Johnson had withheld reprisal following the August 2 attack. "That left him less firmly and effectively anti-Communist than he wanted to be," said Bundy. A second attack, however, provided the president with a new window of opportunity. Johnson had been "patient," which was popular with the electorate. But now the president "could also be firm, and most people would like that even better." The military response to the attacks would be "modest," but the resolution would be available for later use if necessary. With just three months until the election, Bundy noted, "the posture was what mattered."[104] As Bundy later commented about Johnson's maneuvering, the president and his advisers exploited "a moment of high feeling to get a desired legislative result," thus finding a way "of connecting opportunity with action" consistent with Johnson's stature as a top-tier political tactician.[105] Johnson's machinations to connect events in the Gulf of Tonkin to win advantage with the Congress as well as the electorate was "an unassisted triple play," Bundy said, concluding, "It was the right response politically, and the time was right."[106]

Bundy retrospectively questioned his own acquiescence to Johnson's calculations. "In the long run, shouldn't I have stopped him? What did really happen? Fulbright Hearings: *Oy veh*," Bundy remarked in his fragments, using a Yiddish expression probably not uttered frequently in the Johnson White House to describe the subsequent hearings, starting in 1966, of the Senate Foreign Relations Committee, chaired by Senator J. William Fulbright of Arkansas. "Did Congress really commit? Shadow and substance: Does this episode justify a resolution that justifies a seven year war?" Bundy called the Gulf of Tonkin affair "a vaudeville show . . . it's all done with smoke and mirrors." The result, lamented Bundy, was that members of Congress "imprison themselves in what retroactively is exposed as a deception." For Bundy, the Gulf of Tonkin episode reflected "the endless mystery of Lyndon Johnson as a politician." The president passes his resolution and pockets it for future use, but "is outraged when Bill Fulbright has his hearings."[107]

Bundy's reconstruction of the Gulf of Tonkin episode left him pondering several intriguing but ultimately unanswerable questions. What if U.S. naval destroyers had not been patrolling "confusably close" to the scene of recent covert intelligence operations? What if weather conditions had been better? What if the destroyers were elsewhere and the attacks did not occur? "You've got to ask yourself," queried Bundy: in the absence of the attacks, what would Johnson do "to look brave and firm without costing him anything between then and November?"[108]

Bundy posed additional questions that help illuminate his struggle, late in life, to understand events in which he was both a central actor and an eyewitness: Why did the president reach "an instant decision" that the presumptive second attack would serve as the "grounding" for the resolution? What was the consequence of "enmeshing" the primary legislative authorization for the Vietnam War in "an episode which had the serious political flaw that it never happened" or at least was the object of "grave doubt," jeopardizing the perceived "honesty of the administration and the integrity of the President himself"? But for Johnson, Bundy suggested, the White House narrative of the Gulf of Tonkin attacks had become a reality. "People who question the reality are on the other side. They are the enemy."[109] Ultimately the potential authority of the resolution was so great, said Bundy, that Johnson was determined to ensure its passage. The Gulf of Tonkin is a "license for a later expansion of the war. . . . It gives him more power," Bundy continued, and "Lyndon Johnson never in his life turned down an opportunity to enlarge his own power."[110] Most significantly, Bundy concluded, "Tonkin is very Johnsonian. It's not possible to imagine Kennedy doing that. He wouldn't have thought of the legislative parlay."[111]

As he looked back on his White House years, Bundy frequently observed that in 1964, all efforts to conceive a realistic American strategy in Vietnam were held in abeyance because Lyndon Johnson wanted it that way during an election year. As Bundy remembered, "Bob McNamara would probably say . . . there was a time that he felt that the most serious problem in those few years was that we lost the year 1964 because of the election."[112] But did the political calendar truly preclude Bundy from conducting a rigorous examination of his own assumptions and the likely options the administration would face after the election? Although Bundy did not explicitly draw the conclusion himself, the historical record suggests that as national security adviser he largely acquiesced to those political constraints and was disengaged from the vital task of evaluating limited military and diplomatic choices that others, particularly George Ball, attacked with analytical intensity. In this sense Bundy capitulated to what was arguably the triumph of politics over strategy, an outcome he retrospectively blamed on Johnson but perhaps should have also assumed some responsibility for himself.

The record demonstrates that Bundy did not shield himself from the politics of 1964. To the contrary, he chose various moments to plunge into the fray. Why did Bundy lobby Lyndon Johnson to select Robert Kennedy as his running mate? When rebuffed, why did Bundy agree to help push Kennedy into the political wilderness? When asked, why was Bundy so vague in defining military options for Johnson but so forthcoming in proposing political strategies to market the American commitment to Vietnam? Why was Bundy advising the president on the domestic political implications of the neutrality option, warning him that it could alienate a constituency with sufficient leverage "to lose us an election"? Why did Bundy so ostentatiously brandish the threat that if he faltered in Vietnam Johnson would risk the same political fate Harry Truman suffered for the loss of China? Why was Bundy so engaged in planning a congressional resolution to be deployed *before* the election but so inactive in contingency planning for military options *after* the election? His passivity was particularly striking in light of the fact that in the summer of 1964 Ray Cline, the CIA's deputy director for intelligence, privately informed Bundy that the military situation in South Vietnam was so dire that "we will just barely squeak through" the election without a collapse of the regime in Saigon.[113] More broadly, why did a self-described "academic manager" and "political zero" insinuate himself in so many questions where his expertise was questionable at best? Was this the proper role for the national security adviser? Were these not precisely the questions Bundy should have avoided to ensure his own independence and credibility? Bundy did not ask these questions of himself in the course of his retrospective study. Perhaps he should have.

Observed from a different perspective, the political preoccupations of 1964 could have presented Bundy with a significant opportunity, if only he had chosen to seize it. Note Johnson's palpable anxiety when he tells Bundy in the spring of 1964 that "it looks to me like we're getting into another Korea. It just worries the hell out of me. . . . I don't think that we can fight them 10,000 miles away from home. . . . I don't think it's worth fighting for and I don't think we can get out. It's just the biggest damn mess I ever saw."[114] These are the words of a president desperate for choices. If the status quo was going to be maintained in Vietnam through the election, Bundy had more than ample time and institutional authority to coordinate a top-to-bottom review of American military and diplomatic options—an ExComm for Vietnam but conducted in slow motion, over a period of months rather than thirteen days—and with Bundy fully insulated from Congress, where he was not required to testify, and insulated from the din of the political campaign year. Such a review could have examined the full panoply of historic, strategic, and military assumptions about Vietnam while leveraging all of the resources of the national security apparatus Bundy had the power to coordinate.

Bundy believed that the historical legacy of the Korean War informed the mind-set of senior policy makers confronting the challenge of Vietnam in 1964. He noted that approximately thirty-five thousand soldiers had died in the Korean conflict over a three-year period, at a rate roughly comparable to the death toll in Vietnam. Yet there was no protest. Many of his colleagues recalled the Korean conflict as he did, "a hard choice, but incontestably right, both in morals and politics." Bundy said that while Vietnam was different from Korea, "the cases were enough alike to encourage the comparison."[115] But if the precedent of Korea was in fact relevant to decisions about Vietnam, that parallel would seem to suggest the need for deeper analysis. Korea, of course, ended in a military stalemate and triggered the partition of the country and a permanent American military deployment that has continued since 1953. Was that the strategic outcome Bundy anticipated in 1964? If not, then how would he propose the United States fight the war in Vietnam to ensure a different outcome? Beyond precluding what Bundy regarded as an ignominious Cold War defeat, what was his vision for the future of Vietnam? Finally, did Bundy not remember President Kennedy's commentary about Korea and Vietnam from November 1961? In a meeting convened to reject combat troop deployments to South Vietnam, Kennedy recalled the clarity of the aggression in Korea and the support the United States had received from members of the United Nations. The conflict in South Vietnam, the president had argued, was far more obscure.[116]

In 1964 the domino theory also projected a largely unexamined intellectual hegemony over the foreign policy elite. Bundy himself seemed to appropriate its logic in his dire January 6 memorandum to Johnson. The blunt determinism of the domino theory and its broad acceptance in American politics were central to the Vietnam debate. Yet because the domino theory's predictive power was assumed rather than substantiated, why did Bundy not explore it further or assign his staff to examine it more critically? It was a question he turned to only decades after leaving office. "My present view is that it was an extraordinarily unfitting simile, a preventor of discourse," Bundy concluded in 1995.[117] "States are not little oblong blocks . . . lined up next to each other. They do not get pushed around by God-like figures playing a card."[118] "The domino theory," he added, "is a particular formulation—and a rather rigid one—of a broader proposition that in the Cold War every battle lost diminishes you." One consequence yields another: to lose Vietnam is to lose Laos; to lose Malaysia is to lose Indonesia. "The general proposition," he said, "that if you lose in the Cold War it hurts you everywhere is a state of mind about the battle."[119]

The domino theory was first promulgated by President Eisenhower in April 1954. "You have a row of dominos set up," he explained at a news conference held in the midst of the Dien Bien Phu crisis. "You knock over the first one. . . . What will happen to the last one is the certainty that it will go over very quickly."[120] By 1964 the domino theory had the force of doctrine, becoming a de facto feature of the political debate over Vietnam, the teetering domino that could ostensibly unleash communism across Southeast Asia.

Bundy retrospectively faulted himself for not challenging the logic of the domino theory when he had the opportunity to do so as national security adviser. "I did *not* believe in dominoes," he wrote, "but did not try to argue the full case against that notion or its lesser included case: we must not lose another!"[121] In an additional fragment, he surmised that "for LBJ the domino theory was really a matter of domestic politics."[122] Bundy told me, "No serious contender for political office can propose letting go of Vietnam. Not because dominoes will fall, but because *Vietnam must not fall*."[123] And he concluded, "It's an American political problem, not a geopolitical or cosmic matter."[124] Yet because the domino theory had Eisenhower, "a very strong and much feared ex-president as the head of its church," its influence remained considerable.[125] "The metaphor . . . carries a very considerably different weight when it comes rolling down from Gettysburg," where Eisenhower had retired, "tumbling over senators as it comes. That's the domino theory that's actually working."[126]

Despite President Johnson's identification with the domino theory, in June 1964 the CIA produced a major study sharply at variance with the theory's core predictions.[127] Prepared by the respected intelligence analyst Sherman Kent for the Board of National Estimates, the study was known as the "Death of the Domino Theory" memo. In it Kent shared the intelligence community's dubious conclusions about one of the principal justifications for intervention in Vietnam: "We do not believe that the loss of South Vietnam and Laos would be followed by the rapid, successive communization of the other states of the Far East. . . . With the possible exception of Cambodia, it is likely that no nation in the area would quickly succumb to Communism as a result of the fall of Laos and South Vietnam."[128] While Bundy was certainly aware of the CIA estimate—it was recommended to him by his top Vietnam aide, Mike Forrestal—he appears to have disregarded it.[129] A unique opportunity for Bundy to test the assumptions underlying the potential American military escalation in Vietnam had been lost or perhaps simply ignored.

Bundy's core convictions about Vietnam in 1964 left him only one path to follow. Inclined to accept the Cold War parallels to the Korean War, unwilling to question the primacy of the domino theory, and repelled by the premise of withdrawal or a diplomatic extrication through neutralization, the only option left was military escalation. That escalation would likely take the form of either a sustained bombing campaign to deplete North Vietnam's support for the Vietcong insurgency or the deployment of U.S. ground combat forces to reinforce the South Vietnamese army. Of the two options for escalation, bombing would presumably precede the more dramatic and consequential decision to fully Americanize the war. Therefore, in the countdown to the days following the election, bombing was for Bundy the most obvious of the existing strategic options to probe and analyze. Yet the record suggests he made no serious effort to rigorously evaluate its viability. To the contrary, he seems to have simply disregarded pivotal intelligence findings and war-game simulations that could have significantly influenced his thinking.

In early March the State Department's Policy Planning Council produced a lengthy study concluding that sustained air strikes—even if they produced extensive physical destruction—would fail to weaken Hanoi's determination to support the insurgency. In fact, the study predicted that bombing would probably strengthen the control of the North Vietnam-ese regime while doing little to boost morale in the South, an expectation roughly consistent with what Charles de Gaulle had been arguing pri-vately.[130] A second bombing study was produced in April when the Joint Chiefs of Staff organized a complex war game code-named "SIGMA I 1964" to project the outcome of U.S. air strikes. Harold Ford, a CIA ana-lyst, recalled the disturbing results. North Vietnam, he noted, "did not knuckle under to the heightened pressure but counter-escalated by pour-ing more troops into the South." The American team then confronted two grim alternatives. "On the one hand, it could try to seek a military decision by greatly expanding hostilities against [North Vietnam]—which SIGMA I's players judged might risk repeating the Korean experi-ence of massive Chinese intervention. Or Washington could begin deescalating—which the players believed could cost the United States a marked loss of international credibility and prestige."[131] George Ball ap-pears to be the only senior administration official to express concern, asking Dean Rusk in late May why air strikes were under consideration "in the face of a recently played war game that demonstrated the ineffec-tiveness of such a tactic."[132] There is no evidence that Bundy seriously evaluated the SIGMA I results.

Bundy also appears to have disregarded a successor study, SIGMA II, conducted from September 8 to September 17, 1964. Ironically, the na-tional security adviser was among the most senior civilian participants in the exercise, which was administered by Colonel George Lincoln, the head of the Department of Social Sciences at West Point. As the army of-ficer and military historian H. R. McMaster points out, SIGMA II was explicitly designed to test a thesis Bundy repeatedly espoused—the ex-pectation that air power could coerce Hanoi's leaders to abandon their support for the Vietcong insurgency. As McMaster reports, air strikes "had minimal effect and actually stiffened North Vietnamese determination, as the Viet Cong used existing stockpiles and civilian support to sustain the insurgency in the South." By the game's conclusion, the United States had been prompted to deploy more than ten ground combat divisions to Southeast Asia. "The results of SIGMA II," according to McMaster, "suggested that graduated pressure could lead to disaster in Vietnam."[133]

In December, after the election and with Johnson's inauguration approaching, the inevitability of a change in Vietnam strategy prompted Senator Fulbright to publicly warn that it would be "senseless" to enlarge the American role in the war. James Thomson, a thirty-three-year-old China expert Bundy had recruited to his National Security Council staff, was also preoccupied with the risks in expanding the war. "What I fear most of all in this juncture," he wrote to Bundy, "would be our move onto a policy track in Vietnam that could cripple the new administration and tarnish its bright promise."

As recounted by Bundy's biographer Kai Bird, the national security adviser invited Thomson to his office for a private meeting in early December 1964. "I want you to read something," Bundy told Thomson when he arrived. "Sit right here, and read it carefully, and tell me what you think." Thomson sat on the sofa in Bundy's office and pored over a confidential memorandum produced by a working group chaired by Mac's brother Bill, sketching a scenario in which the United States would manufacture a crisis like the Gulf of Tonkin that would trigger a military reprisal but also usher in negotiations for a broad regional peace conference under the aegis of the United Nations.[134] "It was all about a fantastic, escalatory multiple-bombing track to force the North Vietnamese to their knees," recalled Thomson. The strategy, although it envisioned negotiations, made him palpably uneasy.

"Look, sir, I don't know anything about firepower," Thomson explained to Bundy. "But this document is trying to tell us that we can bomb them into submission, and my fear, since I know China, and I have learned something about Indo-China, is that those people we're bombing will survive our taking out everything they've built over these past many years, their infrastructure and so forth." The insurgency will retreat into the jungle, Thomson predicted, evading and enduring a bombing campaign for as long as necessary. Why? "Because they know they have no place to go. And eventually we will go home. And so I'm not sure this is going to work. . . . They know that we know that we will have to go home, someday, quite soon."

Bundy sat in silence, staring at Thomson and pondering his reply. "Well, James," he said finally, "that's a good point. You may well be right. Thank you so much."[135]

Their exchange ended and with it a window of opportunity in 1964 was essentially sealed shut. SIGMA I did not matter. SIGMA II did not matter. The views of an expert like Thomson did not matter. Other well-known estimates questioning the efficacy of bombing from the CIA, the Defense Intelligence Agency, and the State Department's intelligence directorate also did not matter.[136] "As soon as the election was over," Bundy recalled after leaving the White House, "it became apparent, as indeed it had been right through the year that we were living on borrowed time. The President hadn't wanted to make and the government did not press him to make those hard decisions during an election year."[137] Within just three months McGeorge Bundy would recommend to the president that the United States initiate a strategic bombing campaign against North Vietnam.

CONVICTION WITHOUT RIGOR IS A STRATEGY FOR DISASTER

His books were everywhere—piled high on his office desk, stacked on the floor, filling every inch of available shelf space— the pages protruding with pink and yellow adhesive tabs designating passages of special interest. McGeorge Bundy's method was to apply an almost muscular form of research to his retrospective study of Vietnam. He attacked every text with a pen at the ready, carefully annotating a vast and growing literature of the war in his impossibly small handwriting, recording copious notes, questions, critiques, and challenges in the margins of his books and in reams of yellow legal pads. In his own idiosyncratic way, through the accounts he studied, discussed, and sometimes disputed, Bundy was conducting a hidden dialogue with the historians of the Vietnam era, including most of the authors and commentators who would pass judgment on his own treatment of the war.

Cheerfully catholic about the sources he consulted, Bundy was prepared to read anything about the war that was the product of credible historical scholarship or analysis, regardless of its place on the political spectrum. To understand the machinations of the policy-making process, he continuously read from a voluminous library of original documentary materials assembled from archival collections and recently declassified government publications. These sources constituted tens of thousands of pages of empirical evidence describing the inner workings of the U.S. government during his years as national security adviser. To understand the prevailing interpretative debates about Vietnam, Bundy read from among the established histories, such as the work of George Herring, the author of *America's Longest War*, to whom Bundy wrote a friendly letter pointing out a minor error in the summary of a government document of the Kennedy years. And to understand his most passionate critics, Bundy studied a range of narrative and journalistic works, which often carried personal and sometimes scathing attacks on his performance in office.

The Bundy that emerged in the course of this research exercise was not the verbally lacerating and supremely confident debater of the Vietnam years. Neither was he the glib, rapid-fire, silver-tongued dean of Harvard Yard. The Bundy who was openly grappling with unanswered questions about Vietnam was a man in his midseventies and in declining health, slowed and depleted of his prior certitude. He was skeptical. He was probing. He was temperate. And never once in our time together did he express animosity toward his critics or even dispense a disparaging remark about them. To the contrary, he seemed to study his critics with a cool detachment and sustained concentration. Of particular interest to him were the articles and books of David Halberstam.

Bundy had known Halberstam for more than four decades. Their relationship began in the mid-1950s when Bundy was a Harvard professor and dean and Halberstam was a reporter and managing editor of the student newspaper, the *Crimson*. In 1954 the paper was led by a quartet of enormously talented young men. There was Halberstam, who would go on to cover Vietnam for the *New York Times* and win a Pulitzer Prize. J. Anthony Lukas would also go on to become a Pulitzer winner and distinguished author. Richard Ullman would become an eminent professor of international relations at Princeton University. A. J. Langguth, the president of the *Crimson*, would also go on to cover Vietnam for the *New York Times* and decades later would publish, among other celebrated works, *Our Vietnam*, an award-winning narrative history of the war. When Bundy was appointed dean it was Langguth and Halberstam, the first- and second-ranking members of the *Crimson* staff, who would interview him weekly for their coverage of Harvard's academic affairs, accompanied by Lukas and Ullman. The university's president, Nathan Pusey, would also attend and was the ostensible focal point for the weekly interviews. But it was always Bundy who dominated the play and the attention of the young journalists of the *Crimson*.

Halberstam continued to make the Harvard dean his subject long after graduation. In 1969, three years after Bundy stepped down as national security adviser, Halberstam published his seminal *Harper's* magazine profile, "The Very Expensive Education of McGeorge Bundy," which was among the first articles to explore deeply Bundy's role in crafting the Vietnam policies of the Kennedy and Johnson administrations. The *Harper's* article, which ran three times the magazine's normal length, generated a storm of interest among the intelligentsia.

"Bundy was a dual icon," Halberstam recalled in explaining the article's impact. "He had been a dean of Harvard at an unspeakably young age, portrayed constantly in the press as the most cerebral member of the Kennedy Administration other than the President himself, and at the same time the leader of the next generation of the American Establishment."[1] Halberstam was among the first journalists seriously to question the wisdom of Bundy's counsel in the White House. For the former national security adviser, accustomed to glowing press coverage, it was a bruising experience. After the article appeared Bundy kept a file of outraged letters from his friends and loyalists. Bundy himself composed a list of what he regarded as Halberstam's most egregious misstatements—although it included items no more serious than minor factual errors about his family's illustrious ancestral tree. Bundy prudently chose never to send his complaints to the editors of *Harper's*.

"The Very Expensive Education of McGeorge Bundy" quickly became the template for a much longer work of contemporary history Halberstam aspired to write. "The basic question behind the book," Halberstam explained, "was why men who were said to be the ablest to serve the government in this century had been the architects of what struck me as likely to be the worst tragedy since the Civil War."[2] The book that followed, *The Best and the Brightest*, sold 180,000 copies in hardcover and 1,500,000 in paperback.[3] It also defined Bundy for a generation as the very personification of the hubris and arrogance of America's tragic encounter with Vietnam.

Bundy was well aware of the influence *The Best and the Brightest* exerted over elite opinion in the United States and the indelible portrait it had created among an interwoven community of pundits, reporters, academics, and foreign policy and military experts. Early in our collaboration, Bundy and I reviewed a detailed memorandum I had prepared summarizing Halberstam's treatment of him in *The Best and the Brightest*. Bundy himself read the twentieth anniversary edition of the book from cover to cover, toting around a tabbed and annotated paperback copy between his home and office. That exercise confronted Bundy with some of Halberstam's most critical pronouncements about him. Revisiting Halberstam's history may have opened old wounds. "My wife," Bundy confided to me, "thinks that a book about Vietnam is a very bad idea."

Other family members also harbored unrelieved resentment for Halberstam's criticisms. At a small dinner at the Bundys' apartment decades after Halberstam's Vietnam work had been published, one of the guests inadvertently uttered the phrase, "the best and the brightest." Mac's sister

Laurie Auchincloss was aghast, the blood draining from her cheeks immediately. She stood up and announced that in the Bundy family, that phrase had been out of fashion for a good many years. And then she huffily left the apartment. Mac chuckled. Mary did not. Dinner progressed awkwardly, with Mary finding reasons to visit the kitchen regularly. Mac explained to his guests that some members of his family had never resolved their feelings about the war.[4] Vietnam had seemingly become embedded in the Bundy family history. And David Halberstam was the author who had implanted it there.

While some in his family may have detested Halberstam for his uncompromising portrait, McGeorge Bundy clearly did not. He told me that he considered Halberstam "a very brilliant journalist" and that he struggled over the question of how to address some of Halberstam's own hawkish statements about the war, particularly from Halberstam's 1965 book *The Making of a Quagmire*, in which the journalist argued against a precipitous American withdrawal from South Vietnam.[5]

In rereading *The Best and the Brightest*, Bundy was inclined to focus less on how he was depicted and more on the characterization of the two presidents he served. "Thus one of the lessons for civilians who thought they could run small wars with great control," wrote Halberstam of Kennedy, "was that to harness the military, you had to harness them completely; that once in, even partially, everything began to work in their favor. Once activated, even in a small way at first, they would soon dominate the play." Bundy rejected this proposition. During one of our meetings we discussed his comment in the margins of *The Best and the Brightest*. "As if inevitable," he had written derisively.[6] In another passage Halberstam wrote, "The illusion would always be of civilian control; the reality would be of a relentlessly growing military domination of policy." Bundy's response was dubious. "President and Commander-in-Chief Cease to Exist?" he asked.[7] And finally there was this generalization about Kennedy: "What the president was learning . . . (once again, the Bay of

Pigs had been lesson one), was something that his successor Lyndon Johnson would also find out the hard way: that the capacity to control a policy involving the military is greatest before the policy is initiated, but once started, no matter how small the initial step, a policy has a life and a thrust of its own, it is an organic thing. More, its thrust and its drive may not be in any way akin to the desires of the President who initiated it." Again, Bundy rejected Halberstam's conclusion; "Not so," he countered.[8] But not all of Bundy's responses took the form of disagreement. Halberstam was "right," Bundy observed, about the great "sadness" of the war.[9]

As he delved deeper into the Vietnam literature, Bundy turned repeatedly to Halberstam's central thesis, the notion that the council of war—the Joint Chiefs of Staff, the generals in the field, and the civilian advisers like Bundy, McNamara, and Rusk—had essentially captured Vietnam strategy from the president. It was an argument he aggressively contested. From Bundy's perspective, the seminal protagonists of the Vietnam era and the true architects of the war were John F. Kennedy and Lyndon B. Johnson. Everyone else was merely a supporting player. And there was the crux of Bundy's conundrum. How could he make his case without appearing to exculpate himself for his own failures of analysis and advice? A few weeks before he died, Bundy shared his concern with Professor James Blight of Brown University. "Mac said that one of the most difficult—maybe the most difficult— task in his own project is saying what needs to be said but without sounding self-serving," Blight recalled.[10] And how would Bundy respond to the portrait painted by Halberstam—his depiction of a man driven by arrogance and overconfidence in pursuit of an ultimately disastrous policy to Americanize the war in Vietnam? If Bundy had lived to complete his Vietnam memoir—if he could have been brutally honest about his performance in 1965—what lesson could Bundy have drawn from his own self-confessed admissions of failure? It was a question he asked himself in his fragments directly: what are my most significant mistakes in the year America followed the path to war?[11] It was a question he did not fully answer. If there were lessons to be drawn from his experience and self-criticism relating to the pivotal turning points of 1965, that task would be left to others.

❦

On Christmas Eve in 1964 the National Liberation Front (NLF) bombed a U.S. officers' billet in Saigon, killing two American soldiers and injuring thirty-eight others.[12] On December 28 McGeorge Bundy prepared a paper for President Johnson enumerating the arguments for and against reprisal air strikes. "The central problem is and remains the establishment of political stability in South Vietnam and a major decision of this sort should await progress toward stability," he argued. "At the least it should not be taken while the situation is more unstable than ever." Yet that requirement, Bundy noted, could be modified. "We decided in December that we would execute reprisals from now on and this decision was not tied, as other possibilities were, to increased political stability in Saigon." Bundy explained the strategic logic behind bombing. Employing calibrated military force against the Vietcong—inflicting pain in measured increments—would provide the United States with coercive leverage to contain the communist insurgency: "The theory of our policy of reprisal," Bundy advised Johnson, "is that it can help to prevent gradual Viet Cong escalation in South Vietnam. This theory seems as sound now as it was when we decided to follow it."[13]

After concluding discussions with Bundy and Rusk at his ranch in Texas, Johnson decided against authorizing retaliatory air strikes. But the president made it clear that while he doubted the efficacy of bombing attacks he was eager to consider recommendations for the deployment of ground troops. "Every time I get a military recommendation it seems to me that it calls for a large-scale bombing," Johnson vented in a cable to Ambassador Taylor in Saigon. "I have never felt that this war will be won from the air, and it seems to me that what is much more needed and would be more effective is a larger and stronger use of Rangers and Special Forces and Marines, or other appropriate military strength on the ground and on the scene." Johnson essentially instructed Taylor to produce such a proposal. "I am ready to look with great favor on that kind of increased American effort," he explained, "directed at the guerrillas and aimed to stiffen the aggressiveness of Vietnamese military units up and down the line. Any recommendation that you or General Westmoreland make in this sense will have immediate attention from me, although I know that it may involve the acceptance of larger American sacrifice. We have been building our strength to fight this kind of war ever since 1961, and I myself am ready to substantially increase the number of Americans in Vietnam if it is necessary to provide this type of fighting force against the Viet Cong."[14] The cable, dated December 30, 1964, was drafted by Bundy and reflects his handwritten revisions.[15]

Johnson's cable was "important," Bundy retrospectively commented. It communicated the president's desire to generate planning for a "well-designed" ground force campaign and a "readiness" to expand the war within South Vietnam that he pursued "steadily" for the next three years.[16] Because Bundy drafted the cable at the president's request, he had direct exposure to Johnson's unambiguous preference not to rely on air power to turn the tide of the war but rather to commit American combat forces to salvage the regime in Saigon. Thus in the final days of 1964, the national security adviser had a very clear indication of what President Johnson would likely decide in 1965.

What would an American ground combat strategy require? General William Westmoreland, the successor to Paul Harkins as the top U.S. military commander in Vietnam, conducted a comprehensive study of the question with the assistance of his staff. "He arrives at the startling requirement of 34-battalion equivalents of army or marine infantry," Ambassador Taylor reported on January 6, 1965, "together with the necessary logistic support. He considers that the total manpower requirement would approximate 75,000 U.S. personnel."[17] For his own part, Taylor was dubious about whether ground combat forces could defeat the insurgency. "I do not recall in history a successful anti-guerrilla campaign with less than a 10 to 1 numerical superiority over the guerrillas and without the elimination of assistance from outside the country," the ambassador informed President Johnson. That ratio would be virtually impossible to achieve in Vietnam. It was also unlikely, Taylor argued, that the United States could "change national characteristics, create leadership where it does not exist, raise large additional [South Vietnamese] forces or seal porous frontiers to infiltration." Doubting the viability of ground action, Taylor also favored the use of coercive air power. Among the options available to the United States, the "only one which offers any chance of the needed success in the available time . . . is the program of graduated air attacks directed against the will" of the North Vietnamese regime.[18] President Johnson and the U.S. ambassador in Saigon, himself an illustrious former general, were now in fundamental discord about the direction of American military strategy. Johnson, persuaded by the limitations of bombing, favored escalation with ground combat forces, a position supported by General Westmoreland. Taylor, persuaded by the limitations of ground combat forces, favored escalation by bombing.

As the presumptive arbiter and coordinating intermediary behind Vietnam strategy, Bundy was presented with the challenge of resolving this now central debate about the application of American military power. By late January 1965, as consensus continued to elude the administration, Bundy and McNamara submitted what became known as the "Fork in the Road" memorandum to President Johnson. "What we want to say to you is that both of us are now pretty well convinced that our current policy" placed the United States on a "disastrous" losing course in Vietnam, cautioned Bundy. The requirement of achieving political stability in Saigon before escalating the war was unattainable. "The result," he said, "is that we are pinned into a policy of first aid to squabbling politi-cos and passive reaction to events we do not try to control. Or so it seems. Bob and I believe that the worst course of action is to continue in this essentially passive role which can only lead to eventual defeat and an invitation to get out in humiliating circumstances."

Bundy outlined only two alternatives. "The first is to use our military power in the Far East and to force a change of Communist policy. The sec-ond is to deploy all our resources along a track of negotiation, aimed at sal-vaging what little can be preserved with no major addition to our present military risks. Bob and I tend to favor the first course, but we believe that both should be carefully studied and that alternative programs should be argued out before you. . . . McNamara and I have reached the point where our obligations to you simply do not permit us to administer our present directives in silence and let you think we see real hope in them."[19] With the "Fork in the Road" memo Bundy established his own very narrow calculus of American strategic options. The United States could either apply un-specified forms of military action to coerce the insurgency to abandon its cause, or negotiate some kind of settlement, presumably neutralization, an outcome he had long disparaged and deplored.

Bundy retrospectively acknowledged that his memo was designed to push President Johnson out of the zone of indecision that had character-ized the 1964 campaign year. "The relation of Vietnam policy to presi-dential elections is a recurrent theme," he observed, and "one of the largest elements" in the "Fork in the Road" memo. The core message of their brief, he explained, was for those officials who were managing the day-to-day enterprise "to hang on" in Saigon; "1964 has been a lost year. Decisions haven't been taken. Reinforcements have not been supplied. The Gulf of Tonkin Resolution is passed, but nothing happens."[20] Elsewhere, Bundy noted, "The President was pushing the decision ahead of him. . . . I'm sure, too, that there was an element in it from both of us of having learned, through November, December, and January, in a thousand ways, that the President's main action agenda was the 150 laws he was going to pass in 150 days."[21]

Yet the "Fork in the Road" memo did have the desired effect of confronting Johnson with the necessity of making a decision soon about America's course in Vietnam. Bundy's colleague Douglass Cater recalled the president's response to it. "I'd never seen the man in as dejected a mood—he said, 'I don't know what to do. If I send more boys in, there's going to be killin'. If I take them out, there's going to be more killin'. Anything I do, there's going to be more killin'.' And he never put a 'g' on the 'killin',' it was Texas 'killin'.' Then he got up and walked out of the room, leaving us in a somewhat shattered state."[22]

In the first days of February 1965 Bundy was dispatched to South Vietnam to conduct a firsthand analysis of the conditions there, a review personally requested by Ambassador Taylor.[23] It was the first time in his life that the national security adviser had traveled to Southeast Asia or had set foot in South Vietnam, a country whose fate had been subject to his considerable influence for the previous four years. Bundy's initial reports were bleak. "We have pressed throughout the day to see whether any member of Country Team believes that we can prevent continued deterioration in the absence of a 'reasonably effective and stable government,'" Bundy reported in a cable to Washington. He advised Director McCone, "In particular, I think you should tell the President . . . the current situation among non-Communist forces gives all the appearance of a civil war within a civil war."[24] In the course of his visit Bundy met with South Vietnamese religious and political leaders, including General Khanh, who for that month, at least, continued to run the government. When Khanh asked Bundy to clarify U.S. strategy, the national security adviser explained that the American mission was to "assist" in the maintenance of "Vietnamese independence and freedom, but that we only advise and assist." The main burden for the defense of the country, Bundy went on, fell on the South Vietnamese, who needed to work more effectively and cohesively.[25]

On the last day of Bundy's mission, in the early morning hours of February 7, NLF forces simultaneously struck two military targets in Pleiku, a critical swath of territory adjacent to the Cambodian and Laotian borders connecting insurgent infiltration routes to South Vietnam's central highlands. The commando strikes, directed at a South Vietnamese army headquarters jointly protected by U.S. advisers, killed 9 American soldiers, wounded 137, and prompted the evacuation of 76 others.[26] Speculation mounted that the attack was a deliberate provocation designed specifically to coincide with Bundy's mission to South Vietnam. Dang Vu Hiep, a North Vietnamese adviser to the NLF forces operating in the military sector encompassing Pleiku, later disclosed that he and his men did not know about the Bundy mission and that it did not influence the timing of the attacks against the American targets, which had been in preparation for weeks.[27]

Various histories depict Bundy's swift recommendation for reprisal air strikes as a visceral reaction to witnessing later that day the damage of the Pleiku attacks, the explosive force of which dismembered its victims, scattering their limbs and body parts.[28] General Westmoreland, for example, suggested that once Bundy "smelled a little gunpowder," the national security adviser "developed a field marshal psychosis."[29] Bundy dismissed such accounts of an emotional overreaction as exaggerated and incorrect. "I did not 'take charge' . . . as some assert," he wrote. "I was called as a White House staff man in a useful place."[30] Yet some of his colleagues recall the impact the Pleiku episode appeared to have on the national security adviser. Francis Bator, Bundy's deputy for international trade and economics, noted "the standard theory . . . that it was during Pleiku that he sort of caught the religion on Vietnam." Bundy rejected that notion, but Bator recalled, "I'm not so sure—not on the basis of what he said, but I saw his face when he came back from Pleiku, literally when he walked into the Situation Room office, and I had sort of a sense that perhaps he'd become more emotionally caught up in it."[31]

With the support of Ambassador Taylor and General Westmoreland in Saigon, Bundy recommended an immediate reprisal strike against North Vietnam. Back in Washington, President Johnson agreed. According to Bill Colby's notes, the president told a meeting of the National Security Council that "he had kept the shotgun over the mantle and the bullets in the basement for a long time now, but that the enemy was killing his personnel and he could not expect them to continue their work if he did not authorize them to take steps to defend themselves. . . . The President then decided to authorize the strikes."[32]

What Johnson approved in the wake of Pleiku was a single retaliatory attack code-named "Operation Flaming Dart," launched with American fighter jets from the carrier *Ranger* and targeting a North Vietnamese army camp sixty miles north of the seventeenth parallel.[33] But what Bundy and his team sought to engineer was a perpetual bombing campaign, which they described as a generalized and continuing program of "graduated and sustained reprisal." Despite the internal studies and war games demonstrating that coercive bombing was an ineffectual strategy, Bundy and his team pressed ahead, ignoring not only the two SIGMA simulations but also the dubious estimates from the CIA, the Defense Intelligence Agency, and the State Department's bureau of intelligence and research.[34] The national security adviser's objective was to break the will of the insurgency in ways consistent with the expectations of game theory, the study of how to escalate and prevail in dynamic conflict or bargaining situations.[35] The team's proposal was formulated under the guidance of John McNaughton, a Harvard Law School professor who had succeeded Paul Nitze as assistant secretary of defense for international security affairs.[36] McNaughton, an ardent student of game theory, enjoyed Bundy's strong support for importing intellectual precepts of conflict management developed in the classrooms of Cambridge and applying them to the guerrilla warfare of Vietnam.[37]

Bundy summarized his team's formal recommendation in a report drafted on the long return flight from Vietnam. "The situation in Vietnam is deteriorating," he warned, "and without new U.S. action defeat appears inevitable—probably not in a matter of weeks or perhaps even months, but within the next year or so. There is still time to turn it around, but not much." Once again Bundy dismissed the possibility of a diplomatic extrication from the crisis. "The international prestige of the United States, and a substantial part of our influence, are directly at risk in Vietnam," he wrote. "There is no way of unloading the burden on the Vietnamese themselves, and there is no way of negotiating ourselves out of Vietnam which offers any serious promise at present. . . . any negotiated U.S. withdrawal today would mean surrender on the installment plan."

In his report, Bundy was pessimistic about the sustainability of America's client government in Saigon: "There is an appearance of wariness among some military leaders. There is a worrisome lassitude among the Vietnamese generally. There is a distressing absence of positive commitment to any serious social or political purpose. Outside observers are ready to write the patient off. All of this tends to bring latent anti-Americanism dangerously near to the surface. To be an American in Saigon today is to have a gnawing feeling that time is against us. . . . Even in areas which are 'cleared,' the follow-on pacification is stalled because of widespread belief that the Viet Cong are going to win in the long run. The areas which can be regarded as truly cleared and pacified and safe are few and shrinking." One response, Bundy proposed, was to utilize the "unemployed asset" of "versatile and flexible" Special Forces units in ground action under the command of General Westmoreland. Bundy was nonetheless reserved about the American ability to contain the insurgency, which he acknowledged was formidable. "The prospect in Vietnam is grim," he concluded. "The energy and persistence of the Viet Cong are as-tonishing. They can appear anywhere—and at almost any time. They have accepted extraordinary losses and they come back for more. They show skill in their sneak attacks and ferocity when cornered."[38]

Bundy conceded that his recommended military strategy had limita-tions, but he argued that the shortcomings were acceptable because bombing would communicate a necessary message of resolve at home and abroad. "We cannot assert that a policy of sustained reprisal will suc-ceed in changing the course of the contest in Vietnam. It may fail, and we cannot estimate the odds of success with accuracy—they may be some-where between 25% and 75%. What we can say is that even if it fails, the policy will be worth it. At a minimum it will damp down the charge that we did not do all that we could have done, and this charge will be impor-tant in many countries, including our own."[39]

Bundy submitted his memorandum to President Johnson shortly be-fore eleven o'clock on the evening of February 7, ending a thirty-six-hour day that had started that morning in Vietnam.[40] Bundy recalled, "He read it through in his bedroom the night I got back and said to me, 'Well, isn't that all decided?' . . . I forgot what I said I was so surprised at that. . . . It's *terribly* hard to be sure with him exactly when a decision is made."[41] Johnson instructed Bundy to recall all copies of the document from the members of the mission team and declared his preference for there to be no "extensive discussions of my report," Bundy remembered. In his con-versations with reporters, "I did not refer to the existence of any written report."[42]

Thirty years later, the February 7 bombing proposal continued to preoccupy Bundy. He could not explain why Johnson sought to contain it and render it moot. Yet there was an obvious explanation for the presi-dent's dismissive reaction to the graduated and sustained reprisal recom-mendation. Johnson had already indicated his doubts about the efficacy of bombing and his preference for ground combat forces just weeks before, in response to the Christmas Eve terror attacks in Saigon. That view was represented in the December 30 cable that Bundy himself had drafted on behalf of the president.

Of the bombing strategy recommendation, Bundy recalled that Johnson "can hardly hear it before putting it all off-limits."[43] Commenting on his proposal to unleash a campaign of continuous American air power, Bundy sought to "underline" that the bombing option "is what was available at a time when no one—especially not Max Taylor—wanted ground troops" and when there was "no readiness" for a diplomatic negotiation "because of opposite goals and unexhausted hope."[44] President Johnson's treatment of the bombing proposal, Bundy said, "tells us something about what he was doing, which was to move into a program that would have just as few political traces to it and as little public discussion as he could manage. . . . What happened . . . was that he was very determined not to have it become a cause of escalation in the larger sense, and especially not to tickle the Chinese dragon."[45] And in contrast to his national security adviser, the president simply thought bombing would prove futile. As Bundy told me about Johnson: "He used to say, 'Ol' Ho isn't gonna give in to any airplanes.'"[46]

Senator Mike Mansfield seemed to appreciate that Pleiku marked a turning point in the war. "What the answer to the situation is at the moment I do not know nor does anyone else," Mansfield wrote in a letter to Johnson on February 8. "But I am persuaded that the trend toward enlargement of the conflict and a continuous deepening of our military commitment on the Asian mainland, despite your desire to the contrary, is not going to provide one."[47]

"The President," Bundy wrote in reply to Mansfield, "has repeatedly made it clear that we cannot ourselves solve all the problems of South Vietnam. He has also insisted, however, that every possible step be taken to make our support for the Vietnamese people more effective and efficient. . . . The President certainly shares your view that military security should be as effective as possible within the limits of our basic policy decision not to deploy large American combat units for guard duty in Vietnam." Thirty years later, noting the administration's misleading pledge in his letter to Mansfield, Bundy remarked in the margin, "as late *as this*!!"[48]

George Ball also sensed that an inflection point had arrived—the transition to a broad strategy of coercive military force designed to break the determination of the insurgency. He doubted the strategy had any realistic expectation of success. In an implicit challenge to the rigor of Bundy's analysis, Ball argued that short of a "crushing military defeat" concretely imposed on the insurgency, coercive pressure would have little impact. "Hanoi would never abandon the aggressive course it has pursued at great cost for ten years and give up all the progress it has made in the Communization of South Viet-Nam," he wrote in a memo to the president. "For North Viet-Nam to call off the insurgency in South-Vietnam, close the border, and withdraw the elements it had infiltrated into that country would mean that it had accepted unconditional surrender."[49]

Bundy was unresponsive to Ball's critique of his coercive force strategy. He did not advance an argument for why it would compel the capitulation of an enemy that was, by Bundy's own admission, "astonishing" in its energy, persistence, and resilience. In fact, Bundy did not even consider it necessary to posit a precise military objective for the escalation he was advocating. As Ball would later explain about Bundy, "His position—if I now properly recall his explanation—was that since 'we did not know what the answer would be,' we did not have 'to follow a particular course down the road to a particular result.' He was, in other words, qualifying our declared war aim of restoring South Vietnam to the *status quo ante* . . . by opting to leave our objective unformulated and therefore flexible. Though I privately applauded his pragmatism, I could not agree that we should keep charging more deeply into the mire without clearly acknowledging where we were going and on what basis we would call a halt."[50]

Lyndon Johnson now presided over an administration with deeply conflicting perspectives on both the strategic objectives of escalation in Vietnam and its appropriate military form. Bundy favored coercive bombing and its capacity to grind down the enemy. President Johnson was a skeptic about bombing; like General Westmoreland, he favored inserting ground combat forces—deployments that Ambassador Taylor in Saigon considered doomed to failure. Ball believed that either method of escalation—bombing or ground troops—would fail. Added to this mix was the advocacy of former President Eisenhower, who believed the threat of using nuclear weapons had ended the Korean War in 1953.[51] Eisenhower now informed Johnson that if given the opportunity, as commander in chief, "he would use any weapons required, adding that if we were to use tactical nuclear weapons, such use would not in itself add to the chance of escalation."[52]

While the proposal to use tactical nuclear weapons against North Vietnam never gained traction, Bundy nonetheless believed Eisenhower's influence on Johnson was significant. Johnson, wrote Bundy, "deeply and honestly believed" that protecting South Vietnam from communist domination was pivotal to the regional security of Southeast Asia. In this conviction the president enjoyed "the powerful and steadfast support" of two figures whose solidarity Johnson coveted: the former president and war hero Dwight Eisenhower and Secretary of State Dean Rusk, whom Bundy described as Johnson's "totally discreet and loyal cultural cousin." Eisenhower believed that once war was embarked upon, "you must fight to win," and Rusk was persuaded that in a global contest with communist power the United States must remain "reliable" and "a friend who means what he says."

Of the two, Bundy recalled, Eisenhower was even more important to Johnson than Rusk. With the former president's political support, "dissidents were harmless" and their anger could even serve as a foil to the president's own professed moderation. Eisenhower stood by Westmoreland's recommendations as the commander in the field, and he shared the conviction that Southeast Asia must not be allowed to fall under communist hegemony. "For Johnson," Bundy observed, "General Eisenhower was now the most important single political ally."[53]

On February 19, almost two weeks after the Pleiku attack, Johnson finally accepted Bundy's recommendation for a continuing campaign of air strikes in support of a strategy of "graduated and sustained reprisal." But Johnson rejected his national security adviser's advice to announce the decision publicly.[54] And along with Bundy the president shrugged off the grave concerns of the French foreign minister, Maurice Couve de Murville, who "honestly does not think we can avoid defeat in South Vietnam," Bundy reported. "This is of course a comforting conclusion for a Frenchman for obvious reasons."[55]

Johnson similarly rejected counsel coming from within his own cabinet that echoed the French warning. In a pair of February memos, Vice President Hubert Humphrey implored the president to reevaluate the rapidly growing American military commitment to Saigon. "From a political viewpoint, the American people find it hard to understand why we would risk World War III by enlarging a war under terms we found unacceptable 12 years ago in Korea, particularly since the chances of success are slimmer," wrote Humphrey. The vice president argued that Americans recalled the "lessons" of the Korean war, which he identified as a recognition of the limitations of air power, a wariness of the risk of Chinese intervention, respect for the "never again club" precluding the deployment of American combat forces to fight a land war in Asia, and, finally, acknowledgment of the "Eisenhower administration's compromise which represented a frank recognition of all these factors." Humphrey urged Johnson to cut his losses in Vietnam, noting that the president was "in a stronger position to do so than any administration in this century."[56] Johnson was livid over Humphrey's warnings and banished him from Vietnam deliberations for the following year.[57]

A campaign of bombing strikes launched from South Vietnam would make the bases from which they originated high-value targets for the insurgency. Those bases would, of course, require significantly increased protection. Yet Bundy's bombing recommendation failed to address the program's implications for base security and the use of combat forces in South Vietnam. General Westmoreland quickly seized on the national security adviser's oversight, requesting a marine expeditionary brigade to defend the U.S. air base at Da Nang, the central complex of airfields that would serve as the hub for Operation Rolling Thunder.[58] Ambassador Taylor vehemently objected, anticipating that combat force deployments of this type would ultimately send Washington on the path to de facto Americanization of the war.

"Such action would be a step in reversing long-standing policies of avoiding commitment of ground combat forces in South Vietnam," Taylor inveighed in a cable to the Joint Chiefs. "Once this policy is breached it will be very difficult to hold the line."[59] When the first marines hit the ground, Taylor predicted, additional and expanded deployments would be inevitable. "If Danang needs better protection, so do Bien Hoa, Ton Son Nhut, Nha Trang and other key base areas," he pointed out. "Once it becomes evident that we are willing to assume such new responsibilities, one may be sure [the Saigon government] will seek to unload other ground force tasks upon us." If the goal was the defense of the Da Nang air base from retaliatory mortar fire, "it would be necessary for Marines to be in place on [the] ground in considerable strength," with up to six battalions. And what if the Johnson administration deployed ground combat units in a full-scale effort to suppress the insurgency in the jungles and forests of Southeast Asia? Taylor predicted that America would then suffer the same fate as France, "which tried to adapt their forces to this mission and failed; I doubt that US forces could do much better. . . . When I view this array of difficulties I am convinced that we should adhere to our past policy of keeping our ground forces out of a direct counterinsurgency role."[60]

Taylor's warning was rejected. On February 26, Secretary of State Rusk informed the U.S. embassy in Saigon of the imminent deployment of new U.S. forces. A marine battalion landing team, a marine expeditionary brigade command-and-control element, and one helicopter squadron would "proceed to land at once."[61] With the approval of Westmoreland's request for a combat contingent to guard the Da Nang air base, a fundamentally new era of the war had been launched. When 3,500 marines landed in South Vietnam on March 8, 1965, it was the first time U.S. ground combat units had been deployed to the Asian mainland since the Korean War.[62] The ineluctable Americanization of the Vietnam War had commenced.

In the wake of his policy disagreement with General Taylor, Bundy urged President Johnson to dismiss him as the U.S. ambassador to South Vietnam. In a memo, McNamara and Rusk concurred: "Max has been gallant, determined, and honorable to a fault, but he has also been rigid, remote, and sometimes abrupt. We all recognize that Taylor has served an enormously important purpose in keeping American opinion from division and criticism, but our inclination would be to bring him back." Bundy also pressed the president to indicate his response to a possible ground offensive by North Vietnamese or Chinese troops. "The crucial question," he noted, "is, in a sense, whether and when you would authorize landings of a number of U.S. divisions in South Vietnam."[63]

Precisely as Taylor had predicted, the military swiftly adapted to the breach of the no-combat-troop policy with ambitious new proposals. The army chief of staff, Harold K. Johnson, conducted a review mission in South Vietnam to generate recommendations for intensified military action. On March 15, one week after the first U.S. combat troops waded ashore in South Vietnam, he briefed President Johnson and other senior officials on proposals he had been developing with John McNaughton, the assistant secretary of defense who had argued the theoretical merits of "graduated and sustained reprisal." General Johnson stunned the president and his advisers, warning that "it could take 500,000 U.S. troops five years to win the war." According to McNamara, "His estimate shocked not just the president and me but the other chiefs as well. None of us had been thinking in anything approaching such terms."[64]

Although the no-combat-troop policy had been breached, the essential strategic question governing such deployments remained unanswered. How would combat troops alter the basic calculus of the war? Chester Cooper, who had replaced Mike Forrestal as Bundy's staff specialist on Vietnam, confessed his doubts. In response to a memorandum from Taylor positing the inability of any escalation to seal internal frontiers from the Vietcong or destroy their forces, Cooper agreed that the United States would never achieve the ten-to-one or twenty-to-one numerical advantage of combat troops over guerilla soldiers historically necessary to prevail in wars of counterinsurgency. "We cannot count on eliminating the ability of the VC to replenish its manpower and supplies," Cooper cautioned the national security adviser. "We might slow down this support, we might make it more costly, but if we establish its elimination as a criterion for progress, we had better resign ourselves to defeat."[65]

Cooper's warning, like Taylor's even graver reservations, appear to have had little impact on Bundy. On March 16, in advance of a weekly Tuesday lunch President Johnson now convened with the national security adviser, the secretary of defense, and the secretary of state, Bundy sketched his argument for enlarging combat troop deployments to South Vietnam.[66] "In essence," he explained, "there appear to be three things that Hanoi can do: it can stop its infiltration; it can withdraw forces and supplies under its control from the South; it can order its people not to use force against the government in the South. None of these is likely at present, and it is questionable whether any of them will be ordered under the pressure of our air operations alone." Yet Bundy argued that the United States could use ground forces to compel one of "three general possibilities" for "an eventual settlement."

The first was the "effective pacification of a wholly non-Communist South Vietnam." The second was "a somewhat Laotian solution," comparable to what Walter Lippmann had advocated, "in which a government of national unity would have some members from the liberation front and in which de facto VC control in large parts of the countryside would be accepted," requiring a continuing U.S. troop presence. The third was "an explicit partition" of South Vietnam that might allow for a temporary withdrawal of U.S. forces but in which "continuing VC ambition would quickly lead to a situation in which we would have to return." Although Bundy had identified a series of dramatically disparate outcomes, each with radically different requirements for success, he refused to identify one objective as paramount over the others. "It does not appear necessary today to decide among these three alternatives," he argued. "What does appear quite likely is that our eventual bargaining position with respect to all three possibilities will be improved and not weakened if the United States presence on the ground increases in coming weeks. This US ground presence is likely to reinforce both pacification efforts and Southern morale, while discouraging the VC from their current expectation of early victory."[67]

On March 21, in the midst of the transformation of the American commitment to South Vietnam, Bundy reflected on the country's ultimate strategic significance. Even though he had been advocating enlargement of the war, in private notes composed at the time he acknowledged some doubts. "Is our interest economic?" Bundy asked himself. "Obviously not. The arguments on this plane are fatuous. . . . Is our interest military? Not really . . . even a bad result would be marginal on a straight military account. . . . So our interest is political. Real or fancied?" Bundy declared: "A tentative conclusion is that: the whole game is less than it today appears, both in *status and in consequences*, because the level of open conflict is and will probably stay low—and because [both] sides will be able to claim special circumstances whenever they want."

Yet the "cardinal" principle of the Vietnamese intervention, he wrote, was for the United States "*not* to be a Paper Tiger. Not to have it thought that when we commit ourselves we really mean no major risk. This means, essentially, a willingness to fight China *if* necessary. But if it is *not* necessary, the minus far outweighs the plus on any China war. Moreover it is *not* clear that even a *Chinese* war would help us *win* in Vietnam (though it *would* punish the aggressor). The conclusion I draw from this is that it is to our advantage to frame our posture toward our military program so that we have a right to go *anywhere* (and will if sufficiently provoked)—but so that we *also* focus attention where it belongs: on the South. (This implies, among other things, a change in Ambassador.)"

Bundy's projections about the use of American combat troops were conspicuously, if not purposely, vague. "A proper balance of readiness to act and real attention to real problems seems to be the best design for making the result endurable, however much we succeed or fail. For if we visibly *do enough* in the South (whatever that may be), any failure will be, in that sense, beyond our control." Even a failed intervention in Vietnam, Bundy asserted, would be better than no intervention at all. "Questions: in terms of U.S. politics which is better: to 'lose' now or to 'lose' after committing 100,000 men? Tentative answer: the latter."[68]

Bundy's March 21 notes vividly and candidly capture the core conviction about Americanizing the Vietnam War that guided his conduct as national security adviser in the fateful year of 1965. The Johnson administration, he argued, should be driven not by the minimal economic or military interests at risk but rather by the principle of protecting its global credibility, the imperative not to be rendered a so-called paper tiger. Fulfillment of that objective did not require the United States to prevail in Vietnam. To the contrary, a military defeat was acceptable provided Washington lost with some demonstrable cost, perhaps even after deploying 100,000 troops. According to Bundy's presumptive logic, defeat in Vietnam would protect American credibility globally and the credibility of the Johnson administration domestically.

Bundy was not the only foreign policy intellectual in the Johnson administration to identify American credibility as the paramount interest in Vietnam. John McNaughton, the law professor turned defense intellectual, shared the same fixation. In a March 24, 1965, memo he quantitatively ranked the hierarchy of American interests in Vietnam: "70%—to avoid a humiliating US defeat (to our reputation as a guarantor). 20%—To keep SVN (and the adjacent) territory from Chinese hands.[69] 10%—To permit the people of SVN to enjoy a better, freer way of life."[70]

On April 1, Bundy submitted another memorandum to President Johnson elaborating on the merits of an open-ended and unformulated U.S. military strategy in Vietnam. He conceded that if Hanoi continued "to make real headway in the south . . . even a major step-up in our air attacks would probably not cause them to become much more reasonable." Yet air strikes constituted just one of three key sources of coercive leverage to quash the insurgency. The other two, according to Bundy, were U.S. combat forces and the possibility of "economic carrots" that might induce cooperation from Hanoi. "We want to trade these cards," he advised, "for just as much as possible of the following: an end to infiltration of men and supplies, an end of Hanoi's direction, control, and encouragement of the Viet Cong, a removal of cadres under direct Hanoi control, and a dissolution of the organized Viet Cong military and political forces."

Bundy again argued that America's strategic objectives did not have to be precisely defined. "We do not need to decide today just how we wish to mesh our high cards against Communist concessions. But we will need to be in such a position soon."[71] Bundy did not explain why he presumed the communist guerrilla fighters would capitulate, why they would be likely to offer "concessions," or why they would "trade" their fierce commitment to the insurgency for an easing of air strikes or in return for economic rewards. In fact, he made no effort to sketch any causal linkage between the forms of leverage he enumerated and the acts of submission they were designed to induce. "All I do here is to list our desiderata," he wrote in 1981, long before he embarked on a serious study of the war. "I don't say how much of them we can get." While admitting the difficulty of realizing all of the diverse objectives identified in his memorandum, Bundy wondered why it was "wrong to try for 'just as much as possible'?"[72]

Johnson was "full of determination," Bundy noted, when he, Rusk, and McNamara met with the president on the afternoon of April 1.[73] Johnson approved an 18,000-to-20,000-man increase in U.S. military support forces and the deployment of two additional marine combat battalions and a marine air squadron. More significantly, Johnson agreed to change the marines' mission from base security to active offensive counterinsurgency combat operations against the Vietcong.[74] With this decree the Americanization of the war was arguably an accomplished fact. Not only was the Kennedy no-combat-troop policy decisively reversed, the mission of U.S. forces was now the active participation in offensive counterinsurgency operations.

Although embarked on a dramatically different strategy in Vietnam, Johnson was determined to limit disclosure of the new combat mission for American forces. As Bundy noted on April 6 in National Security Action Memorandum 328, "The President desires that . . . premature publicity be avoided by all possible precautions. . . . The actions themselves should be taken as rapidly as practicable, but in ways that should minimize any appearance of sudden changes in policy, and official statements on these troop movements will be made only with the direct approval of the Secretary of Defense, in consultation with the Secretary of State."[75] Speaking at Johns Hopkins University in Baltimore on April 7, Johnson attempted to play down the rapidly shifting U.S. mission in Vietnam. "In recent months attacks on South Vietnam were stepped up," he explained. "Thus, it became necessary for us to increase our response and to make attacks by air. This is not a change of purpose. It is a change in what we believe that purpose requires."

In the Johns Hopkins speech, Johnson dangled the notion of a broad development program for North Vietnam, featuring a Vietnamese version of the Tennessee Valley Authority. "The vast Mekong River," he insisted, "can provide food and water and power on a scale to dwarf even our own TVA."[76] Johnson also offered direct talks with Hanoi, a proposal that went nowhere.[77] During the previous month, Bundy recalled, the president was determined to prevent administration officials from even discussing the possibility of unconditional negotiations with the North Vietnamese. This was a further example of Johnson's "characteristic habit" of protecting "his options in a time of decision-making."[78] Bundy said he was among those in the administration lobbying Johnson for a more open explication of the war's requirements and costs. "I had a terrible fight over getting as much as we got said in Baltimore," Bundy recalled in 1994. "I had been pestering him about how you've got to explain this war and unexplained wars are no way to fight."[79] This nascent tension—Johnson's propensity for obfuscation and Bundy's advocacy of transparency—would grow more pronounced in the weeks to follow.

In a meeting with senior civilian advisers and the Joint Chiefs on April 13, the president approved the immediate deployment to South Vietnam of the 173rd Airborne Brigade for security and counterinsurgency combat operations.[80] From Saigon, Ambassador Taylor sharply objected. "This comes as a complete surprise," he protested, "in view of the understanding . . . that we would experiment with the Marines in a counter-insurgency role before bringing in other US contingents. . . . I recommend that this deployment be held up until we can sort out all matters relating to it."[81] In a second cable that day, Taylor observed, "Recent actions relating to the introduction of US ground forces have tended to create an impression of eagerness in some quarters to deploy forces into [South Vietnam] which I find difficult to understand. . . . The mounting number of foreign troops may sap the [government's] initiative and turn a defense of the . . . homeland into what appears a foreign war." He concluded: "The net effect may be not an expediting of victory but its retardation. I mention these countervailing factors to make the point that it is far from an unmitigated advantage to bring in more US forces."[82]

This time Bundy was sensitive to Taylor's dissent. He urged President Johnson not to issue a series of new combat directives developed in White House discussions and drafted by McNamara. "My own judgment," Bundy reported, "is that direct orders of this sort to Taylor would be very explosive right now because he will not agree with many of them and he will not feel that he has been consulted."[83] Yet Bundy soon fell into line.

"On further troop deployments," Taylor was informed in a cable cleared by Bundy, Rusk, and McNamara on April 15, "President's belief is that current situation requires use of all practicable means of strengthening position in South Vietnam and that additional US troops are important if not decisive reinforcement. He has not seen evidence of negative result of deployments to date." The cable solicited Taylor's concurrence with an experiment in the combined operation of three American and three South Vietnamese combat battalions; the introduction of a brigade force into the Bien Hoa–Vung Tau area; and the deployment of "battalion or multi-battalion forces into 2 or 3 additional locations along the coast . . . to experiment further with US forces in a counter-insurgency role, in addition to providing security for the Base."[84]

Taylor's skepticism remained unabated. "Mac, can't we be better protected from our friends?" he plaintively asked Bundy. "I know that everyone wants to help but there's such a thing as killing with kindness. In particular, we want to stay alive here because we think we're winning—and will continue to win unless helped to death."[85]

The momentum for an enlarged American escalation grew stronger. On April 19 and 20, Ambassador Taylor, General Westmoreland, and other senior officials met in Honolulu to chart the next phase of U.S. combat force deployments. The group collectively recommended a 150 percent increase of U.S. troops in South Vietnam, from the current level of 33,500 to 82,000.[86] As Taylor recalled, "By that time I knew what the President wanted. He was going to get all the ground forces in the field the commander wanted, and get them in there as fast as he could."[87] McNamara presented the Honolulu recommendations to President Johnson in a White House meeting attended by Bundy, who according to minutes of the discussion, "pointed out that the program outlined in the McNamara paper is quite different from the course of action heretofore considered, and should be carefully studied."[88]

A flabbergasted George Ball responded more forcefully. "This transforms our whole relation to the war," cautioned Ball, foreshadowing "*a much larger number* of casualties."[89] In an emotional plea he implored Johnson not to take "a hazardous leap into space without further exploring the possibilities of a settlement." Yet Ball had set himself up for one of Johnson's classic political machinations. "All right, George," challenged the president. "I'll give you until tomorrow morning to get me a settlement plan. If you can pull a rabbit out of the hat, I'm all for it!"[90]

Despite the odds Ball did try to maneuver the seemingly impossible: a plan for withdrawal from Vietnam that Lyndon Johnson would endorse. In a long memorandum sent to the White House that evening, Ball advised the president to reverse course in Vietnam by seeking a coalition government and extracting U.S. forces. "Distasteful as it is, we must face the hard fact that large and articulate elements in the intellectual community and other segments of United States opinion do not believe in our South Vietnamese policy," he argued. "In fact, to many Americans our position appears far more ambiguous—and hence far more dubious—than in the Korean war."[91] Ball met with the president the following morning. "I had not, I soon realized, 'pulled a rabbit out of the hat'—at least not a rabbit strong enough to fight off the hounds of war baying at its heels," Ball recalled.[92]

Once more an imperfect extrication plan advocated by Ball became the straw man in the Vietnam debate. What was needed, of course, was a realistic evaluation of the prospects for a ground war waged against the different elements contributing to the insurgency. On April 20 the intelligence community concluded in a classified estimate that even an increase of U.S. combat strength in excess of 80,000 troops would fail to deter the Vietcong, North Vietnam, or China from engaging in or supporting the war: "They would likely count on time being on their side and try to force the piecemeal engagement of US troops under conditions which might bog them down in jungle warfare, hoping to present the US with a de facto partition of the country." The estimate determined that the Vietcong, North Vietnam, and China "all rate the staying power of their side as inherently superior to that of their enemies."[93]

Yet again, a penetrating intelligence analysis of the profound limitations of escalation—this time via combat forces—was essentially ignored. Neither Bundy nor any of his senior administration colleagues used the estimate as a catalyst to debate the plausibility that even substantial American ground troop deployments could coerce communist forces into reversing course or negotiating a settlement favorable to the United States. On April 22 Secretary of State Rusk informed Ambassador Taylor of the imminent escalation to 82,000 troops under U.S. command in South Vietnam.[94]

President Johnson did his best to evade the media. At a press conference on April 27, Johnson was asked whether there could be "circumstances in which large numbers of American troops might be engaged in the fighting of the war rather than in the advising and assistance to the South Vietnamese?" Johnson's reply was curt. "Our purpose in Vietnam," he said, "is . . . to advise and assist those people in resisting aggression." In his account of the press conference, the historian Brian VanDeMark points out that "Johnson neglected any mention of the Marines' combat mission, or of the 50,000 additional forces."[95] In 1995, when he reviewed VanDeMark's account, Bundy commented: "This was all wrong and I knew it but did not make as good a fight against it as I wish I had."

The American combat troop deployments in the spring of 1965 were made despite sustained political paralysis in Saigon and the South

Vietnamese army's continuously deficient military performance. Following a flurry of intrigues and maneuvers within the government, in May a military coup mounted by the so-called Young Turks—led by Air Marshal Nguyen Cao Ky and General Nguyen Van Thieu—toppled the civilian government formed by Phan Huy Quat, marking the fifth change of government since the overthrow and assassination of President Diem in November 1963. On the battlefield, the Vietcong—now strengthened by as many as four regiments of North Vietnamese regulars—decimated the government's army in battles north of Saigon and in the central highlands.[96] And the first practical test of Bundy's "graduated and sustained reprisal" strategy suggested just how misguided Washington was in its assumptions about the potency of bombing. Following an intense internal debate, President Johnson ordered a brief, unpublicized bombing pause on May 13.[97] The U.S. ambassador in Moscow, Foy Kohler, was instructed to inform North Vietnam that in return for a halt to air strikes the United States expected a reduction in armed action by the Vietcong.[98] The administration's gesture was comically rebuffed. "Kohler had a tough time getting his message to the North Vietnamese Ambassador," Bundy reported to the president. "The North Vietnamese Embassy refused to receive the message on the ground that we did not have diplomatic relations and suggested that Kohler deliver it through the Soviet Government. . . . The Soviets refused to play this role, and Kohler eventually got the message delivered by handing it to an employee at the North Vietnamese Embassy who accepted it. Kohler also gave a copy to the Soviets who refused to pass it on, but did not pass it back."[99] Johnson lamented Hanoi's silence. "No one has even thanked us for the pause," he complained.[100] When the United States resumed bombing on May 18, Hanoi's foreign ministry repudiated the pause as "a deceitful maneuver designed to pave the way for new US acts of war."[101]

The American escalation in the spring of 1965 roused doubt and noisy dissent among the intelligentsia. Bundy, supremely confident in his status as the administration's debater in chief, was eager to respond to the growing ranks of Vietnam critics, especially from an alienated academic community. Johnson, equally confident in his skills as a political strategist in chief, believed that his national security adviser should not draw unfavorable attention to the administration's Vietnam policy through high-profile arguments with intellectual and media elites. The breakdown of his relationship with the president, Bundy wrote in one of his draft fragments, was most vividly demonstrated by their dispute over his participation in a public debate over Vietnam policy. Without informing Johnson, Bundy had accepted an invitation to speak at a "national teach-in," an event convened by some of the administration's most vocal critics. When the president found out, he pressed Bundy to withdraw. "I told him that it would be a defeat for our side if I were to back out," Bundy recalled, "and went on preparing for the debate."[102]

Scheduled for May 15 in Washington, the debate would see the former Harvard dean face off against a panel of scholars in a forum organized by a group of professors from the University of Michigan. Bundy's public appearance was scuttled, however, when Johnson abruptly dispatched him to the Dominican Republic, where twenty-two thousand U.S. Marines had landed in response to a growing crisis between the ruling military junta and supporters of Juan Bosch, the democratically elected but deposed former president. Bundy was appended to a mission led by Thomas Mann from the State Department and Cyrus Vance from the Pentagon. Bundy thought at the time that he was being sent along to provide "reinforcing credibility," but what the president really wanted was the national security adviser's absence from the Washington debate.[103]

By early June official opinion from Saigon had turned sharply pessimistic about the prospects for Bundy's strategy of "graduated and sustained reprisal." Ambassador Taylor reported, "We do not believe that any feasible amount of bombing of the North is of itself likely to cause [North Vietnam] to cease and desist in its actions in the South."[104] Two days later

Taylor informed Washington that the South Vietnamese army was plagued by desertions, poor training, and weak leadership and in some cases had "broken under pressures and fled from the battlefield." In contrast, Vietcong forces, despite sometimes "severe losses . . . have shown a remarkable recuperative ability." To prevent a collapse of the entire war effort, Taylor finally conceded, "it will probably be necessary to commit U.S. ground forces to action."[105] The former general, who had advocated U.S. combat troop deployments under Kennedy but became a staunch opponent of ground forces under Johnson, had finally succumbed.

While eighty-two thousand combat troops had been authorized for action in Vietnam, the larger strategic concept that would govern their mission was still, remarkably, undetermined by Bundy and the other strategists in the administration's war council. "How do we get what we want?" President Johnson asked on the afternoon of Saturday, June 5, when he dropped in on a lunch meeting of the national security adviser and other senior officials.[106] The consensus, Bill Bundy reported, still supported "a defensive and long-term strategy, premised on the rational belief that a frustrated and pained Hanoi must in time call it off."[107] McNamara was less sanguine. "We're looking for no more than a stalemate in the South," he grimly told President Johnson. "Can we achieve it? I don't know. The communists still think they're winning."[108]

On June 7 General Westmoreland informed McNamara that even the enlarged force levels agreed to that spring would not be adequate. Westmoreland requested an immediate increase of 41,000 combat troops, to be followed by 52,000 later. His plan called for augmenting the thirteen American battalions already committed to South Vietnam with nineteen more U.S. battalions and ten from allied countries. Under Westmoreland's proposal the total combat troop commitment would grow from 82,000 forces under U.S. command to 175,000, and the general's combined command would grow to forty-two battalions, and by the end of the month to forty-four battalions.[109]

"The basic purpose of the additional deployments," Westmoreland explained, "is to give us a substantial and hard hitting offensive capability on the ground to convince the VC they cannot win."[110] Even with a more than 100 percent increase in combat forces—following the previous 150 percent increase of April—the top American commander in Vietnam still could not ensure an outcome better than the stalemate McNamara had recently predicted. Neither could Westmoreland articulate a more plausible strategy other than the administration's prevailing assumption, explicit in Bundy's bombing proposal and all of the phases of escalation, that military force should be applied as a means of persuasion, "to convince" a remarkably resilient enemy that "they cannot win." What Westmoreland's analysis omitted, along with every other plan for escalation considered at the time, was a rigorous examination of the strategic implications for the United States if the Vietnamese communists were *not* deterred, if their forces were *not* demoralized, and if despite severe losses they simply refused to quit.

The dramatic scale of Westmoreland's proposal triggered a sharp administration debate. According to McGeorge Bundy's private notes of a June 10 White House meeting, McNamara argued that South Vietnam's collapse could be averted with a commitment of U.S. troops significantly smaller than that proposed by Westmoreland—roughly ninety-five thousand men or eighteen battalions—a number slightly more than half of the general's request.[111] Bill Bundy recalled that "Rusk concurred, and Taylor made the case that this appeared to be about right to prevent serious losses of territory and lead in the direction of a stalemate in the South."[112] But Richard Russell, the chairman of the Senate Armed Services Committee, favored Westmoreland's plan. "Driblets," Russell declared, "were not the answer; if a division in the highlands would help, or bombing the SAM sites, these things should be done."[113] According to McNamara's notes, President Johnson posed several threshold questions to the group, including one that the administration had studiously left unanswered throughout the series of escalations in 1965. "How do we extricate ourselves?" he asked. "Hope for a settlement," Johnson was told, "lay in stalemating the Viet Cong and keeping the North under pressure."[114]

༄

As he revisited the narrative of 1965, the year the Johnson administration Americanized the Vietnam War, McGeorge Bundy was confronted with his own role in conceiving a calamitous shift in strategy. It was a question he did not come to easily. Other elements of the war's progression were less threatening and more amenable to his retrospective mode of argument. Kennedy's policy rejecting combat troops in Vietnam; Johnson's manipulative political style; George Ball's inability to win the argument against Americanization; Bundy's own emphasis in 1965 on greater public debate—these were the subsidiary themes of the war he was predisposed to address. His own failures of analysis and advice would prove far more difficult to articulate. But Bundy did not totally reject the task of self-criticism. He struggled with it, sporadically asking himself difficult questions and producing insights that, while only partially developed, were nonetheless incisive and illuminating.

"What are my worst mistakes?" Bundy asked himself in one of his draft fragments. The answer, in retrospect, was clear: "Not to press the study of the prospects of success, of one side's strength and one side's weakness, especially in 1965. Not to examine what could be done to make the best of a bad business while not escalating."[115] With this admission Bundy indirectly acknowledged the essential irony of his tenure as national security adviser. In response to the crisis in Vietnam, the administration's preeminent intellectual demonstrated a fundamental lack of rigor in his analysis of the ends and means of American strategy. It was a failure he struggled to understand in his draft fragments. "What causes the mistake: i) Underestimate of the enemy, ii) The failure to examine [the] plan (White House did not know what it was doing . . .)."

Bundy said that this outcome was "partly my fault," but added that blame should also be attributed to the Pentagon and the U.S. country team in Saigon. A common failure of analysis across the government, he observed, was the inability to grasp "how the enemy would take it and come back for *more*."[116]

Bundy's self-criticism was, of course, justified. He did underestimate the resilience of the enemy. He did fail to examine the plan for military action. And he did fail to anticipate that the American escalation would be met with a furious countervailing escalation by the forces of the National Liberation Front and the North Vietnamese army. Reduced to its essence, in 1965 Bundy pursued a strategy that presumed the ascending application of military force would deprive the insurgency of victory and that the ensuing stalemate and its associated costs would eventually compel the Vietnamese communists to compromise their objectives. But this was little more than an unexamined assumption. There was no analysis or evidence to validate Bundy's expectation that Ho Chi Minh and his fervent followers would capitulate. Bundy also failed to insist that the national security bureaucracy quantify the policy implications of a coercion strategy. How many bombs would it take to dilute the will of the insurgency? How much disruption and destruction would the United States have to impose on their lines of supply and reinforcement? How many U.S. troops would be required to persuade the Vietnamese communists that they could not prevail? How many casualties would be required to compel them to quit? How many years would it take? Where, exactly, was the tipping point—the threshold of pain and loss that would extract a fundamental reversal in Vietnamese nationalist ambitions?

Bundy acknowledged that he believed the United States would not "fail to prevail" if American troop deployments ultimately matched what he called the "Korean level"—a view he shared with other administration strategists.[117] He also acknowledged that his fatal flaw was the conviction that he could employ military force as a means to achieve a political end, in this case the negotiated abandonment of the Vietnamese communist cause. In scattered notes conveying his struggle to identify the roots of a disastrous military strategy, Bundy wrote, "LBJ and the rest of us don't ask how much Ho can endure." Perhaps, Bundy speculated, Johnson feared losing his case in favor of a "long hard war" if the question were publicly debated. Bundy struggled with the reasons for his own failure to challenge Johnson and in apparent frustration concluded: "Anyway, we don't have the debate and we don't ask the necessary how-strong-is-the-adversary question. We think of ourselves as propping up Saigon, which will do better and do its share and somehow do—enough."[118]

There was a fundamental imprecision to Bundy's argument for escalation in 1965. He marched ahead with the expectation that an undefined degree of coercive military pressure would extract an undefined form of political capitulation over an undefined period of conflict. This expectation came back to haunt him. As he retrospectively studied his assertion in his March 16, 1965, memorandum that larger combat troop deployments would strengthen "our eventual bargaining position" with the Vietcong, Bundy archly observed: "Yes, but suppose there's no bargain available?"[119] More broadly, Bundy came to dismiss the whole premise of negotiated settlement in Vietnam. There was no "peaceful path" to a negotiated agreement, Bundy contended in one of his fragments, and "no way" for the United States to exercise leadership to achieve "a peaceful compromise." He noted that "what Hanoi would accept would never satisfy Saigon, and vice versa"—and that Washington, "if only for its own political reasons," could not compel the regime in Saigon to follow a path leading "only to early collapse."[120]

Massive ground force deployments would fail to compel the North Vietnamese to the bargaining table. So would Bundy's bombing strategy, which would accomplish nothing with respect to its objective of extracting negotiated concessions from North Vietnam. To the contrary, as multiple intelligence analyses had predicted, bombing had the opposite effect. Nguyen Khac Huynh, a Foreign Ministry official focusing on U.S. affairs who later served on his country's delegation at the Paris peace talks, emphasized the role bombing played in solidifying North Vietnam's determination to continue and escalate its guerrilla war effort. "The bombing was the key factor," he said, "and the cessation of bombing was our key demand. You must understand that the U.S. bombing of the North was a serious challenge to our sovereignty. Our only choice was whether to submit or resist. Under these circumstances, every Vietnamese citizen would have felt ashamed if we sat down and talked with you under the pressure of bombing. This is the reason why so long as you continued to bomb the North, there could be no negotiations."[121]

Tran Quang Co, who served as first deputy foreign minister, would make the case that the American bombing campaign was critical to national morale in North Vietnam. "Never before did the people of Vietnam, from top to bottom, unite as they did during the years that the U.S. was bombing us. Never before had Chairman Ho Chi Minh's appeal— that there is nothing more precious than freedom and independence— go straight to the hearts and minds of the Vietnamese people."[122] The limited utility of bombing and the massive determination and endurance of Vietnamese communist forces should never have been in doubt to Bundy and other senior administration officials. After all, it was one of the principal insights generated by the SIGMA war-game exercises in which the national security adviser had participated.

Bundy knew from his discussions with Johnson in the final days of 1964 and from the cable he drafted to Saigon on December 30 that the president doubted the utility of air strikes and favored the deployment of ground forces to South Vietnam. "Is McGB wrong on air campaign of '65?" Bundy asked himself thirty years later. "Not because '65 air is wrong, but because they make the *next steps easier*?"[123] Westmoreland's swift appropriation of bombing as a pretext to deploy combat forces certainly appears to have fused perfectly with Johnson's predisposition at the time to deploy ground troops. This intersection of a field commander's opportunism and a president's known preferences should have been obvious to Bundy but ironically was not.

"My own belief" in 1965, Bundy declared, "was in support and training and supplies" for the South Vietnamese army, consistent with the legacy of the American relationship with Saigon from the beginning. And Bundy supported the application of airpower, he noted, because the South Vietnamese "could not do that for themselves in 1964."[124] Commenting on his strategy of graduated and sustained reprisal, Bundy called it "an example of the difficulties in getting a strong President to do it your way, not his." He believed that the memorandum he had drafted on the long flight home from South Vietnam might have opened the door for a substantive dialogue within the administration about both "politics and tactics that were only intermittently and fragmentarily" acknowledged in later years. But Lyndon Johnson did not desire such a discussion "for reasons I did not understand then," a fact illustrated by the "early death" of Bundy's memorandum.[125] But given his exposure to Johnson's clearly articulated doubts about bombing and his preference to deploy ground combat forces, why was Bundy surprised that his paper would receive an ambivalent response? And why did he not anticipate that a bombing campaign would lead rapidly to a ground war?

By Bundy's own admission, the senior figures in the Johnson administration's war council did little to address the unanswered questions embedded in the drift to Americanization of the war. "No one asks ahead of time what kind of war it will be and what kind of losses must be expected," he wrote. "The military of 1965 are almost trained *not* to ask such (cowardly?) questions."[126] Bundy believed Johnson did not want such an inquiry. "It would leak; it might not tell him what he wanted to hear; he could not *control* it."[127] But as national security adviser it was Bundy's responsibility to compel the Pentagon to demonstrate the rigor of its recommendations to the president, even if Johnson himself was disinclined to stand up to his military advisers. Why did Bundy back away? The record, both historical and retrospective, suggests two answers.

As his contemporaneous notes from March 1965 demonstrate, Bundy was fixated with the imperative for the United States *not* to be, as he put it, "a paper tiger," a global power that failed to make credible commitments. It was a preoccupation that also had domestic implications, as illustrated by Bundy's remarkable calculation that it would be better, in the context of American politics, to deploy one hundred thousand combat forces to South Vietnam and lose rather than send no troops at all. If he had completed his Vietnam reappraisal, Bundy would have been obligated to acknowledge that his fixation with credibility—an overarching conviction that animated all of his Vietnam recommendations—was actually corrosive to his judgment. Determined to militarily sustain South Vietnam for some undefined duration but not necessarily to prevail, Bundy encouraged a policy of dramatic escalation without defining the scope of the U.S. commitment, the factors that would ensure its success, or the conditions that would allow the United States to cut its losses and extricate itself from the war.

Bundy's retrospective reflections suggest another source of his intellectual passivity regarding the escalation decisions of 1965. On questions of Vietnam policy, he was disinclined to challenge the prevailing consensus, particularly if it enjoyed the president's support. By this time, Bundy concluded, "I think my own role has become that of the staff officer who knows the big decision is made and is working to help in its execution." He added that because he supported an enlarged American effort to defend the regime in Saigon, he was predisposed to assist President Johnson to "do it his way; he's the boss."[128] It is also clear that Bundy was disinclined to challenge Johnson because his conviction—crystallized so vividly in his March 21, 1965, notes—that it was better to fight and lose in Vietnam than not fight at all.

Bundy wondered if there could have been a different outcome in 1965, one in which the consensus for Americanizing the war actually did not include President Johnson. "You could ask that question very well in the context of 1965, and there you would, I think, be in a position where the President, if he had said, 'No boys, I'm sorry. If it means a couple of hundred thousand troops and a permanent commitment to bomb, I'm going to go with George Ball against Dean Rusk. I know that Bob McNamara and Mac Bundy are more on Dean Rusk's side than they are on George Ball's, but I kind of think they'll go with me.' Whatever the President decides will stick. And . . . we wouldn't have made difficulties for President Johnson."[129] Bundy's admission is revealing. If Lyndon Johnson in 1965 had viewed Vietnam more in the way John Kennedy had in 1961, Bundy would have subordinated his own convictions to the president's very different determination that the war in Vietnam should not become an American enterprise.

Johnson, of course, never experienced such an epiphany. As Bundy looked back at 1965, it was his own lapse in rigor, his own analytical lassitude, that was most palpable. "Suppose you *had* been alert and *had* directed that the necessary staff work was done and *had* persuaded Dean Rusk and Robert McNamara—what then in 1965?" Bundy asked himself. Should the administration have coldly conceded that South Vietnam could not be saved? This could have perhaps been the realist conclusion of Bundy's retrospective logic. The "doves" of 1965, he asserted, labored under a weakened argument predicated on the "fancifully hopeful" expectation that there existed a negotiated diplomatic settlement that could end the war in Vietnam and achieve a grand compromise with communist power. It was therefore necessary in our research, Bundy suggested to me, for us to identify in 1965 proponents of a dispassionate realpolitik solution to America's quandary. He wanted to know "who said straight out—it's a loser—so lose it as cheaply as you can."[130]

Bundy himself was not predisposed to wage such a difficult bureaucratic battle in 1965. He lacked the determination to do so because his core convictions—a confidence in the power of coercion, a fixation with credibility, and a predisposition to support the president's political calculations—each gravitated against the analytical activism the moment demanded. Instead Bundy watched as the Johnson administration launched an open-ended deployment of ground combat forces to South Vietnam to compete in an unconstrained contest of endurance, casualties, and numbers. This was, Bundy wrote, "a major error *and we failed even to address it.*"[131]

NEVER DEPLOY MILITARY MEANS IN PURSUIT OF INDETERMINATE ENDS

"**W**hat can we say is the most surprising?" McGeorge Bundy asked himself in a fragment he composed on February 3, 1996, as he and Mary returned from a holiday in the Caribbean. His answer: "*The endurance of the enemy.*" It was a dynamic of the war that fascinated him. Bundy marveled at the leadership of the insurgency, its political strength inside South Vietnam, the stamina of the armed forces of the Vietnamese communists, and the social cohesion that bound these variables together into an equation that allowed a small power, among the poorest countries in the world, to triumph over the United States.[1]

In strictly military terms, over the long course of the war between 1965 and 1973, the United States imposed massively asymmetrical damage on the forces of the North Vietnamese army and the cadres of the National Liberation Front in the South. Yet the Vietnamese communists drove American forces from the battlefield, toppled the Saigon regime, and ultimately prevailed over a global superpower. Bundy searched for some kind of metric to illustrate the rough order of magnitude separating American and North Vietnamese casualties. Acknowledging a degree of imprecision to his formulation, he projected that the communists' battle losses were about ten times the size of American losses, yet they were imposed on a population roughly one-tenth as large. By his calculation, for every million North Vietnamese, there were roughly fifty thousand combat deaths. "Yet we were more than willing to leave the field when we did in the time of Nixon," he observed.[2]

More than three decades after the United States embarked on the full-scale Americanization of the war, Bundy was still struggling to understand how the Johnson administration had committed itself to a strategy that would devolve into a contest of endurance Americans were destined to lose. "Most histories of the war," wrote Bundy, establish that the U.S. ground combat operations were predicated "on a strategy of attrition." The capture and control of territory, although part of American military strategy, did not define its central purpose. The core function of U.S. combat troops was different. "Their mission," according to Bundy, "was to bring the enemy ground forces to battle and wear them down."[3]

Attrition was not clearly understood in the summer of 1965 to be the military strategy that would come to dominate Americanization of the war. As Bundy noted, attrition also "is not extensively explained by those who adopted it, but the best account we have is from General Westmoreland in his memoirs."[4] There, Westmoreland stated that "the military strategy employed in Vietnam, dictated by political decisions, was essentially that of a war of attrition." While acknowledging that since World War I attrition had fallen into "disrepute," Westmoreland argued that it was an appropriate strategy in Vietnam, "against an enemy with relatively limited manpower."[5] Thus, beginning in 1965 the United States deployed considerable and escalating numbers of ground combat forces in a protracted effort to grind down the enemy—depleting its numbers, breaking its will, and compelling its surrender or negotiated settlement on terms favorable to the United States.

That strategy was, of course, a great failure. The commitment of American ground combat forces in South Vietnam to a contest based on attrition was "plainly . . . a major error *and we failed even to address it*," as Bundy wrote in one of his previously noted draft fragments. Thirty years later he was not sure how he should have addressed it, "given LBJ's method." Yet he admitted that this was not an excuse and that "we should have got this issue clear."[6] The failure of the policy-making process was a collective one, Bundy observed, encompassing the president and his top advisers. "LBJ and the rest of us don't ask how much Ho can endure," Bundy conceded, speaking of the North Vietnamese leader, Ho Chi Minh. The United States, he added, conceived of its role as sustaining the South Vietnamese regime, which was expected to perform better militarily, carry its share of the burden, "and somehow do—enough." The administration's senior strategists, however, "don't ask the how-do-we-finish this question."[7] "It was a loser," Bundy concluded about the attrition strategy. "But it was also a most formidable indicator of which side cared the most. Because in strategic military terms we quit first."[8]

The questions flowing from the military decisions of 1965 were compelling: Why did Bundy fail to grasp the limitations of America's incipient attrition strategy? Why did he fail to anticipate that the war would become a protracted stalemate with no plausible expectation for the capitulation of the Vietnamese communists? Why did he resist challenging President Johnson more forcefully during the fateful period when the ends and means of American combat troop deployments were under debate? The answers to such questions were not obvious. As Bundy retrospectively noted, those who advocated or acquiesced to an attrition strategy did not foresee that military failure could result even from "numerical success."[9] He pointedly asked himself, "Do we discuss whether we are in fact well-equipped to conduct a war of attrition? I don't think that question is ever presented to Lyndon Johnson in the whole of the year in which that strategy is adopted."[10]

∽

On June 14, 1965, in what the *Pentagon Papers* later called "a textbook display of tactical ineptitude," forces of the South Vietnamese army were "frittered away piecemeal" and crushed in an engagement at Dong Xoai.[11] With a decision about a troop escalation imminent, Lyndon Johnson reached out to former President Eisenhower for his counsel. Eisenhower advised not only supporting South Vietnamese forces in action but also urged direct offensive action by American troops. "We have got to win," he said.[12] In a hectoring exchange with the press on June 17, Johnson asserted that the Tonkin Gulf resolution provided him with the authority to order such direct action. "That language," he insisted, "just as a reminder to you, said the Congress approves and supports the determination of the President as Commander-in-Chief to take all—all—all necessary measures to repel any—any—any armed attack against the forces of the United States and to prevent further aggression."[13]

George Ball understood that the administration was on the precipice of a major expansion of its commitment to South Vietnam. "In raising our commitment from 50,000 to 100,000 or more men and deploying most of the increment in *combat roles* we are beginning a new war—the United States *directly* against the Viet Cong," Ball warned President Johnson. "Perhaps the large-scale introduction of American forces with their concentrated fire power will force Hanoi and the Viet Cong to the decision we are seeking. On the other hand," he presciently cautioned, "we may *not* be able to fight the war successfully enough—even with 500,000 Americans in South Vietnam—to achieve this purpose." Ball confronted President Johnson with lessons from recent history. "The French fought a war in Viet-Nam, and were finally defeated—after seven years of bloody struggle and when they still had 250,000 combat-hardened veterans in the field, supported by an army of 205,000 Vietnamese."[14]

But as before, Ball's dissent was aggressively countered by the administration's hawks. When President Johnson met with Bundy, McNamara, Rusk, and other senior advisers on the afternoon of June 23, the principal question remained the size and scope of new American combat troop deployments, not their strategic purpose or military viability.[15] While the administration had been flirting with the idea of another bombing pause or even taking the Vietnam issue to the United Nations, those options gained little support. Ball, resolute in his pessimism, urged Johnson to set a ceiling of one hundred thousand men and to consider cutting American losses in Vietnam and shifting Washington's focus to the defense of Thailand. Rusk and McNamara strenuously objected. If South Vietnam fell, they reasoned, Thailand would be lost, too. Rusk envisioned a wave of falling dominoes—even India would collapse under the control of the Chinese communists, he predicted, and the only secure areas left for American allies would be the NATO countries Australia, New Zealand, and the Philippines.[16]

As the administration debate continued, General Westmoreland delivered a bleak report from the front. "The struggle has become a war of attrition," he declared on June 24.[17] "Short of decision to introduce nuclear weapons against sources and channels of enemy power, I see no likelihood of achieving a quick, favorable end to the war. . . . I am becoming more convinced every day that US forces in appropriate numbers must be deployed to permit the Vietnamese with our help to carry the war to the enemy."[18] The next day, guerrilla fighters launched one of their most spectacular terrorist acts yet, exploding a bomb in the My Canh floating restaurant. Forty-four people were killed, including thirteen Americans. In a separate incident, the Vietcong executed an American serviceman, Sergeant Harold G. Bennett.

Against this backdrop of gathering anxiety, McNamara circulated a draft memorandum that would set the terms of debate over further escalation. He formally joined the Joint Chiefs in urging the president to approve General Westmoreland's proposed expansion to a forty-four-battalion force in South Vietnam—thirty-four U.S. maneuver battalions and ten third-country maneuver battalions totaling approximately 175,000 men. In arguing for Westmoreland's recommendation from June 7, McNamara's draft once again posited that the projection of superior power by the United States would eventually break the will of North Vietnamese and insurgent forces. "Our objective is to create conditions for a favorable settlement by demonstrating . . . that the odds are against their winning," McNamara reasoned. A major escalation of U.S. forces, he argued, would force the insurgents "to accept a situation in the war in the South which offers them no prospect of an early victory and no grounds for hope they can simply outlast the US."[19]

As the Johnson administration prepared to decide whether it should more than double its combat troop commitment in South Vietnam, General Earle Wheeler, the chairman of the Joint Chiefs of Staff, asked General Westmoreland directly: Would the escalation be sufficient to break the insurgency?[20] Westmoreland's response was unequivocal and shocking. The "direct answer to your basic question is 'no,'" he declared, admitting that the forty-four battalions would not "provide reasonable assurance of attaining the objective."[21] Thus on the eve of the largest and most fateful expansion of the U.S. ground force commitment to Vietnam, the architect of that troop surge told the chairman of the Joint Chiefs of Staff that it simply would not be sufficient to achieve the stated American goal of persuading the insurgency that its victory was impossible. An enduring question of historical significance is why General Westmoreland's reply was acceptable to either himself or his superiors in the Pentagon. If the military means proposed to break the will and capacity of the insurgency were inadequate, why was the forty-four-battalion proposal being pursued at all?

The CIA shared a similarly pessimistic view of the prospects of a coercive show of strength through ground force escalation. "We doubt if it will be possible to demonstrate '. . . that the odds are against their winning' unless and until they are in fact losing—which, as the memorandum rightly notes, is not now the case." The CIA analysis noted that the most important prerequisite for success would be "actually beginning to turn the tide" against the Vietcong, but this was not assured. "Obviously we cannot do this if [U.S. and South Vietnamese] forces sustain a series of shattering setbacks during the next few weeks."[22]

George Ball seized on the inherent uncertainty surrounding the forty-four-battalion deployment and its implicit strategic assumptions. "There is no assurance that we can achieve our objectives by substantially expanding American forces in South Viet-Nam and committing them to direct combat," he argued. "On the contrary, we would run grave risks of bogging down an indeterminate number of American troops in a protracted and bloody conflict of uncertain outcome. The risk is so great, in fact, that those who advocate this course must sustain the burden of proof that commitment of American forces to combat will assure our objectives at an acceptable cost." Warning that "a deep commitment of United States forces in a land war in South Viet-Nam would be a catastrophic error," Ball concluded, "If ever there was an occasion for a tactical withdrawal, this is it."[23]

The stage was now set for what should have been the seminal debate of the Vietnam War. McNamara had thrown his support behind an enormous expansion of the American commitment. General Westmoreland, the principal architect of the forty-four-battalion strategy, clearly conceded that the new American combat commitment could not assure the achievement of its stated objective. And Ball was warning of an impending catastrophe. Where was Bundy positioned at this juncture? Frustrated by a deteriorating relationship with President Johnson, he was on the precipice of resigning as national security adviser. Ironically, Bundy's differences with Johnson had little to do with the substance of Vietnam policy.

For Bundy, icon of the Establishment and the administration's fiercest debater, silence in response to criticism of the White House policy in Vietnam and Southeast Asia was untenable. The critics of the war, Bundy recalled, "were people with whom I was used to being in communication, and many of them, at least, were feeling deliberately cut-off from and rejected by an administration with whom they were trying to communicate in good faith. And so we had a whole office for the purpose of receiving and communicating with men of good will whose sentiments were more moderate on the dove side, or whatever you want to call it, than the administration position."[24] Still angry that Johnson had spirited him out of the country for his commitment to debate the war on May 15, Bundy launched an end run around the president. Although he knew that Johnson would be infuriated, Bundy agreed to appear on a one-hour prime-time television debate to be broadcast without commercial interruption by CBS News on the evening of June 21.

"I informed him after the decision had been made and told him I just couldn't live with myself if I didn't do it," Bundy explained in a 1969 oral history. "I felt that this was a case where I'd better not ask him, he would say no, and then . . . he would be damaged in the long run. My own pride would obviously be engaged, but I hoped that wasn't the dominant fact. People would say the administration is afraid to meet its opponents, and this would be more destructive. The President temperamentally just didn't see it that way."[25] What Bundy never said but should have retrospectively acknowledged was that his decision to go around Johnson's back to appear on the CBS Vietnam debate was tantamount to submitting his letter of resignation. Bundy's relationship with the president and his role within the administration would never be the same.

The CBS forum was held live before an audience at Georgetown University and had been promoted by the network as a "Vietnam Dialogue: Mr. Bundy and the Professors." Once announced, it was impossible for Bundy to withdraw without exposing the administration to ridicule.

Thus the national security adviser had boxed in the president and elevated the Vietnam debate into a national media event.

"The next hour is an important one we think in the history of television," said the host, Eric Sevareid, "and quite possibly an important one in the current history of this country. On the other side of the world the United States is at war. However you title or define it, it is war. Vietnam has cost America somewhat around a billion and a half dollars so far, and several hundred lives." The war had sparked opposition, Sevareid explained, particularly on college campuses. "Their protest was expressed in a series of teach-ins around the country this spring. These culminated in a big gathering here in Washington on May fifteenth. The government official who the protesters most wanted to hear and to question was Mr. McGeorge Bundy, Special Assistant to President Johnson for National Security Affairs. Mr. Bundy was then unable to appear. But he is here tonight."[26]

Bundy was joined on stage by five prominent academics, including his principal opponent, Professor Hans Morgenthau of the University of Chicago, one of the world's preeminent theorists of international relations. A German intellectual who had fled his native country in 1937 amid Hitler's rise to power, Morgenthau was renowned as the progenitor of the modern realist school of world politics. Distrustful of ideology and dismissive of legalistic and moralistic approaches to the conduct of statecraft, Morgenthau believed that the international system was inherently anarchic and defined by the balance of power among nations, which flourished or perished according to their ability to differentiate between vital and peripheral interests. Morgenthau had argued that Vietnam was not a vital interest to the United States and that the domino theory was a dubious foundation upon which to base American foreign policy. He maintained that nationalism was among the most potent phenomena of political life and had succeeded in disrupting the British, French, Dutch, Portuguese, Austro-Hungarian, and Ottoman empires. If the United States persisted in its commitment to Vietnam, he concluded, it would suffer a similar fate.[27]

The CBS debate was uneasily anticipated in the Bundy family. Mary Bundy gave her husband some sage advice, Mac told his staff in the White House. "Try to be tonight the man I married and not the man I almost didn't marry."[28] But once the debate was under way, Bundy reverted to familiar forms of argument, mixing the rhetoric of commitment with prep school debating tactics designed to undermine Morgenthau's credibility. Quoting President Johnson, Bundy insisted that the United States had made

> a national pledge to help South Vietnam defend its independence. To dishonor that pledge, to abandon this small brave nation to its enemy and to the terror that must follow would be an unforgivable wrong. . . . We are also there . . . to strengthen world order. Around the globe, from Berlin to Thailand, are people whose well-being rests in part on the belief they can count on us if they are attacked. To leave Vietnam to its fate would shake the confidence of all these people in the value of the American commitment.

Yet Bundy concentrated his most strenuous arguments not to explain the administration's strategy to defend Vietnam—he was silent on Johnson's military plans—but rather to attack Morgenthau for previous comments the professor had made about the Marshall Plan and about Laos, topics that, of course, were irrelevant.

For his part, Morgenthau challenged Bundy's claim that America's prior commitment to South Vietnam was binding on all future administrations. Noting that Washington had installed the Diem regime, Saigon's first government, Morgenthau observed that "the state of South Vietnam is in a sense our own creation. . . . We have contracted with ourselves, and I do not regard this as a valid foundation for our presence in South Vietnam." Morgenthau cited Alexander Hamilton, who in 1793 "laid down the principle that no nation is obligated to endanger its own interests, let alone its own existence, in order to come to the aid of another nation." In Vietnam, Morgenthau went on, "it would be very difficult for us to win a military victory and even if we win it, it means nothing politically." Morgenthau reminded the audience that the desertion rate in the South Vietnamese army was 30 percent (and in some areas even higher), hardly an inducement to enlarge the American military commitment. The wise course in Vietnam, he argued, would be for the United States to emulate France's historical example of divesting itself of its colonial obligations. "And certainly if you look at the prestige of France today, it is certainly higher than it was when France fought in Algeria, and certainly is higher than when France fought in Indochina."[29]

When he read in the press that Bundy had agreed to the CBS debate, Johnson was enraged. "Do you see this?" Johnson roared to his aide Bill Moyers. "Bundy is going on television—on national television—with five professors. That's an act of disloyalty. He didn't tell me because he knew I didn't want him to do it." Johnson told Moyers that he should inform Bundy that the president would be "pleased—mighty pleased," to accept the resignation of his national security adviser. Moyers was dumbstruck. "On second thought, maybe I should talk with him myself," said Johnson. The president paused. Moyers watched him uneasily. "No, you go do it," said Johnson.

Moyers did not act on the president's instruction. One evening soon after Bundy's CBS appearance, Moyers was with Johnson in the presidential bedroom. The president asked Moyers to get his pajamas from the next room. "And after you've got my pajamas," Johnson added, "go downstairs and fire Bundy." Moyers protested, but in the end he went to the White House basement in search of the national security adviser, only to discover that Bundy had left for the night. The next morning, Moyers was grilled by the president. "You didn't fire Bundy, did you?" said Johnson. "I know you didn't. He called this morning and didn't say anything about it. Go down and do it now." Moyers descended once again to Bundy's basement office, where he found the national security adviser at his desk. "The President sent me down to fire you," Moyers explained. Bundy momentarily looked up from his papers. "Again?" he asked. Bundy then returned to his work.[30]

Bundy warmly recollected how Lady Bird Johnson tried on more than one occasion to mend the frayed relationship between the president and his national security adviser. Her method was to telephone with an unanticipated dinner invitation. "Mary *dear*," she would say to Bundy's wife, "Lyndon and I were just saying to each other last night that it's been so long since we've seen the dear Bundys. And what we wonder, and hope so much, is whether you and Mac could come to a little dinner for four tonight." Like other confounding elements of his relationship with the president, Bundy found it difficult to read Lyndon Johnson's intent in these gatherings. "What I *don't* know to this day," he recalled thirty years later, "is whether *she* said: 'I'm going to fix this and he won't stop me if I've already invited Mary.' Or whether *he* said: 'I can't talk to the bastard in the office, but maybe we can talk to him if you ask him over?' Or some mixture of the two."[31] To the end of his life, Bundy continued to feel a debt to Lady Bird Johnson. "My wife will not let me say anything that will make Mrs. Johnson furious or miserable," Bundy explained. "And she would be right."[32]

Mrs. Johnson's efforts at reconciliation were to no avail. By the summer of 1965, Bundy recalled, his relationship with Lyndon Johnson had devolved into an "unseemly guerrilla warfare" between the president of the United States and one of his most important counselors. As for Bundy's conviction that the Johnson administration should provide a more transparent public explanation of its escalation plans, the president was simply incredulous. "You mean," Johnson said, "that if your mother-in-law—your very own mother-in-law—has only one eye, and it happens to be right in the middle of her forehead, then the best place for her is in the livin' room with all the company!" That one-eyed creature, of course, was the Americanization of the Vietnam War.[33]

Johnson's resistance to explaining and defending the administration's policy exasperated Bundy. The president attempted "to execute a major new deployment"—the first allocation of an enlarged combat troop mission—"with as little public explanation as possible," Bundy wrote in one of his draft fragments. "It was not a change in policy," Bundy recalled Johnson saying, "only a change in what policy required." Johnson convened a press conference, Bundy noted acidly, "at noon, when no one was watching TV." In his public remarks about the war, the president "emphasized good works—a TVA for the Mekong River, for example—not the dispatch of fighting units on a new and different scale." Bundy said he was never sure what the president expected to accomplish and predicted that Johnson's tactics would backfire. If the new offensive were not "more quickly decisive than we had any clear reason to expect," Bundy said, there would be disturbing consequences when the public "looked back and asked themselves if they had been led openly into this war or somehow bamboozled into it."[34]

The president's effort to manage elite opinion increasingly put the administration in the awkward position of trying to spin commentators who were far too discerning to be taken in by the White House line. One particular irritant to Johnson continued to be Walter Lippmann, whose columns were read around the world. Johnson held the wholly unrealistic expectation that his national security adviser could neutralize Lippmann's savage criticism of the administration's conduct of the war. When Bundy inevitably failed at this task, the president tried himself. Johnson's clumsily executed effort to persuade Lippmann of his "unswerving dedication to peace" in Southeast Asia—despite his decision to escalate the war—ended in predictable failure. Bundy recalled that "far from converting Lippmann," Johnson simply convinced the columnist that the presi-

dent was "a practiced liar who took him for a fool."[35] In this case of Johnson's maneuvering with Lippmann, "it *bites* him terribly when he
tries . . . to change the picture of reality." Bundy argued that this pattern
of Johnson "trying to manipulate the press . . . doesn't change the course
for the war, but it does have a very bad effect on the interconnection of
confidence between the government and the country." Johnson's machinations with the media drove Bundy to distraction. "When I get frustrated in the summer of '65, it's partly because of this constant wear and
tear of Lyndon Johnson wanting to arrange the way the world sees him."
Bundy added: "What drives me *crazy* is that I *know* I'm right and I know
he doesn't pay any attention to what I'm telling him."[36]

Johnson's effort to manipulate the chattering class was unsubtle. The
president "doesn't feel the least bit disturbed when he says, 'You know,
Bundy, you're Walter Lippmann's friend, and you're Joe Alsop's friend, and
I need them both.' " Bundy knew that if that premise were ever presented
to either columnist, they would call it a "looney" presumption by Johnson.
"But that's what he had done all his life," Bundy observed, "make a majority out of people who disagreed."[37] Bundy acknowledged that every president, including giants like Lincoln and Roosevelt, sought to communicate
in a way that achieved the greatest political impact. Yet Johnson aspired
for more. The president had "this really quite funny internal belief" that
he could reshape facts to serve his interests. Johnson believed that "if he
could get it stated *his* way in the papers it would *be* that way." This trait of
Johnson's was "genuinely not present" with Kennedy, whom Bundy remembered as far more dispassionate about the media. "Yes, he wants a
good press," Bundy said of Kennedy, "but it never occurs to him that getting a good press is getting a good reality."[38] Johnson, in contrast, "thought
he was the greatest manager of the press that ever happened. Every time he
tried to manage the press he kicked himself smartly in the shins. He probably would have used a slightly more vivid physical metaphor."[39]

In unguarded moments Bundy conveyed an antipathy for Lyndon

Johnson nourished by deep and unresolved resentments. He often described Johnson as a compulsive liar. "He couldn't tell the truth, it was an act against nature," said Bundy. "He had to tell what fit his immediate objectives. . . . If you know more than your legislative rival about which six swing votes are going to swing and for what reason, you win." To disclose such information honestly was equivalent to "giving away the family jewels. . . . Somewhere in Texas he learned that the truth was not good for you if you told it too freely."[40] Bundy sought to explain Johnson in terms familiar from his own New England upbringing. "Lyndon Johnson's view of the truth is like a Boston trustee's view of capital," he said. "It's much too valuable ever to be used."[41]

In the aftermath of the CBS debate and the collapse of his relationship with Johnson, Bundy decided he had to get out of Washington as soon as he could. "I had not learned how to be a useful assistant to this man," Bundy concluded. He cited as his reason to leave "a deep and irregular" difference of perspective "about the ways and means of public discussion," and specifically made the point that his departure was in no way over "the merits of choices" in Vietnam.[42] Bundy had supported the notion of grooming Bill Moyers to be his successor. The previous winter Bundy had pressed Johnson to allow Moyers to "come in as a Deputy in this office with a prospect of succession as and when a vacancy occurs," despite the fact that Moyers had no expertise in national security. Bundy called Moyers "the ideal man for this job. . . . I do know that he has an abiding interest and talent for foreign affairs. I believe he would be extremely good at this job, and I think he would like it."[43] Johnson had not accepted Bundy's proposal. In late June 1965 there was no sympathetic successor waiting in the wings and Bundy was months away from announcing his resignation. Although the national security adviser had reached the breaking point in his relationship with President Johnson, neither man could afford a public dustup, particularly as a major escalation decision loomed.

"The commitment" to Saigon, Bundy explained to the president on

June 27, "is primarily political and any decision to enlarge or reduce it will be political. My own further view is that if and when we wish to shift our course and cut our losses in Vietnam we should do so because of a finding that the Vietnamese themselves are not meeting their obligations to themselves or to us. This is the course we started on with Diem, and if we got a wholly ineffective or anti-American government we could do the same thing again."[44]

Bundy once more dismissed critics who believed the United States was now emulating the disastrous course France followed in Vietnam. "The central fact of French involvement in Vietnam was the persistent *seven-year effort to re-establish French colonial rule*," Bundy argued. The Johnson administration was committed to a different cause. "U.S. forces are present in rapidly growing numbers to help resist the Communists at the request of successive Saigon governments."[45] Bundy's distinction was, of course, irrelevant to the fundamental question of whether American combat troops would be able to prevail over the same fiercely committed and highly effective insurgent forces that had toppled the French—and who also viewed the United States as an imperial occupying power. As he formulated his differing positions in the last days of June, a note Bundy drafted to himself captures again his central conviction and the dominant requirement of any policy the United States would then pursue. "We need to take a look at the role of U.S. . . . . *You have to have made enough of an effort*."[46]

Although Bundy had just submitted a tough and hawkish memo to the president implying support for a major escalation in Vietnam, on June 30 he confided his concerns about the Westmoreland plan to Secretary of Defense McNamara. "The draft memorandum to the President of June 26 seems to me to have grave limitations," Bundy began. "It proposes a doubling of our presently planned strength in South Vietnam, a tripling of air effort in the north, and a new and very important program of naval quarantine. It proposes this new land commitment at a time when our troops are entirely untested in the kind of warfare projected. . . . My first reaction is that this program is rash to the point of folly."

Bundy challenged the assumption that conventional combat forces would be effective in containing the insurgency. "I see no reason to suppose that the Viet Cong will accommodate us by fighting the kind of war we desire. Fragmentary evidence so far suggests that they intend to avoid direct contact with major US forces and concentrate their efforts against the Vietnamese Army." Moving to "a 200 thousand-man level" of support, Bundy warned, was "a slippery slope toward total US responsibility and corresponding fecklessness on the Vietnamese side." What was the upper limit? Bundy asked. "If we need 200 thousand men now for these quite limited missions, may we not need 400 thousand later? Is this a rational course of action? Is there any real prospect that US regular forces can conduct the anti-guerrilla operations which would probably remain the central problem in South Vietnam?" Bundy questioned the ultimate strategic objective to be served by the wholesale transformation of the war. "If it is to get to the conference table, what results do we seek there? Still more brutally, do we want to invest 200 thousand men to cover an eventual retreat? Can we not do that just as well where we are?"[47]

With his incisive and provocative memo, Bundy had finally challenged the partially developed assumptions and arguments for the Americanization of the war. Yet the impact of his critique was largely vitiated by the fact that it was directed toward McNamara rather than the president or the broader team of advisers responsible for strategy in Vietnam. Bundy retrospectively defended his decision to convey his doubts to the secretary of defense alone and not to others in the administration. At this point in the decision-making process, "the only way of affecting particular choices of tactics . . . was to argue with Bob McNamara," Bundy stated. Conceding his unwillingness to challenge Johnson directly, Bundy observed that the president had limited his own role to the enforcement of limits on such key issues as the number of troops to be deployed, the choice of whether to call up the reserves, and guidelines for bombing. All other matters were left to the discretion of the secretary of defense. A staff officer cannot reach beyond the president's degree of engagement, explained Bundy, and therefore it was Robert McNamara in the summer of 1965 who had defined the "choices within LBJ's boundaries."[48]

One of the choices not being considered in 1965 was the use of nuclear weapons against Hanoi. To some readers, Bundy's memo seemed to allude to the possibility with his observation that President Eisenhower had manipulated the nuclear threat in the Korean War. "It is within our power to give much more drastic warning to Hanoi than any we have yet given," he suggested. "If General Eisenhower is right in his belief that it was the prospect of nuclear attack which brought an armistice in Korea, we should at least consider what realistic threat of larger action is available to us for communication to Hanoi. A full interdiction of supplies to North Vietnam by air and sea is a possible candidate for such an ultimatum."[49] Robert McNamara subsequently interpreted this passage as illustrating Bundy's support for nuclear blackmail against Hanoi.[50] This was probably not the case; the only "realistic threat of larger action" explicitly cited in Bundy's memorandum is an air and sea blockade of North Vietnam. "I remember no mention of U.S. nuclear weapons in the context of Vietnam while I was in the White House," Bundy later recalled, adding that "American public opinion made the use of nuclear weapons politically unacceptable" throughout the duration of the conflict.[51]

As the two stark choices confronting Lyndon Johnson in Vietnam crystallized—the forty-four-battalion plan advocated by Westmoreland and McNamara or the withdrawal option espoused by Ball—a third course was proposed. It was the so-called middle way envisioned by Bill Bundy, who proposed a force level of eighteen battalions and 85,000 men. "In essence," he explained, "this is a program to *hold on* for the next two months, and *to test* the military effectiveness of US combat forces and the reaction of the Vietnamese Army and people to the increasing

US role. . . . The program *rejects* withdrawal or negotiating concessions in any form, and equally rejects a present decision to raise our force level above 85,000."[52]

McGeorge Bundy anticipated Johnson's likely response to the three recommendations. In a July 1 memorandum framing the president's options, Bundy wrote: "My hunch is that you will want to listen hard to George Ball and then reject his proposal. Discussion could then move to the narrower choice between my brother's course and McNamara's. The decision between them should be made in about ten days, which is the point at which McNamara would like a final go-ahead on the air mobile division." Bundy enumerated several "disputed questions" at the center of the Vietnam debate—questions the administration had still not resolved as it approached an imminent decision to more than double its ground troop commitment to South Vietnam: "What are the chances of our getting into a white man's war with all the brown men against us or apathetic? . . . What would a really full political and public relations campaign look like in both the [Bill] Bundy option and the McNamara option? What is the upper limit of our liability if we now go to 44 battalions?"[53]

In later years, Bundy was sensitive to the frequently repeated charge that his apparent rejection of Ball's withdrawal arguments was a deliberate preemption of a critically necessary debate and contradicted the skeptical analysis Bundy himself had advanced in his June 30 memorandum to McNamara. As the historian Brian VanDeMark noted, "Addressing the President, Bundy suppressed his thoughts about eventual disengagement and many of his concerns about escalation." Reviewing VanDeMark's conclusion, Bundy wrote: "Important—Prediction, *not* advocacy."[54] Bundy explained that he wrote a memorandum advising the president to choose between two different levels of escalation, but not negotiated withdrawal "because I think that's the real choice seen by President Johnson. I still think so, that LBJ was clearly *not* going to *not* hold the ground." At the same time, Johnson wanted to create the illusion of a deliberative process: "He wanted everybody to hear him hearing the whole argument. He wanted the record to be every argument was made and every voice was heard. And a memo that tells him where he's going to come out is an extremely unpleasant part of the surrounding documentation."[55]

With his marginalization of the Ball memorandum, Bundy may have simply been anticipating the president's preference for one of the core escalation options presented to him. Yet Bundy had a reputation for skillfully aborting dissent when he deemed it necessary, and he was a practiced expert at maneuvering for advantage among competing bureaucracies. Bundy had, for example, previously undermined the secretary of state. "He is not a manager," Bundy advised the president about Dean Rusk in early 1965. "He has never been a good judge of men. His instincts are cautious and negative. . . . the Secretary has little sense of effective operation. He does not move matters toward decision with promptness. He does not stimulate aggressive staff work. He does not coordinate conflicting forces within his own department."[56]

While Johnson's predisposition to escalate combat troop deployments was obvious to Bundy, acknowledging so was problematic. "He didn't like to be found out," he said of the president. "It was sort of not part of the function of the staff officer to tell him what he was thinking." For Johnson, "the staff officer who found out what he was thinking when he was trying to look as if he was thinking something else was a nuisance." Bundy pointedly observed that the president "was *terrified* of anybody understanding him better than he understood himself."[57]

Johnson continued to reach out to key constituencies, probing where the balance of opinion could be found. Just minutes before meeting with his senior Vietnam advisers on July 2, the president consulted Eisenhower. "Do you really think we can beat the Vietcong?" Johnson asked. It was hard to say, replied Eisenhower, because it was unknown how many insurgents are from North Vietnam and how many are drawn from within the population of South Vietnam. After further discussion, Eisenhower advised Johnson to proceed with a troop buildup as soon as possible. "We are not going to be run out of a free country we helped to establish," Eisenhower declared.[58] Immediately following his telephone conversation with the former president, Johnson met at the White House with McNamara, Rusk, Ball, and McGeorge Bundy. According to the only account of the discussion, "Like a Judge, the President expected to mull over the pleadings, and gave no direct indication what his final decision would be."[59]

While Johnson tried to strike a posture suggesting contemplative indecision on the question of further escalation, he nonetheless dropped various hints to observers paying close attention. Bundy eagerly reviewed research on Johnson's public statements about the war in 1965. The president, he observed, often made his case to the nation "in funny places at funny times," such as his remarks in the White House Rose Garden to the National Rural Electric Cooperation Association on July 14, 1965. It was a singularly powerful speech, Bundy observed, but one that rarely emerged in histories of the Vietnam War.[60] In his address, a folksy Johnson begins by invoking the virtues of electricity. "Of all the work that I have been privileged to do in my public career," the president said, "nothing has been more gratifying to me than my association with the rural electrification program." By the end of his remarks, however, Johnson's subject is Vietnam rather than the electrical grid. "The American people have invested more than any other people in history to preserve peace and freedom, not just for ourselves, but for all mankind. . . . Three Presidents—President Eisenhower, President Kennedy, and your present President—have made a commitment in the name of the people of the United States, and our national honor is at stake in Southeast Asia. And we are going to protect it, and you just might as well be prepared for it, and we can do it better if we are united. . . . We do not expect the road to be smooth, and you just be sure it is not going to be short. But we do intend that the end result shall be a better world where men of all lands and all colors and all cultures can enjoy in their lifetime something of the advance that we have known in our lifetime."[61]

As Johnson spoke in the Rose Garden, McNamara was departing for South Vietnam. His mission, Bundy retrospectively concluded, was to negotiate a deal with the U.S. military commander in Saigon on the minimum size of the forthcoming escalation—a role that was more political than substantive. Johnson had dispatched the secretary of defense "to build a consensus on what needed to be done to turn the tide—not to cover a retreat," Bundy wrote. While the president was prepared for various policy options to be "praised and damned, and even analyzed," his overarching priority was to achieve agreement, absent a fractious debate, on a course of action that would sustain South Vietnam from collapse but not disrupt his legislative agenda in Congress.[62]

The consensus on troop levels was brokered according to a familiar method. Bundy often remarked that President Johnson had learned his most important political lessons as Senate majority leader in the 1950s. And he continued to think that way, approaching his cabinet officers and field generals as if they held crucial votes that would determine pending legislation. Therefore Johnson would need the support of "Senator McNamara," "Senator Rusk," and the rest of his advisers. Among the most important was his top commander in Vietnam. "Senator Westmoreland is like the leader of a block of some twenty senators and you haven't got a good majority without him," Bundy surmised.[63]

By July 1965, wrote Bundy, "LBJ was play acting with everyone but McNamara and maybe Rusk." Upon his return from Saigon, McNamara presented troop numbers that "were the smallest numbers that Westy would support," perhaps with the assent of the Joint Chiefs as well. For Bundy, the realization crystallized that "what LBJ wanted was Westmoreland's vote. He was Senate-Leader-of-a-Commander-in-Chief, I finally decided, years later."[64]

Bundy recalled a secret back channel the president used to bargain with

Westmoreland, "a private defense wire system" through Deputy Secretary of Defense Cyrus Vance that allowed McNamara to apprise Johnson of his discussions in Saigon while keeping the State Department and the rest of the government in the dark. In these private cables, "McNamara reports what Westy wants, and what he thinks Westy will accept. . . . And what in effect has happened is that Johnson has not committed himself to anyone else until he has Westy signed up. He hasn't decided anything about that number except that it's . . . the smallest number that will sign up Westy, and it's quite a big number."[65]

The Vance cable, a subject of intense interest since a partial summary of it appeared in the *Pentagon Papers*, was declassified in 1988.[66] It reveals that Cyrus Vance, in his capacity as acting secretary of defense, informed McNamara on July 17 of President Johnson's approval of Westmoreland's plan for a total force of forty-four battalions.[67]

"What is being worked out" in the McNamara-Vance back channel, Bundy explained, "is a position that will be solid along the line that runs from the President to the Secretary of Defense to the Commander in the field. And if you have those guys all on one side, you're in fine shape." Many histories of the Vietnam War, Bundy pointed out, depict the debate in the summer of 1965 incorrectly. One of the difficulties he had with a large part of the standard history is that it acts "as if the President really was trying to decide between George Ball and Bob McNamara—when what he was really doing was trying to work out how to get a decision that he had already worked out *with* McNamara, in a way that would maximize everybody's sense that they had been consulted."[68]

Political stagecraft—creating the appearance of deliberation when a decision had already been made—was the presumptive purpose of the White House meeting Johnson convened on the morning of July 21. Addressing the administration's war council, McNamara presented the main elements of the Westmoreland plan, which had essentially been accepted by the president four days earlier through his back channel via

Vance. Westmoreland's recommendation was to raise American troop levels in South Vietnam to 175,000, an increase of more than 100,000, and his proposal for thirty-four U.S. combat battalions also anticipated the eventual call-up of 235,000 men in the reserves and National Guard. The escalation plan that was circulated in advance of the meeting once more reiterated the prevailing strategic purpose of the proposed surge in combat forces—to demonstrate to the Vietcong and the North Vietnamese that they could not overcome the immense military might of the United States. Yet McNamara conceded that the American strategy so far had failed. "There are no signs that we have throttled the inflow of supplies for the VC or can throttle the flow while their materiel needs are as low as they are. . . . Nor have our air attacks in North Vietnam produced tangible evidence of willingness on the part of Hanoi to come to the conference table in a reasonable mood." He further observed that the Vietnamese communists "seem to believe that South Vietnam is on the run and near collapse; they show no signs of settling for less than a complete take-over."[69]

McNamara concluded that the United States had only three strategic options. Not surprisingly, two of those options would leave the United States in a deplorable geopolitical position. President Johnson could choose to "cut our losses and withdraw under the best conditions that can be arranged—almost certainly conditions humiliating the United States and very damaging to our future effectiveness on the world scene." Alternatively, Johnson could hold steady at roughly the current level of seventy-five thousand troops, but that would leave the United States terminally weakened and "almost certainly would confront us later with a choice between withdrawal and an emergency expansion of forces, perhaps too late to do any good." The only viable choice, McNamara argued, was a substantial expansion of offensive U.S. military pressure against the Vietcong and Hanoi—supplemented by vigorous diplomacy. Such an approach, he predicted, "would stave off defeat in the short run and offer a good chance of producing a favorable settlement in the longer run," although it would also render "any later decision to withdraw even more difficult and even more costly than would be the case today."

McNamara was vague, however, in delineating the causal logic of his proposed strategy, positing the escalation not as the military means to a military objective but simply as an end in itself. "The forces will be used however they can be brought to bear most effectively. . . . The strategy for winning this stage of the war will be to take the offensive—to take and hold the initiative."[70]

Preliminary discussion among the president's advisers seemed to anticipate that McNamara's recommendation would be accepted. "What is the timing on how we should proceed?" asked Rusk.

"There ought to be a statement to the American people no later than a week," said McNamara.

"It is quite possible," Bundy added, "that the message to Congress will be a message to the public."

George Ball was troubled by the presumptive acquiescence he observed to McNamara's recommendation. "It is one thing to ready the country for this decision and another to face the realities of the decision," he explained. "We can't allow the country to wake up one morning and find heavy casualties. We need to be damn serious with the American public."[71]

President Johnson, eager to project a ruminative state of mind, arrived after forty minutes of discussion and unleashed a wave of questions ranging from the existential to the logistical. "What has happened . . . that requires this decision on my part?" he asked his advisers. "What are the alternatives? . . . Have we wrung every single soldier out of every country we can? Who else can help? Are we the sole defenders of freedom in the world? Have we done all we can in this direction? The reasons for the call up? The results we can expect? What are the alternatives? . . . Let's look at all our options so that every man at this table understands fully the total picture."[72]

A circuitous exchange followed. "Is anyone of the opinion we should not do what the memo says?" asked Johnson. "If so, I'd like to hear from them."

This was Ball's cue to register his dissent. "I can foresee a perilous voyage," he said, "very dangerous—great apprehensions that we can win under these circumstances. But let me be clear, if the decision is to go ahead, I'm committed."

Dean Rusk regretted the failure to act earlier. "What we have done since 1954 . . . has not been good enough," he said. "We should have probably committed ourselves heavier in 1961."

Henry Cabot Lodge, who would return as the U.S. ambassador to South Vietnam at the end of the summer, bemoaned the dysfunctional nature of the regime.[73] "There is no tradition of a national government in Saigon," he said. "There are no roots in the country. Not until there is tranquility can you have any stability. I don't think we ought to take this government seriously. There is no one who can do anything. We have to do what we think we ought to do regardless of what the Saigon government does."

"George," the president asked Ball, "do you think we have another course?"

"I would not recommend that you follow McNamara's course," Ball contentiously replied.

McNamara argued that the seventy-five thousand U.S. troops already deployed to Vietnam were inadequate, "just enough to protect the bases—it will let us lose slowly instead of rapidly. The extra men will stabilize the situation and improve it. . . . There is no major risk of catastrophe."

President Johnson probed the military. With more Americans in combat, he suggested, there would be greater losses. "The more men we have," countered General Wheeler, "the greater the likelihood of smaller losses." He provided no substantiation in support of his claim, prompting an incredulous Johnson to pose his question differently.

"What makes you think if we put in 100,000 men Ho Chi Minh won't put in another 100,000?" Johnson asked.

"That means greater bodies of men—which will allow us to cream them," Wheeler assured the president.[74] The meeting ended without resolution.

When discussion resumed that afternoon, George Ball was given the floor to present his challenge to the Pentagon escalation plan. "We can't win," he contended. "The most we can hope for is a messy conclusion." There remained the threat of China's intervention, Ball noted, and the possibility of replicating the "galling" stalemate of the Korean War, when public support plummeted as casualties mounted. If the Vietnam conflict was "long and protracted we will suffer because a great power cannot beat guerrillas. . . . Every great captain in history is not afraid to make a tactical withdrawal if conditions are unfavorable to him. The enemy cannot even be seen; he is indigenous to the country." There was serious doubt, Ball argued, that an army of Westerners could fight Orientals in the Asian jungle and prevail.[75]

"This is important," Johnson interrupted. In the absence of intelligence, could American forces successfully fight the enemy in Vietnam's jungles and rice paddies? Ball certainly doubted it. Continuing to prop up the Saigon regime, he warned, was tantamount to "giving cobalt treatment to a terminal cancer case." Ball proposed that the United States devise a political strategy to stimulate a withdrawal of its military forces from South Vietnam. "The least harmful way to cut losses in South Vietnam is to let the government decide it doesn't want us to stay there," he said, echoing what Senator Richard Russell had told the president a year earlier. The United States could then focus its energies, Ball proposed, on the defense of other regional allies such as Thailand, South Korea, and Taiwan.[76]

"Wouldn't all those countries say Uncle Sam is a paper tiger—wouldn't we lose credibility breaking the word of three presidents—if we set it up as you proposed?" Johnson asked. "It would seem to be an ir-reparable blow. But I gather you don't think so."

"The worst blow," Ball replied, "would be that the mightiest power in the world is unable to defeat guerrillas."[77]

Bundy now jumped into the debate, once again citing the potential of a coercion strategy to grind down the insurgency. He charged that adopt-ing Ball's recommendation for withdrawal "would be a radical switch without evidence that it should be done. . . . His whole analytical argu-ment gives no weight to loss suffered by the other side." But Bundy tem-pered his challenge to Ball with a qualification. "A great many elements in his argument are correct," said Bundy. "We need to make clear that this is a somber matter—that it will not be quick—no single action will bring quick victory. I think it is clear that we are not going to be thrown out."

"My problem," Ball shot back, "is not that we don't get thrown out, but that we get bogged down and don't win."

Ball had identified the essential weakness in Bundy's position. An es-calation of combat forces designed to impose losses and stalemate on the insurgency did not ensure victory. To the contrary, a strategy predicated on the application of coercive military force to exhaust rather than van-quish the enemy risked a protracted and ultimately indeterminate con-flict. But Bundy refused to engage Ball's counterargument, once more invoking the credibility imperative. "The world, the country, and the Vietnamese would have alarming reactions if we got out," he said.[78] Achieving victory was apparently less important than the perception of pursuing it. "There will be time to decide our policy won't work after we have given it a good try," Bundy insisted.

"We won't get out," Ball retorted. "We'll double our bet and get lost in the rice paddies."[79] Reviewing Ball's prediction three decades later, Bundy conceded: "He's right." In 1965, however, Bundy rejected Ball's withdrawal option as "disastrous." It would be better to maintain the present commitment and "waffle through" than withdraw. The country, he observed, was of a mood to accept grim news.[80]

In contrast to the doubt that consumed George Ball, Secretary of State Rusk did not betray an iota of ambivalence. "Dean has a real sort of moral feeling," Bundy recalled, "that if you *said* you will defend somebody, not only do you have an obligation of principle as a statesman to not go back on your word, but you also have the pragmatic obligation not to, because if you do, your word goes down in value on every currency of every other account."[81] Rusk believed that the American commitment to the Southeast Asia Treaty Organization was sacrosanct. "SEATO is five rather obscure initials to the American public—and even to Lyndon Johnson," Bundy said. "But the fact that Dean Rusk sees it as a moral and political pillar makes President Johnson feel good."[82] He added, "Dean Rusk is a patriot. He hasn't got a private interest in the world and he despises people who do. Lyndon Johnson has been accommodating . . . meshing, puzzling out, making things happen out of the assemblage of private interest all his life. So in that sense they were in different worlds."[83]

What struck Bundy most in looking back on the discussion of July 21, 1965, he told me, was a quality of unreality to the deliberations, because Johnson had already communicated his approval of Westmoreland's forty-four-battalion strategy to McNamara on July 17. The essential decision had already been sealed. Johnson "wants to be *seen* having careful discussions," said Bundy, "and he does indeed want to *hear* what everybody is saying, because that becomes a part of the way a majority leader controls events—you've got to know what the opposition's *thoughts* are—so he finds out." But the president showed little interest in the arguments for withdrawal "because George Ball . . . can't show him anything that doesn't translate as defeat in the politics of the United States. And he doesn't really expect George to do that because he doesn't see how it can be done himself."[84]

Bundy posited that one strong indication that the large group meetings in July were not Johnson's actual forum to debate and make a decision was the inclusion of his loyal domestic policy aide, Jack Valenti, who was instructed to compose a full record of a discussion for which the outcome was already known.[85] Johnson, he concluded, wanted his decision making to remain opaque. "He lives this extraordinarily lonely final decision proposition, because if he tells you ahead of time what his final decision is, he's given away his freedom to change his mind."[86] As Bundy described it, Johnson had a distinct aversion to unregulated group deliberations. He preferred engaging a "power element" in individual dialogue. "So that he knows one-on-one what Eisenhower is advising. He knows one-on-one what Russell is advising. What Ball is advising." These disaggregated discussions helped Johnson to manage a series of independent relationships with key advisers and constituencies. Yet the result of this method, Bundy lamented, was that "the principal players do not engage in anything you can really call an exchange of views."[87] In the final analysis, Bundy discounted what any of Johnson's advisers could contribute to the debate of the summer of 1965. He didn't believe that a full analysis would have made a difference. "That was prevented by him and the process he used was really for show and not for choice."[88]

In a revealing coda to Johnson's stagecraft, the following day the president convened a group of fourteen civilian and military advisers—a collection of so-called wise men—for further discussion of the military options. Explaining that he wanted a thorough debate, the president nonetheless hinted at the real purpose for the meeting. "Remember," he explained, "they're going to write stories about this like they did the Bay of Pigs—and about my advisers." President Johnson told the group that Bundy had been instructed to compose a memorandum summarizing the questions most critical to the debate about Americanizing the war. "Some congressmen and senators think we are going to be the most discredited people in the world," Johnson said. "What Bundy will now tell you is not his opinion, nor mine—I haven't taken a position—but what we hear."[89]

"The argument we will face," said Bundy, "is, one, for ten years every step we have taken has been based on a previous failure. All we have done has failed and caused us to take another step which failed. As we got further into the bag, we got deeply bruised. Also we have made excessive claims we haven't been able to realize.

"Two, also after twenty years of warning about war in Asia, we are now doing what MacArthur and others have warned us about. We are about to fight a war we can't fight and win as the country we are trying to help is quitting.

"Three, there is a failure on our own to fully realize what guerrilla war is like. We are sending conventional troops to do an unconventional job.

"Four, how long—how much? Can we take casualties over five years—aren't we talking about a military solution when the solution is really political? Why can't we interdict better? Why are our bombings so fruitless? Why can't we blockade the coast? Why can't we improve our intelligence? Why can't we find the VC?"[90]

Robert McNamara pointed to Bundy's paper and said, "I think we can answer most of those questions posed."[91] The meeting soon ended, however, and nowhere in the record is there any indication that the questions identified by Bundy were rigorously examined by those advocating Americanization of the war—including, most notably, by Bundy himself.

&

Amid the breakdown of his relationship with Johnson and the escalation decisions of the summer of 1965, Bundy reached out to the president of Harvard University, Nathan Pusey, to explore the possibility of returning to academic life. While that notion percolated, the Ford Foundation came calling, offering Bundy its top job and providing a graceful exit from Washington in the winter of 1966. Bundy called it "a most interesting job," sufficiently attractive to explain his departure. "So I got out of the White House without embarrassment to the President," he wrote, "and our personal relations in fact improved with distance."[92] Moyers would not be chosen as Bundy's successor. Johnson instead appointed Walt W. Rostow, a passionate believer in the domino theory and a relentless advocate of the war in Vietnam who, decades after the fall of South Vietnam, continued to insist that the United States had in fact won a wider geopolitical victory to prevent the spread of communism in Southeast Asia.[93]

Bundy emphasized his support for Lyndon Johnson's Americanization of the war while he served as national security adviser. "Once the choice of 1965 was made I supported it, in and out of office," he recalled. "My reason for leaving was different," he said, relating not to the scope of the troop deployment "but on the way the Administration, and in particular the President himself, did and did not explain" America's new mission in Vietnam.[94] It was the president's lack of transparency that angered Bundy rather than the strategy to Americanize the war—a strategy he privately questioned with McNamara but otherwise publicly endorsed. As Bundy struggled to explain in one of his fragments, "You must make it plain that while you wanted choices spelled out to the public, you yourself were in favor of ground combat reinforcement in 1965. You did also favor a real examination of alternatives, which did not happen."[95]

As he revisited the decision to Americanize the war, Bundy summarized the convictions that predisposed him to avoid the hard debate that was critically necessary. He wrote in one of his draft fragments that he was guided by three principal beliefs in the summer of 1965. First, he rejected "giving up" in South Vietnam. Second, he asserted that he was "not for big troop decision either" and pointed to the reservations he had enumerated in his June 30 memorandum, which characterized the Westmoreland escalation as "rash to the point of folly." Third, Bundy opposed "bucking debate." He added that it remained his contention that the

United States and Saigon could make it work. "This was wrong. But so were the other two visible options: no good peace—and no victory were available."[96] Bundy faulted himself for his own analytical disengagement. "*My mistakes*: I do not get further in to Vietnam staff work to see to it that the requirements and prospects of both JFK's way and LBJ's way are explained," Bundy wrote. He faulted himself for engaging only "in a glancing way" with Johnson and McNamara and particularly for his "deeper failure" to follow up on his June 30 memorandum to ask whether sending more troops would work. Bundy further stipulated that to be a true arbiter of military strategy in the summer of 1965 would have required "the ability and determination to try to help President Johnson *against* his will."[97]

As the administration's premier academic and the principal coordinating agent for the formulation and management of national security strategy, Bundy was the one senior official in the Johnson administration with both the institutional mandate and the intellectual gravitas to force a real examination of the military implications of an open-ended deployment of U.S. combat forces to South Vietnam. That exercise did not occur. In fact, it was never even attempted. As Bundy acknowledged, the decision-making process of 1965 failed to incorporate a "real analysis and debate on the underlying questions" posed by the massive enlargement of the war. Specifically, would the public support a protracted and potentially stalemated ground force war? Or, as Bundy provocatively rephrased the question, "How many would have wanted, supported, pressed for the war that actually happened?" If President Johnson had been confronted with this proposition, Bundy asked, "What ways of avoiding it would have been studied and debated (Can you do it? Will the country accept it? etc., etc.)."[98]

In explaining his disengagement with what he retrospectively called the "will-it-work" question of Americanizing the war, Bundy invariably returned to the quality and character of Lyndon Johnson's leadership. "The process of decision, explanation, and defense is unsatisfactory, frustrating, destructive and impossible to fix," he recalled in one of his fragments. "No one knows but LBJ himself what the issues are, what his questions are aimed at—why he is deciding as he is—or *whether* or *when*—so if we really get to help him it is almost by accident."[99]

Bundy grappled with the task of how to characterize his relationship with Lyndon Johnson. In a letter he wrote in 1994, Bundy described Johnson as "kind and mean, open and closed, brave and timid, sensitive and unfeeling, careful and rash, trusting and suspicious, self-centered and generous." The thread that united these disparate qualities, he reflected, was Johnson's colossal ambition as a political actor.[100] And while Bundy could not cloak the antipathy he felt for Johnson's methods, it was also clear that he held a reverence for the presidency. Bundy struggled mightily but inconclusively to reconcile this conflict.

What appeared to trouble Bundy most, as he searched for lessons in Lyndon Johnson's leadership as commander in chief, was his conclusion that the president conceived of military strategy as a function of political calculations, particularly the need to sustain a consensus among General Westmoreland, the Joint Chiefs of Staff, and the civilian leadership of the Pentagon on the scope of the troop escalation in the summer of 1965. In this sense, as Bundy noted, Johnson was more of a Senate-majority-leader-in-chief cobbling together a legislative coalition than a commander in chief defining a clear military mission and the resources required for its success. Bundy was right to observe in Johnson a predilection to play politics with his advisers—feigning studied indecision with some, silencing or bargaining quietly with others, and staging ostentatious scenes of deliberative debate for everyone when the essential choice had already been made. While Bundy retrospectively blamed such machinations for his own relative disengagement from the crucial decisions of the summer of 1965, perhaps there were deeper and less thoroughly examined reasons to explain his passivity in the evaluation of the Westmoreland escalation recommendation.

One of the consistent themes of Bundy's Vietnam counsel as national security adviser was his support for military action uncorrelated to concrete military outcomes. Again and again, Bundy demonstrated a willingness, if not an eagerness, to deploy military means in pursuit of indeterminate and primarily political ends. "Laos was never really ours after 1954. South Vietnam is and wants to be," Bundy told President Kennedy his first year in office, arguing for the first deployment of ground combat forces in defense of the Saigon regime. Although the mission of U.S. forces was left undefined in Bundy's recommendation, he urged its approval because the commitment of combat troops "has now become a sort of touchstone of our will."[101] In May 1964 Bundy urged Johnson to make a "resolute and extensive deployment" of combat troops "on a very large scale . . . to maximize their deterrent impact and their menace" and to launch "an initial strike against the north." Yet Bundy had also admitted that "there were several holes in this discussion, most notably on action in South Vietnam and on the precise U.S. objectives."[102] In August 1964 Bundy presented a memorandum describing Vietnam military contingencies involving naval harassment, air interdiction in Laos, and fleet maneuvers in the Gulf of Tonkin. "The object of any of these," he explained, "would be more to heighten morale and to show our strength of purpose than to accomplish anything very specific in a military sense."[103]

Bundy's bombing recommendation in February 1965, as George Ball claimed, reflected the national security adviser's intent "to leave our objective unformulated and therefore flexible," a principle of military planning Ball deemed untenable.[104] In arguing for a strategy of "graduated and sustained reprisal" Bundy conceded that bombing "may fail" and that its odds for success were between 25 and 75 percent. "What we can say is that even if it fails, the policy will be worth it," Bundy assured President Johnson. "At a minimum, it will damp down the charge that we did not do all that we could have done, and this charge will be important in many countries, including our own."[105] It appeared that Bundy valued the efficacy of bombing less than the appearance of commitment it signified.

Bundy had a similar perspective on the deployment of ground forces. His private notes of March 21, 1965—in which he identified the "cardinal" principle for the United States in Vietnam as "*not* to be a Paper Tiger"—demonstrate that Bundy was fixated not on prevailing militarily but on maintaining America's credibility in the Cold War. The American combat troop commitment did not have to advance a compelling military strategy or have a real prospect of success. It simply needed to dramatize the proposition that the United States was prepared to pay a real cost in blood and treasure to maintain its position of global leadership. "For if we visibly *do enough* in the South (whatever that may be), any failure will be, in that sense, beyond our control," Bundy wrote. Even losing the war after committing one hundred thousand troops would be a better outcome for "U.S. politics" than not having deployed any combat troops at all.[106]

Perhaps for Bundy during his White House years the perception of credibility trumped every other aspect of military strategy in Vietnam. Perhaps the repeated imprecision of his military recommendations and seeming indifference to their realistic prospects for success reflected a basic calculation that although the United States must fight in Vietnam, it was not necessary to win. In the end, Bundy's notes of March 21, 1965, anticipated exactly what would happen when the president deployed the first one hundred thousand men to Vietnam, with hundreds of thousands more to follow: America would fight and lose, but its credibility, in some form, would be preserved for having maintained an enormously costly commitment. Although Bundy did not come to the conclusion himself, if pressed perhaps he would have admitted that in 1965 he and President Johnson secured roughly the outcomes each found most critical. As Bundy frequently observed, Johnson wanted a bureaucratic consensus on combat troops relating to a number, not a strategy or use.

And Bundy wanted a military commitment that evinced U.S. credibility even if it did not hold real promise of winning the war. Thus both the president and his national security adviser achieved what was paramount to them in the summer of 1965. And the United States was launched on the path to a protracted, inconclusive, and unintended war of attrition in Vietnam.

As Bundy would later recall, the summer of 1965 was a fateful moment when grave strategic and tactical misjudgments converged. "The Kennedy rule," he wrote, "is washed rapidly away; the number of troops is negotiated with Westy through RSM; no strategy is discussed . . . the JFK No-No is forgotten . . . and the U.S. is committed to a war of attrition with a most formidably determined and disciplined enemy." These first choices facilitated further combat force deployments, thus resolving the essential strategic question of Vietnam. The path to an open-ended war of attrition had been opened, "no longer shut by the commander-in-chief."[107]

As he immersed himself in the essential decisions of Vietnam more than thirty years after the Americanization of the war, Bundy arrived at three conclusions at variance with his advocacy as national security adviser. He dismissed the notion that there was a geopolitical imperative to fight the war, a conviction he had fervently held in the White House. He rejected the premise that there was ever any possibility that the North Vietnamese would relent in their drive to unify the country or would negotiate a compromise settlement with the United States, a potential outcome he postulated in 1965. And he acknowledged that the massive military deployments initiated in 1965 were doomed to fail and held no plausible expectation for a military solution to the conflict.

The "geopolitical argument" for Americanizing the war was "primarily regional," Bundy noted, observing that Indonesia, the largest "domino" in Southeast Asia, "fell firmly the other way—against the Communists—late in 1965." (This was a reference to the rout of the Communist Party there at the hands of a right-wing military junta led by General Suharto.)[108] "So that result was *not* achieved by the battles of 1966 and after." Yet according to Bundy's calculation, 95 percent of the casualties suffered by the United States in Vietnam occurred after the Indonesian domino had toppled to the right rather than to the left. He contended that the case of Indonesia demonstrates that American casualties in the Vietnam War were not necessary for the maintenance of regional security. "The U.S. had done what it could for the *region* by the end of 1965," he declared, noting that military deaths through the end of that year were 1,594, versus a total of 58,191 killed by the time the war ended in 1973.[109]

In notes about a possible introduction to the Vietnam book, Bundy enumerated some of the arguments he would *not* make. His focus would not be on the negotiated settlement that Washington could have secured, he said, "because I deeply believe that peaceful compromise was never available."[110] Moreover, the Johnson administration could not pay the political price for compelling the Saigon regime to accept a settlement that would lead to its own dissolution. "Better to simply go home," he concluded.[111]

The adoption of attrition as the de facto U.S. military strategy was determined, in part, by the absence of other viable options. As Bundy noted, the use of nuclear weapons was never seriously considered and was taken off the table. A ground invasion of North Vietnam was similarly dismissed because of its potential to trigger war with China. Destroying the dikes that crossed North Vietnam would flood the country, create a humanitarian crisis, and not necessarily staunch support for the insurgency in the South. Thus with the source of the war in the North subject only to air and sea actions that would prove ineffectual, contesting the guerrilla war in the South became the preponderant focus of U.S. strategy.[112] As Westmoreland argued, "only by seeking, fighting, and destroying the enemy could that be done."[113]

Despite the theory behind Westmoreland's attrition strategy, in reality it devolved into an open-ended "search and destroy" mission that ceded the initiative to the enemy. Bundy reasoned that if American troops could not enter the enemy's territory, and if the adversary could not be forced to defend its positions within South Vietnam, "then he must be sought and engaged on his terms and defeated engagement by engagement." The pursuit of victory therefore amounted to the accumulation of "one small campaign after another," in which the defining metric of progress became "the number of casualties inflicted." In a military contest defined by such structural limitations, he concluded, "the strategic objective was to reduce enemy strength to the point where the enemy would be willing to leave his neighbor alone. As we all know that point was never reached."[114]

By the metric of attrition, U.S. forces did in fact succeed in imposing severe losses on the insurgency. As Westmoreland observed, "No American unit in South Vietnam other than a few companies on the offensive or an occasional small outpost ever incurred what could fairly be called a setback. That is a remarkable record."[115] In his retrospective reflections, Bundy noted Westmoreland's conclusion and its irrelevance to the outcome of the war. Although the United States did not seek a war of attrition, the failure of this strategy would not have been anticipated given the much greater losses absorbed by North Vietnamese and NLF forces.[116] Scholars have projected that the military under Hanoi's command suffered five hundred thousand battle fatalities by 1968 and between two and three million additional losses by 1975.[117]

Through its campaign of attrition, the United States presumed that a crossover point would be reached, when the accumulated pain of war would compel the insurgents to relent. But in practice this coercion strategy simply created an endurance contest. In that competition it was not the will of the Vietnamese communists that was broken. For each year of combat from 1965 to 1973, Bundy observed, the United States inflicted far greater casualties on the enemy than it absorbed. Yet despite this dramatic disparity, it was the United States that withdrew its forces "home without victory." As Bundy starkly confessed, "We had followed a losing strategy—one that led us not to success but to the acceptance of failure."[118] "Attrition is a brutal measuring stick," he affirmed. "Its use is not advertised and its authorship not eagerly claimed."[119]

Bundy frequently cited the battle of the Ia Drang Valley as an engagement that epitomized the inverted strategic logic of the American attrition campaign. In October 1965 America's First Air Cavalry confronted forces of the North Vietnamese army in the Central Highlands of South Vietnam, where General Westmoreland believed communist troops were attempting to slice the country in two. In more than a month of fierce combat, American forces leveraged their massive advantage in firepower, dropping 500-pound bombs from B-52 aircraft, launching 50,000 helicopter sorties, and firing 33,108 rounds of 105 mm ammunition and 7,356 aerial rockets. Well over 1,500 North Vietnamese soldiers were killed while the United States recorded 200 deaths.[120]

Although heralded at the time as a major U.S. victory, the Ia Drang battle foreshadowed the future course of the war. Communist troops suffered losses dramatically disproportionate to those absorbed by the United States. Yet they were not intimidated by the American show of strength, their commitment to the war remained undiluted, and U.S. forces were compelled to endure a grinding contest that imposed significant costs that would be continually replicated. As Bundy observed, "In terms of the reservoirs of strength, you can say . . . that Ia Drang is then repeated for three or four years, until the Americans are exhausted—*not* the Vietnamese."[121] Bundy argued that the same dynamic that led to President Johnson's acceptance of an attrition strategy also prevented the administration from examining its failure, because "the ways and means of going forward with it are both adopted and delimited by this senatorial process of politics."[122] The attrition strategy thus contributed to one of the great ironies of the war. In the end, one of the protagonists in Vietnam was ultimately coerced to abandon the battle, beaten not militarily but persuaded that victory could not be achieved at an acceptable price. Bundy's conviction that coercion would prevail was correct, but its impact was applied in reverse. It was Washington, not Hanoi, that was forced to abandon an unwinnable war.

Some students of the Vietnam conflict contend that America's military program was compromised by excessive civilian micromanagement from the Johnson White House. A stronger argument, however, can be made for the contrary case. It was not the intrusion of civilian war planners but rather the absence of rigorous oversight that created the conditions for the strategic quagmire that followed. General Bruce Palmer Jr., a former deputy to William Westmoreland, perceived a systemic failure to evaluate the viability of the military's proposals. "In the end the theater commander—in effect, General Westmoreland—made successive requests for larger and larger force levels without benefit of an overall concept and plan," he observed. The Joint Chiefs of Staff and the armed services leadership "in turn could only review these force requirements in a strategic vacuum without a firm feel for what the ultimate requirement might be, and without knowing what level of commitment would be acceptable to the American people and their elected leaders." He added, "Not once during the war did the JCS advise the commander-in-chief or the secretary of defense that the strategy being pursued most probably would fail and that the United States would be unable to achieve its objectives." Bundy intended to quote Palmer but also pose a question: "Did we ask them?"[123]

How far would Bundy have gone in holding himself accountable for the lack of rigor that characterized the evaluation of military strategy? In scattered notes to himself, Bundy could be blunt and categorical in his judgments. Reviewing a study of the war by the political scientist Larry Berman, Bundy noted a memorandum he sent to President Johnson on

May 4, 1967, more than a year after he had stepped down as national security adviser. "The fact that South Vietnam has not been lost and is not going to be lost is a fact of truly massive importance in the history of Asia, the Pacific and the U.S.," Bundy wrote. Looking back on that assurance nearly thirty years later, he observed, tersely: "McGB all *wrong*."[124] Bundy was also prepared to be sharply critical of Johnson for authorizing a muddled military mission. He proclaimed his "deep conviction" that in the pursuit of a flawed strategy in Vietnam, "the decisive errors were those made or approved by the President as commander-in-chief."[125]

When in 1995 he finally decided to address the unresolved questions of the Vietnam War, Bundy registered a starkly different point of view from his years in power. He called Vietnam "a war we should not have fought" and conceded that "on the overall issue—are you for the war or against it, in 1965 and after, the doves were right." Bundy would therefore try to explain "the ways in which the executive branch continuously got that great choice wrong—not because it wanted the long hard war it got, but because it would repeatedly reject the hard alternative of 'losing to the Reds.'" It can be argued that the former national security adviser's admissions of misjudgment about the war and the military failure it perpetuated reflected a profound personal transformation. With respect to the question of Vietnam, undoubtedly his most consequential encounter with history, Bundy in retrospect had embraced a quality he had lacked when in high office three decades earlier. He had finally learned humility.

Bundy expected that his inquiry would be constrained in scope. Noting that he had tackled "comprehensive modern history" in *Danger and Survival*, his 1988 study of statecraft and nuclear weapons, he identified a more limited but no less meaningful agenda for his study of Vietnam— his desire to confront two seminal questions he had consciously avoided for three decades: "first, how did this tragedy happen, and second what could be learned from it to guide America in the future?"[126] The lessons Bundy studied most passionately related to the presidents he served,

Kennedy and Johnson, and the very different ways they conceived of and managed American strategic interests in Southeast Asia. Bundy believed those differences were so great that within the contrast between the two presidents one could observe how history might have rendered a different fate for the United States in Vietnam.

INTERVENTION IS A PRESIDENTIAL CHOICE, NOT AN INEVITABILITY

In the years following the assassination of President Kennedy, when Vietnam became America's longest war and the nation's first to culminate in defeat, McGeorge Bundy was frequently asked a compelling but seemingly unanswerable question. "I have never thought it wise to speculate in public as to what John Kennedy would have done about Vietnam had he lived," Bundy explained to the Massachusetts Historical Society in 1978. "The public record shows him constantly asserting two propositions that could not have coexisted easily in later years: that we must not quit there and that in the end the Vietnamese must do the job for themselves. . . . Just what he would have done we shall never know."[1] Bundy made the same argument to an audience at Hofstra University in 1985. "Those propositions," he said, "together with his clear determination not to be drawn into large-scale ground-based action could not have co-existed in 1965. I don't know what he would have done."[2]

Yet in private discussions Bundy was far more forthcoming. In 1964—several years before Vietnam would assume the profile of a debacle—Bundy suggested in the oral history conducted by the Columbia University political scientist Richard Neustadt that Kennedy had a dispassionate and independent perspective regarding the challenge in Vietnam.[3] Bundy speculated that Kennedy would not have fallen captive to the intellectual constraints of the domino theory, that he harbored serious doubts about the viability of the war effort in South Vietnam, and that he questioned Vietnam's relevance to the U.S. national interest and domestic politics.

"He was not a domino theorist, I take it?" Neustadt asked Bundy.

"He was not prepared to be an anti–domino theorist," Bundy replied, "but he certainly was not in the sort of straightforward way 'you lose this and all is gone' kind of fellow. . . . If he had been he wouldn't have been a neutralizer of Laos."[4] On the question of Vietnam, Bundy mused, "If you had poked President Kennedy very hard," he would have called it "essential to have made a determined effort . . . because we mustn't be the ones who lost the war, someone else has to lose this war." But Kennedy doubted the chances for success in Vietnam, Bundy added. "I don't think he would have said to you that *he* saw any persuasive reason to believe that this was certainly going to succeed. I think he was not so much a pessimistic man as a man who built no realities on hopes." Bundy went on to say that the president supported Robert Kennedy's efforts to develop a counterinsurgency capacity in South Vietnam and that he "liked" and was "amused" by the "methodical belligerence" of Walt Rostow, the former deputy national security adviser whom Kennedy had transferred from the White House to the State Department. "But he wasn't so sure himself. He was deeply aware of the fact that this place was in fact 'X' thousand miles away in terms both of American interest and American politics."[5]

Some former Kennedy advisers who in later years expressed views comparable to Bundy's in 1964 were accused of trying to burnish the slain president's posthumous reputation and distance him from a foreign policy disaster. In the case of Bundy's exchange with Neustadt, however, he was speaking just a year after the assassination and before the war's dramatic escalation and ultimate loss. During 1964, only 149 Americans were killed in action in Vietnam, a small fraction of the fatalities that would follow the Americanization of the war beginning in 1965.[6]

In his final years, as he revisited the history of the Vietnam War through the prism of the Kennedy and Johnson presidencies, Bundy arrived at a firm judgment that he shared with me and discussed with various colleagues. It was a judgment consistent with aspects of his commentary in 1964. Bundy had become convinced that President Kennedy would not have deployed ground combat forces to Vietnam and thus would not have Americanized the war. With the 1964 election behind him, Kennedy would have arrived at a point of decision on Vietnam in 1965 just as his successor did, Bundy explained in one of our work sessions. "And what he wanted to do about Vietnam—shorthand, in political terms—was flush it. He didn't want it to be a big item. And he didn't think it was a big test of the balance of power. It was a test of American political opinion, but he could stand that in a second term."[7] In a discussion with another colleague, James Blight of Brown University, "Mac said there were no missed opportunities," Blight noted. "None, except the 'opportunity' that was irretrievably lost when Kennedy was felled and replaced by Johnson. He said he believes both sides of the argument: Had Kennedy lived, there would have been no Vietnam War as we know it; and with Johnson in the White House, it was (in combination with Hanoi's total intransigence) destined to unfold like the tragedy it became."[8]

As he maintained throughout our work together, Bundy emphasized that the two figures of greatest consequence for America's tragic encounter with Vietnam were the two presidents he served, Kennedy and Johnson. "Their choices, including what they chose *not* to decide, were the most important, and however much others tried to help, each of these men had a final authority and responsibility that each understood," he wrote in a draft fragment.[9] No U.S. combat troops could be deployed without the explicit approval of the commander in chief, Bundy stressed, and neither Kennedy nor Johnson ever failed to understand that the ultimate responsibility and authority for Vietnam decisions "was his and his alone."[10] While Bundy declared his respect and affection for the two presidents he served, "each becomes larger, though also more *tragic*, as his role in Vietnam becomes better understood," he said.[11] Bundy argued that the no-combat-troop policy imposed by Kennedy was of fundamental significance for America's history in Vietnam. "If Lyndon Johnson had not reversed that decision," Bundy wrote, "the Vietnam War as America came to know it could not have happened."[12]

The historical record demonstrates that during his years as national security adviser Bundy was never confident that the United States could achieve a battlefield victory in Vietnam, and such a military strategy was never his priority. He similarly doubted, at the time and retrospectively, that the South Vietnamese army—even with robust and continued American assistance—could defeat the communist insurgency. "It seems highly likely that this course would have failed," Bundy acknowledged, ending—as Americanization of the war did or as a negotiated settlement would have—with Hanoi in control of a united Vietnam. But the human costs of the war would have been substantially contained, and the United States would still have been seen supporting an ally with the arms and advisers it required to survive. Insisting that the South Vietnamese army fight its own ground combat operations was an entirely legitimate demand, Bundy pronounced. "That had been the Kennedy policy of 1961, and it could have been the policy of 1965."[13]

Bundy never completed his description of the different course he believed Kennedy would have pursued in Vietnam if he had lived to serve a second term. But he did leave behind a partial outline of his argument. "A Major Element of the Book: What if JFK Lives," Bundy registered in a draft fragment, asking himself what would have been Kennedy's position in 1965. "We don't *know* and we don't need to *know* to consider the alternative," he went on. "A possibility is enough." He underscored that Kennedy would have been in a position where his prohibition against combat troops had been in force and effectively working for him for close to four years.[14] And he thought about some guidelines for how he would want to address the conjecture concerning Kennedy in a second term: "How does a President explain a 'defeat' without a commitment of U.S. ground troops? We have to admit (a) that it is very hard and (b) no one can be sure JFK would have done it." Finally, Bundy offered this admonition: "In particular we must not suppose a 'happy' ending. What we have to face is what JFK did not: the real problem of 1965."[15]

*

The debate about Kennedy and how he would have confronted the crisis in Vietnam in a second term of his presidency—a debate known in academic circles as the "counterfactual" question—continues to roil the community of scholars who study the Vietnam War. Some, like James Galbraith of the University of Texas, consider Kennedy's announcement of the withdrawal of one thousand U.S. advisers in October 1963 to be the genesis of an incipient extrication strategy from Vietnam.[16] Bundy did not comment on the significance of this withdrawal plan nor did he ever suggest that Kennedy had implemented an extrication strategy prior to the assassination. What Bundy did assert was that after the president's 1961 decision to reject combat troop deployments to South Vietnam, his counselors never again produced such a formal proposal, a claim the documentary record appears to substantiate. And Bundy repeatedly asserted that in a second term Kennedy would have maintained his no-combat-troop policy and would have resisted pressures to Americanize the war.

Bundy also believed that Kennedy would have maintained the status quo in Vietnam during the 1964 presidential election. "I feel morally certain that 1964, as an election year, would have been a dampener of change in Vietnam for JFK, just as it was for Lyndon Johnson: a good thing *not* to talk about . . . in the course of a campaign," Bundy said. "What we were doing when the President died was to try to make the post-coup process work." Bundy regretted Kennedy's reticence on Vietnam, arguing that although Kennedy was right and Johnson was wrong on the question of Americanizing the war, both presidents were wrong for not transparently explaining their policies to the public at large. Yet Bundy also acknowledged the inherent advantages of toeing the rhetorical line in 1964, observing that politicians from both political parties supported the goal of maintaining the independence of South Vietnam as a noncommunist state. "The question is: what are you going to do about it?" he asked. "And what are you *not* going to do?" And, he pointedly noted, what do you do to avoid appearing "less of a hawk than your more respectable opponents or predecessors"?[17]

Bundy speculated in the 1964 Neustadt oral history that in contrast to the combat troop proposals of Maxwell Taylor and Walt Rostow, President Kennedy would have continued during the election year to support the counterinsurgency training of South Vietnamese troops favored by Robert Kennedy. "It was felt that if you applied the techniques used in Malaya and really put your mind to it and operated with energy you had a darn good chance," Bundy told Neustadt. "At the very least you couldn't say you couldn't do it, and that the level of commitment you were undertaking, which was carefully limited, below what Taylor and Rostow recommended, had quite a sufficient promise of success so that it didn't make sense to quit."[18]

Based on Bundy's assumption that Kennedy would not have withdrawn or escalated in Vietnam during the 1964 election year, what evidence would be relevant to understanding the course Kennedy might have followed in 1965? If Bundy wanted to bolster his thesis that Kennedy would not have Americanized the war, he could have cited the abundant evidence of the president's consistently held aversion to deploying U.S.

combat troops in Southeast Asia—evidence that predated his presidency and, of course, extended into his time as commander in chief.

Despite his support for the Diem regime, Kennedy in the 1950s had publicly cited the disastrous French experience in Indochina as a cautionary rationale for the United States never to fight a ground war there.[19] His doubts about a combat-troop commitment to South Vietnam only deepened after he became president. In the summer of 1961, Kennedy invited General Douglas MacArthur to Washington for meetings with selected senior advisers and members of Congress. In Robert Kennedy's account, General MacArthur said "that we would be foolish to fight on the Asiatic continent and that the future of Southeast Asia should be determined at the diplomatic table."[20] According to Kenneth O'Donnell, MacArthur told the president, "There was no end to Asia and even if we poured a million American infantry soldiers into that continent, we would still find ourselves outnumbered on every side."[21] Alexis Johnson, the deputy undersecretary of state, was skeptical of MacArthur's conclusion. "Nevertheless, it made a very deep impression on the President," he recalled. "I think that for the rest of the time he was in office this view of General MacArthur's . . . tended to dominate very much the thinking of President Kennedy with respect to Southeast Asia."[22] Maxwell Taylor had a similar recollection. MacArthur's analysis made "a hell of an impression on the President," he said, "so that whenever he'd get this military advice from the Joint Chiefs or from me or anyone else, he'd say, 'Well, now, you gentleman, you go back and convince General MacArthur, then I'll be convinced.' But none of us undertook the task."[23]

Kennedy shared his reservations with others outside his administration. In October 1961 he had lunch with the *New York Times* columnist Arthur Krock at a moment when a majority of his senior advisers were coalescing around the first proposal to deploy ground combat troops to Vietnam. "The President still believes in what he told the Senate several years ago," Krock wrote in his diary, "that United States troops should not be involved on the Asian mainland, especially in a country with the difficult terrain of Laos and inhabited by people who don't care how the East-West dispute as to freedom and self-determination was resolved. Moreover, said the President, the United States can't interfere in civil disturbances created by guerrillas, and it was hard to prove that this wasn't largely the situation in Vietnam."[24]

Preoccupied with the possibility of escalation in Vietnam, John Kenneth Galbraith, the U.S. ambassador to India, sent Kennedy an anxious memorandum in April 1962. "We have a growing military commitment. This could expand step by step into a major, long-drawn out indecisive military involvement," he warned. "We should resist all steps which commit American troops to combat action and impress upon all concerned the importance of keeping American forces out of actual combat commitment."[25] Kennedy discussed Galbraith's memorandum with Averell Harriman and asked that it be forwarded for comment to Robert McNamara as well. "The President," according to notes of the discussion, "observed generally that he wished us to be prepared to seize upon any favorable moment to reduce our involvement, recognizing that the moment might yet be some time away."[26] Kennedy told Roger Hilsman at around the same time that he doubted the efficacy of direct American military action against North Vietnam, acknowledging the strategic disadvantages to the United States of the highly developed "Ho Chi Minh Trail" that enabled the North Vietnamese to resupply the Vietcong in the South. "No matter what goes wrong," said Kennedy, "or whose fault it really is, the argument will be that the Communists have stepped up their infiltration and we can't win unless we hit the north. Those trails are a built-in excuse for failure, and a built-in argument for escalation."[27]

In developing his argument further, Bundy could have also cited Kennedy's pledge to Senator Mike Mansfield to withdraw from Vietnam in a second term. Mansfield, the Senate majority leader, was an outspoken skeptic on the administration's Vietnam policy. After returning from a tour of South Vietnam in early 1963, Mansfield reiterated his concerns during a congressional leadership breakfast at the White House. Afterward the president asked Kenneth O'Donnell to invite Mansfield to his office for a private discussion. "The President told Mansfield that he had been having serious second thoughts about Mansfield's argument and that he now agreed with the Senator's thinking on the need for a complete military withdrawal from Vietnam," O'Donnell recounted. He added that Kennedy stipulated one essential qualification: " 'But I can't do it until 1965—after I'm reelected,' Kennedy told Mansfield. Kennedy stated— and Mansfield accepted—the president's explanation that if he announced a withdrawal of American military personnel from Vietnam before the 1964 election, there would be a wild conservative outcry against returning him to the Presidency for a second term."[28] Mansfield subsequently confirmed the accuracy of O'Donnell's account of his meeting with President Kennedy.[29]

"In 1965, I'll become one of the most unpopular Presidents in history," Kennedy told O'Donnell after the meeting. "I'll be damned everywhere as a Communist appeaser. But I don't care. If I tried to pull out completely now from Vietnam, we would have another Joe McCarthy red scare on our hands, but I can do it after I'm reelected. So we had better make damn sure that I *am* reelected."[30] Kennedy confided a similar sentiment to Charles Bartlett, a trusted friend in the press corps. "We don't have a prayer of staying in Vietnam," Kennedy told Bartlett. "Those people hate us. They are going to throw our asses out of there at almost any point. But I can't give up a piece of territory like that to the Communists and then get the people to reelect me."[31] But Kennedy realized that expulsion of the American mission from South Vietnam was in fact a viable exit strategy. At a press conference on May 22, 1963, the president had pledged to "withdraw the troops, any number of troops, any time the Government of South Vietnam would suggest it."[32] Asked privately how he would engineer an American withdrawal, Kennedy made the same point more bluntly. "Easy," he told his political advisers. "Put a government in there that will ask us to leave."[33]

The objective of reducing U.S. military personnel in South Vietnam was established in National Security Action Memorandum 263, which Bundy issued on October 11, 1963. According to Deputy Secretary of Defense Roswell Gilpatric, "McNamara indicated to me that this was part of a plan the President asked him to develop to unwind the whole thing."[34] Years later Gilpatric told an audience at the Kennedy Library that the president personally disclosed his intention to disengage from Vietnam in his second term.[35]

In making his argument, Bundy could have noted reports from other senior officials who discussed with President Kennedy his intent to devolve the U.S. commitment in Vietnam and the limitation he consistently imposed against the deployment of ground combat troops. "Having discussed military affairs with him often and in detail for fifteen years," wrote James M. Gavin, a former general and ambassador to Paris, "I know he was totally opposed to the introduction of combat troops in Southeast Asia."[36] Roger Hilsman concurred: "Kennedy told me, as his action officer on Vietnam, over and over again that my job was to keep American involvement at a minimum so that we could withdraw as soon as the opportunity presented itself."[37] Hilsman also said, "On numerous occasions President Kennedy told me that he was determined not to let Vietnam become an American war."[38] According to the former Pentagon analyst Daniel Ellsberg, Robert Kennedy told him in October 1967, "Of course no one can know what my brother would have done in 1964 or 1965, but I do know he was determined not to send ground troops. He would rather do anything than that." The former attorney general said that a tour of Vietnam with his brother in 1951 had disillusioned them with the French position in Indochina.[39]

Michael Forrestal, Bundy's own Vietnam specialist on the NSC staff, engaged in a continuing dialogue with Kennedy about Vietnam—one in which the president privately told him that that the odds against an American victory over the Vietcong were 100 to 1.[40] It was Forrestal who, on November 21, 1963, had one of the last known discussions with Kennedy about Vietnam. They met as Forrestal was departing for Phnom Penh to reassure Prince Norodom Sihanouk of Cambodia that the United States continued to support his country's neutrality. Forrestal recalls that after their meeting the president "did what he sometimes did at the end of the day, or when he was a little tired. He asked me to stay a bit." Kennedy was preoccupied. "You know when you come back I want you to come and see me," he instructed Forrestal, "because we have to start to plan for what we are going to do now in South Vietnam. I want to start a complete and very profound review of how we got into this country, and what we thought we were doing, and what we now think we can do. I even want to think about whether or not we should be there." Forrestal stressed that he had "a very clear recollection" of his conversation with President Kennedy, "and, of course, the following morning when I arrived in Saigon, actually it was night out there, or two o'clock in the morning, he was killed."[41]

Bundy could have argued that while Kennedy's private comments to political intimates may be notable, the president's record of decision making in office is even more powerful evidence of his intent in a second term. In Laos, as in Vietnam, Kennedy rejected his advisers' recommendation to deploy combat forces. As the historian Fredrik Logevall observes, Kennedy "quickly came to doubt the intrinsic importance of Laos to US security. He worried about its difficult geography; about the likely lack of public support for a long-term commitment; about the lack . . . of an 'exit strategy' for any such commitment. Instead he opted for a diplomatic solution, despite warnings that he would pay a domestic political price for it. . . . The Laos case is further evidence of JFK's opposition to large-scale interventions in that part of the world, even when senior associates called for them."[42] And it was not only his senior advisers who promulgated the strategic centrality of Laos. No less a figure than President

Dwight Eisenhower, the hero of World War II, advised Kennedy that Laos was the single greatest test he would face as president.

Kennedy's record of rejecting proposals to deploy ground combat troops to Vietnam is unambiguous and consistent throughout his presidency. Yet, is that evidence sufficient to conclude he would have maintained the no-combat-troop policy in a second term? Would Kennedy in 1965 have leveraged his political power and authority as commander in chief to act on his convictions? Or would external pressures have compelled him to follow the same path of escalation as his successor, Lyndon Johnson?

The premise that such "structural forces" would have compelled Kennedy to Americanize the war represents a competing school of thought among scholars that Bundy would have had to confront to advance his thesis. Adherents of this view are varied and their arguments diverse. George Herring, for example, argues that America's entanglement in Vietnam stemmed from "a world view" and "the policy of containment—which Americans in and out of government accepted without serious question for more than two decades."[43] A corollary of the containment doctrine and another powerful political force was President Eisenhower's admonition to prop up potential falling dominoes.

Another argument attributes America's fate in the war to its complicity in the Diem coup of November 1, 1963, which is said to have solidified and perpetuated an enduring American commitment to defend whatever regimes would follow in Saigon.[44] Garry Wills argues that Kennedy's investment in his administration's counterinsurgency strategy and the doctrine known as "flexible response" would have paralyzed the president from acknowledging its shortcomings. "Any withdrawal," Wills speculates, "would have been a confession that his overarching strategy . . . was feckless; it could not deal with precisely the kind of problem it was framed for."[45] Other interpretations from the structural forces school identify a fixation with "credibility"—the quintessential Bundy conviction—as the driving force behind Americanization of the war. As Jonathan Schell suggests, "A collapse in credibility in the sphere of limited conflict would cast doubt on the credibility of American power in other spheres of competition as well, including even the all-important nuclear sphere." In this zero-sum conceptual framework of the Cold War, a reversal for the United States "in any part of the world, no matter how small, could undermine the whole structure of American power."[46]

To this list of constraints two more may be added: domestic politics and bureaucratic politics. If Kennedy allowed Vietnam to fall, would he not be vulnerable to vicious Republican attacks similar to what Truman endured when China was lost to communist revolution in 1949? And even if Kennedy did want to chart a different course in Vietnam, how could he hope to carry his senior advisers with him, who almost without exception urged Lyndon Johnson to launch massive ground troop deployments in 1965?

These are the arguments cited by historians and political scientists to explain why Kennedy would have been compelled to Americanize the Vietnam War: an ideological worldview and a fixation with falling dominoes; an entangling coup; an implacable commitment to his administration's counterinsurgency techniques; the premium placed on the credibility of the containment doctrine; the threat of debilitating right-wing political attacks; and the opposition of senior advisers committed to combat in Vietnam. Would these constraints—either individually or collectively—have decisively limited Kennedy's capacity for action in Vietnam? Bundy's analysis could have neutralized each of these arguments.

Was Kennedy an orthodox adherent to the domino theory? As Bundy himself observed in 1964, at a time when the tensions of the Cold War remained acute, if Kennedy had been persuaded by Eisenhower's worldview, he would have resisted the neutralization in Laos and would have presumably acquiesced to the CIA plot to reclaim Cuba via proxy forces at the Bay of Pigs. But Kennedy did not allow either Laos or Cuba to define his national security strategy. And in late 1961 he rejected the argument that a failure to deploy U.S. combat troops to defend South Vietnam could risk, in the words of Robert McNamara, "the fairly rapid extension of Communist control, or complete accommodation to Communism, in the rest of mainland Southeast Asia right down to Indonesia."[47]

Would Kennedy have allowed the Diem coup to entrap him into providing unqualified support for all of the dysfunctional successor regimes that followed in South Vietnam? The fact that Kennedy allowed one government in Saigon to be toppled with his assent seems to suggest that if a successor regime could not manage the war effectively, his calculations in the future would be comparably realistic and, if necessary, brutal. As several of Kennedy's advisers have observed, the president viewed the most expedient exit from Vietnam to be via the installation of a government in Saigon that would seek a U.S. withdrawal. As noted previously, to impute a sense of guilt as the animating force behind Kennedy's decision making in Vietnam or elsewhere is a dubious conclusion without substantiation in his record as commander in chief.

Would a fear of acknowledging the shortcomings of the U.S. counterinsurgency program have locked Kennedy into persisting with a failed approach? An affirmative answer to this question depends on Kennedy's susceptibility to patently irrational logic—the expectation that he would have pursued a losing course in Vietnam simply to prove he had a winning strategy. It is difficult to reconcile such strident egotism and rigidity with Kennedy's actual performance in office. The debacle at the Bay of Pigs once again provides a useful example. In the first months of his presidency, Kennedy initially accepted the recommendation of the CIA, the Joint Chiefs, Bundy, and others to launch the exile invasion. But when the mission teetered on the brink of failure and Kennedy was implored to authorize the air support the architects of the plan knew to be essential to its success, he refused. He accepted defeat rather than escalate the crisis. He then claimed responsibility for the disaster, fired the leaders of the CIA responsible for its planning and execution, subordinated the influence of the Joint Chiefs for the remainder of his term, and consolidated national security decision making in the White House. He also admitted the enormity of his mistake. "Not only were our facts in error," Kennedy said, "but our policy was wrong because the premises on which it was built were wrong."[48] It is highly questionable that this same president would cling to a failing counterinsurgency program simply to save face. Kennedy had shown himself willing to concede error or shortcoming when necessary. In fact, he consistently found opportunities to turn such failures to his advantage, as the Bay of Pigs case demonstrates.

Did Kennedy conceive of Cold War "credibility" as indivisible? Did he believe that in the great game of containment a loss or concession in one geopolitical contest would doom him in another? If Kennedy held such beliefs then he would not have privately agreed to remove the Jupiter missiles from Turkey to resolve the Cuban missile crisis—a covert trade with the Soviet Union that hardly seems the act of a credibility absolutist. To the contrary, Kennedy's public victory in the missile crisis gave him a surfeit of political credibility both at home and abroad—credibility that Lyndon Johnson had never earned and that could have been drawn upon by Kennedy on a different course in Vietnam. Once again, Kennedy's prior record is instructive. When in November 1961 Bundy essentially demanded an affirmative decision to deploy combat forces to Vietnam because that commitment had become a "touchstone of our will" and an emblem of U.S. credibility, Kennedy the realist rejected his national security adviser's counsel.[49]

Could Kennedy survive the likely attacks from Republicans if South Vietnam fell under communist rule? As Bundy argued, Kennedy would have wielded significant political capital to mitigate the costs of a loss in Vietnam. Assuming that he would have run against Senator Barry Goldwater in the 1964 election—and assuming, as Bundy did, that he would have maintained the status quo in Vietnam during an election campaign—1965 would then have been a year of great political advantage and opportunity.

Kennedy, like Johnson, would have defeated his opponent by a significant margin, routing a Republican who was far to the right of the country's political consensus. Kennedy, like Johnson, would have controlled comfortable majorities in the House and Senate. But unlike Johnson, Kennedy would not have entered his term with an ambitious domestic agenda of Great Society initiatives for which he would have required Republican support. Unlike Johnson, Kennedy would be in his second full term, invulnerable to an electorate he would never again face. Unlike Johnson, Kennedy would be, as Bundy called him, "the champion of the missile crisis," a president with significant stature in the realm of foreign affairs. Kennedy would be in a position to rely on his repeated insistence that the war was a Vietnamese enterprise—always theirs to fight and win.

This was Kennedy's message to Taylor and Rostow on the eve of their 1961 mission; it was also the bottom line he repeated to Walter Cronkite in a nationally televised interview in September 1963, when he said, "In the final analysis it is the people and the [South Vietnamese] government itself who have to win or lose the struggle. All we can do is help."[50] If a faltering South Vietnam could not prosecute the war successfully, Kennedy could legitimately argue that the United States should not shoulder the burden for them. And even though Kennedy also told Cronkite, "I don't agree with those who say we should withdraw," and reaffirmed the American commitment to assist the Saigon regime, it is also the case that six weeks later he announced the withdrawal of the first one thousand U.S. advisers from South Vietnam.[51]

Finally, could Kennedy manage his own administration and ameliorate potentially sharp internal resistance from his advisers to a policy that might result in the loss of South Vietnam? The answer appears obvious. If in 1961 an isolated and encircled Kennedy, still wobbling from the humiliation of the Bay of Pigs, could overrule McNamara, Bundy, Taylor, Rostow, the Joint Chiefs, and his other advisers on the question of combat troops to Vietnam, then it follows that in 1965 Kennedy could certainly do so again. McNamara, who reversed his support for combat troop deployments in 1961 and lobbied aggressively for an extrication scenario in late 1963, would likely have supported the president's same effort in 1965. According to the historian Howard Jones, in a second Kennedy term the president planned to replace Secretary of State Dean Rusk with Robert McNamara, for the purpose of devolving Washington's commitment to Saigon. Jones cites as his source John Kenneth Galbraith, the president's confidant on the question of Vietnam. McNamara has also said that Robert Kennedy asked him to move to the State Department in a second term.[52] While it can be assumed that Bundy would have recommended combat troop deployments to Kennedy in 1965 just as he did to Johnson, it can also be assumed that Kennedy, confident in his contrary view, would have rejected Bundy's proposal—just as he rejected Bundy's counsel in the Cuban missile crisis. Perhaps more than any other single episode in the Kennedy presidency, the missile crisis makes it abundantly clear that as commander in chief Kennedy would have no reservations about rejecting the advice of any influential player in his national security bureaucracy.

*

With his conclusion that Kennedy would not have reversed his 1961 decision prohibiting the deployment of ground combat forces, Bundy joined other former administration officials who came to believe that Kennedy was determined not to Americanize the Vietnam War. That conjecture was shared most notably by Robert McNamara, who said in his 1995 memoir, "Having reviewed the record in detail, and with the advantage of hindsight, I think it highly probable that, had President Kennedy lived, he would have pulled us out of Vietnam. I think he would have come to this conclusion even if he reasoned, as I believe he would have, that South Vietnam and, ultimately, Southeast Asia would then be lost to Communism."[53] This view was also held by the historian and Kennedy adviser

Arthur M. Schlesinger Jr., who wrote, "Kennedy had no intention of dispatching American ground troops to save South Vietnam." Bundy called Schlesinger's conclusion "*correct* and *crucial*."[54]

In the weeks before he died, Bundy continued to develop aspects of his thesis about Kennedy and Vietnam in conversations with colleagues who were also immersed in the study of the war's complex history. As noted previously, he engaged in spirited weekend arguments with his brother Bill, who had, of course, served with him through the pivotal Vietnam decisions and was himself an accomplished historian. This was a shift from prior decades, when the former national security adviser had reflected a rigid determinism about the Johnson administration's path to Americanization. In a 1969 letter to his brother, Mac Bundy said the United States had acted out of necessity: "There had to be a war," he wrote.[55] But by 1995 and 1996 his perspective had changed, and he strongly argued that resourceful presidential leadership in a second Kennedy term could have defined a different fate for the United States.

"The missile crisis gave Kennedy more than enough room to maneuver his way out of South Vietnam," Bundy told James Blight and Janet Lang of Brown University in August 1996. "By 1963, the Bay of Pigs was a long way behind him. He had proved himself, in the eyes of the allies and the American people. In a second Kennedy Administration, the U.S. advisers would have been withdrawn and Kennedy would have endeavored to justify it just as he had all along—it's not our war, it's their war. If South Vietnam can't win it, we can't win it for them."[56] Bundy and I discussed the same theme on September 11, 1996, five days before he died.

As Bundy argued, Kennedy was consistent in his conviction that the United States could not fight the war on behalf of the Saigon regime. "The best evidence we have on that," he said, was the president's September 1963 interview with Walter Cronkite, in which Kennedy insisted, "In the final analysis it is their war." Bundy emphasized that this was "not an inherited view" from the Eisenhower administration, but rather Kennedy's personal conclusion stemming from "his own study of the third world and his own intellectual exposure to the forces at work in newly independent countries."[57] Bundy noted that the president reiterated his position in a press conference about ten days after the Cronkite interview. "Kennedy said it in about the same way but a little more sharply: 'We have a very simple policy in that area. . . . In some ways I think the Vietnamese people and ourselves agree. We want the war to be won, the Communists contained and the Americans to go home. That is our policy.' "[58] Bundy also speculated that in a second term Kennedy would have engineered another major shift in America's Asia strategy—one that Richard Nixon ultimately consummated—the normalization of relations with communist China. Bundy recalled discussing the question with Kennedy while traveling overseas with him, part of an "informal process" of designating "which subjects were second-term business. The one that sticks in my head is the opening to China."[59]

In the pursuit of a deeper understanding about America and the Vietnam War, Bundy focused on the power of presidential leadership. "We should pay attention to the leaders, and not get lost in the maze of memos authored by the assistants, such as himself," Blight and Lang remembered Bundy saying. "He is convinced that the Vietnam war cannot be understood apart from an understanding of Lyndon Johnson—a deep understanding—and the ways he differed from Kennedy," Blight observed.[60]

Among those differences, Bundy told me, was the far greater confidence Kennedy had in his own judgment and his record of achievement thwarting communist ambitions in West Berlin and Cuba as well as neutralizing Laos. There were other critical differences. "Kennedy didn't have a legislative agenda anything like the length and strength of what Lyndon Johnson generated," said Bundy.[61] And Kennedy would not have pursued the same opportunistic electoral and congressional gambits that were so compelling to Johnson. "There *never* would have been a Gulf of Tonkin" legislative action undertaken by Kennedy, Bundy insisted. "He didn't want a resolution that told him to make war."[62] He pointedly asked whether President Kennedy, who in a second term "had finished the electoral course and was free to make his own judgments . . . [would] have wanted a half million men in Vietnam."[63] His conclusion was clear: "I think he would not have expanded the war. He would have found a way to negotiate it. He would not have a U.S. ground war."[64]

On questions of war and peace, Bundy observed about five weeks before he died, Kennedy "does not have to fear any man as a greater authority." In contrast to Johnson, a reelected Kennedy would have approached the decisions of 1965 as a successful national security leader without a grand liberal domestic agenda or the 1968 election ahead of him and with formidable global accomplishments behind him. "So he does not have to prove himself in Vietnam," Bundy wrote. "He can cut the country's losses then. He can do it by refusing to make it an American war."[65] In our extensive discussions and in his draft fragments, Bundy argued that the Vietnam War could have been averted by President Kennedy's determined choice.

This is perhaps the most important lesson that we can derive from a great disaster. To his enduring credit and despite his own self-proclaimed failures of advice and counsel, Bundy's retrospective struggle to understand the path to war in Vietnam may help current and future generations better understand the indispensable centrality of the commander in chief's leadership. As Bundy's final reflections on Vietnam illuminate, intervention is a presidential choice, not an inevitability.

NOTES

INTRODUCTION: LEGEND OF THE ESTABLISHMENT

1. Author's notes of Gordon Goldstein interview with McGeorge Bundy, September 11, 1996.
2. John Kifner, "McGeorge Bundy Dies at 77; Top Adviser in Vietnam Era," *New York Times*, September 17, 1996.
3. Walter Isaacson, "The Best and the Brightest: McGeorge Bundy, 1919–1996," *Time*, September 30, 1996.
4. Kai Bird, *The Color of Truth: McGeorge Bundy and William Bundy, Brothers in Arms* (New York: Simon and Schuster, 1998), p. 403.
5. Ibid., p. 405.
6. These works include David M. Barrett, *Uncertain Warriors: Lyndon Johnson and His Vietnam Advisers* (Lawrence: University Press of Kansas, 1993); Larry Berman, *Lyndon Johnson's War: The Road to Stalemate in Vietnam* (New York: W. W. Norton, 1989) and *Planning a Tragedy: The Americanization of the War in Vietnam* (New York: W. W. Norton, 1982); Lloyd C. Gardner, *Pay Any Price: Lyndon Johnson and the Wars for Vietnam* (Chicago: Ivan R. Dee, 1995); Leslie H. Gelb and Richard K. Betts, *The Irony of Vietnam: The System Worked* (Washington, D.C.: Brookings Institution Press, 1979); Doris Kearns Goodwin, *Lyndon Johnson and the American Dream* (New York: St. Martin's Press, 1976 and 1991); George C. Herring, *America's*

Longest War: The United States and Vietnam, 1950–1975, 3rd ed. (New York: McGraw Hill, 1996); Stanley Karnow, *Vietnam: A History* (New York: Viking, 1983); Neil Sheehan, *A Bright Shining Lie: John Paul Vann and America in Vietnam* (New York: Random House, 1988); Brian VanDeMark, *Into the Quagmire: Lyndon Johnson and the Escalation of the Vietnam War* (New York: Oxford University Press, 1991); and Marilyn B. Young, *The Vietnam Wars: 1945–1990* (New York: HarperCollins, 1991).

7. Andrew Preston, *The War Council: McGeorge Bundy, the NSC, and Vietnam* (Cambridge, Mass.: Harvard University Press, 2006). The Cold War context myth, Preston notes, should be attributed to Ernest R. May, *Lessons of the Past: The Use and Misuse of History in American Foreign Policy* (New York: Oxford University Press, 1973).

8. Bird, *Color of Truth*, p. 407.

9. James C. Thomson Jr., "A Memory of McGeorge Bundy," *New York Times*, September 22, 1996.

10. Arthur M. Schlesinger Jr., "A Man Called Mac," *George*, December 1996.

11. "JFK's McGeorge Bundy—Cool Head for Any Crisis," *Newsweek*, March 4, 1963, p. 21.

12. Bird, *Color of Truth*, p. 34.

13. Ibid., p. 36.

14. Ibid., p. 52.

15. Ibid., pp. 43–45.

16. David Halberstam, "The Very Expensive Education of McGeorge Bundy," *Harper's*, July 1969, p. 25. See also "JFK's McGeorge Bundy," p. 21.

17. Halberstam, "Very Expensive Education," p. 25; and David Halberstam, *The Best and the Brightest* (New York: Random House, 1972), p. 52.

18. Bird, *Color of Truth*, p. 59.

19. Halberstam, "Very Expensive Education," p. 25.

20. On Bundy's portentous Skull and Bones moniker, see Alexandra Robbins, *Secrets of the Tomb: Skull and Bones, the Ivy League, and the Hidden Paths of Power* (Boston: Little, Brown, 2002), p. 127, cited in Preston, *War Council*, p. 2.

21. "JFK's McGeorge Bundy," p. 22.

22. Bird, *Color of Truth*, p. 96.

23. Ibid., pp. 100–101.

24. Gordon Goldstein interview with McGeorge Bundy, November 21, 1995, p. 26.

25. Gordon Goldstein interview with McGeorge Bundy, December 5, 1995, p. 21.

26. Ibid., p. 23.

27. Bird, *Color of Truth*, p. 106.

28. Gordon Goldstein interview with McGeorge Bundy, September 19, 1995, p. 31.

29. Bird, *Color of Truth*, pp. 107–8.

30. Halberstam, *Best and the Brightest*, pp. 56–57.

31. McGeorge Bundy, ed., *The Pattern of Responsibility: From the Record of Dean Acheson* (Boston: Houghton Mifflin, 1951), p. xiii.

32. Ibid., p. viii.

33. "JFK's McGeorge Bundy," p. 22.

34. Halberstam, *Best and the Brightest*, p. 58.

35. Henry Kissinger, *White House Years* (Boston: Little, Brown, 1979), pp. 13–14.

36. Bird, *Color of Truth*, p. 146.

37. "JFK's McGeorge Bundy," p. 20.

38. Max Frankel, "The Importance of Being Bundy," *New York Times Magazine*, March 28, 1965, p. 32.

39. Halberstam, "Very Expensive Education," p. 22.

40. Ibid.

41. "The Use of Power with a Passion for Peace," *Time*, June 25, 1965, pp. 26–27.

42. Preston, *War Council*, p. 30.

43. "Use of Power," pp. 26–27.

44. Ibid., p. 28.

45. F. Champion Ward, David E. Bell, Harold Howe II, Marshall Robinson, and Mitchell Sviridoff, letter to the editor, *New York Times*, September 30, 1996.

46. Halberstam, "Very Expensive Education," p. 22.

47. "Vietnam: Bundy and Hoffman," WGBH broadcast transcript, March 14, 1968, pp. 2–3.

48. Bird, *Color of Truth*, p. 399.

49. Ibid., p. 397.

50. McGeorge Bundy, "American Policy and Politics: Examples from Southeast Asia," speech at Council on Foreign Relations, New York, 1971, pp. 1, 5.

51. Ibid., p. 2.

52. Ibid., p. 7.

53. Ibid., p. 18.

54. Ibid., p. 19.

55. Ibid., pp. 13–14.

56. Bird, *Color of Truth*, pp. 401–2; and Thomson, "Memory of McGeorge Bundy."

57. David Talbot, "And Now They Are Doves," *Mother Jones*, May 1984, p. 33, cited in Bird, *Color of Truth*, p. 403.

58. Robert S. McNamara with Brian VanDeMark, *In Retrospect: The Tragedy and Lessons of Vietnam* (New York: Times Books, 1995), p. xx.

59. "Mr. McNamara's War," *New York Times*, April 12, 1995.

60. B. Drummond Ayres Jr., "Belated Regrets About Vietnam Create a Consensus of Antipathy," *New York Times*, April 15, 1995.

61. Mary McGrory, "Too Late," *Washington Post*, April 13, 1995.

62. Townsend Hoopes, "Robert McNamara's 'Mea Culpa,'" *Washington Post*, April 27, 1995.

63. Richard Cohen, "McNamara: Better Late Than Never," *Washington Post*, April 13, 1995.

64. Jonathan Alter, "Confessing the Sins of Vietnam," *Newsweek*, April 17, 1995.

65. McGeorge Bundy to Robert S. McNamara, March 3, 1994.

66. McGeorge Bundy to Robert S. McNamara, March 25, 1994.

67. McGeorge Bundy to Robert S. McNamara, February 8, 1995, and February 14, 1995.

68. *MacNeil/Lehrer NewsHour*, April 17, 1995.

69. "Papers of McGeorge Bundy, JFK's National Security Adviser, Donated to the John F. Kennedy Presidential Library," press release, John F. Kennedy Presidential Library & Museum, July 23, 2004.

70. Bundy Fragment, January 29, 1996. (Most of the Bundy Fragments were given numbers by Georganne V. Brown, who worked with McGeorge Bundy at the Carnegie Corporation. Some of the Fragments have a title, others are identified only by date and there are a few Fragments without a number, title, or date.)

71. Bundy Fragment No. 99, First Draft Introduction.

72. Bundy Fragment No. 99, Second Draft Introduction.

73. Bundy Fragment No. 99, Third Draft Introduction.

74. Bundy Fragment No. 99, Second Draft Introduction.

75. An alphabetical list of former policy makers who have written about Vietnam would include George W. Ball, *The Past Has Another Pattern: Memoirs* (New York: W. W. Norton, 1982); Clark Clifford with Richard Holbrooke, *Counsel to the President: A Memoir* (New York: Random House, 1991); Lyndon B. Johnson, *The Vantage Point: Perspectives of the Presidency 1963–1969* (New York: Holt, Rinehart and Winston, 1971); Henry Kissinger, *The White House Years* (Boston: Little, Brown, 1979); Henry Cabot Lodge, *As It Was: An Inside View of Politics and Power in the '50s and '60s,* (New York: W. W. Norton, 1976); Robert S. McNamara with Brian VanDeMark, *In Retrospect: The Tragedy and Lessons of Vietnam* (New York: Times Books, 1995); Richard Nixon, *RN: The Memoirs of Richard Nixon* (New York: Grosset & Dunlap, 1978); W. W. Rostow, *The Diffusion of Power: An Essay in Recent History* (New York: Macmillan, 1972); Dean Rusk, as told to Richard Rusk, *As I Saw It*, ed. Daniel S. Papp (New York: W. W. Norton, 1990); Maxwell D. Taylor, *Swords and Plowshares* (New York: W. W. Norton, 1972); William C. Westmoreland, *A Soldier Reports* (Garden City, N.Y.: Doubleday, 1976).

76. Bundy Fragment No. 99, Second Draft Introduction.

77. Gordon Goldstein interview with McGeorge Bundy, January 17, 1996, p. 15.

78. Gordon Goldstein interview with McGeorge Bundy, September 19, 1995, p. 20.

LESSON ONE: **COUNSELORS ADVISE BUT PRESIDENTS DECIDE**

1. Gordon Goldstein interview with McGeorge Bundy, November 28, 1995, pp. 28, 30.

2. Bundy Fragment No. 86.

3. Bundy Fragment No. 94.

4. Ibid.

5. Bundy Fragment No. 99, Fourth Draft Introduction.

6. Ibid.

7. Ibid.

8. Gordon Goldstein interview with McGeorge Bundy, November 21, 1995, p. 29; and Bundy Fragment No. 99, Fourth Draft Introduction.

9. Arthur M. Schlesinger Jr., *Journals: 1952–2000*, ed. Andrew Schlesinger and Stephen Schlesinger (New York: Penguin Press, 2007), p. 101.

10. Gordon Goldstein interview with McGeorge Bundy, January 17, 1996, p. 21.

11. Bundy Fragment No. 93.

12. Theodore C. Sorensen, *Kennedy* (New York: Harper and Row, 1965), p. 253.

13. Bundy Fragment No. 93.

14. Ibid.

15. Halberstam, *Best and the Brightest*, p. 60.

16. Ibid., p. 59; and Bird, *Color of Truth*, p. 153.

17. David Talbot, *Brothers* (New York: Free Press, 2007), p. 44.

18. Bird, *Color of Truth*, pp. 194–95; and Piero Gleijeses, "Ships in the Night: The CIA, the White House and the Bay of Pigs," *Journal of Latin American Studies* 27 (February 1995): pp. 37–42.

19. Michael R. Beschloss, *The Crisis Years: Kennedy and Khrushchev, 1960–1963* (New York: Edward Burlingame Books/HarperCollins, 1991), pp. 104–5.

20. Richard Reeves, *President Kennedy: Profile in Power* (New York: Simon and Schuster, 1993), p. 70.

21. Bird, *Color of Truth*, pp. 196–97.

22. Richard N. Goodwin, *Remembering America: A Voice from the Sixties* (Boston: Little, Brown, 1988), pp. 176–77, cited in Preston, *War Council*, p. 64.

23. Beschloss, *Crisis Years*, p. 106.

24. Schlesinger, *Journals*, p. 109.

25. Preston, *War Council*, p. 75.

26. Gordon Goldstein interview with McGeorge Bundy, September 22, 1995, pp. 2–3. For a study of Rostow in power, see David Milne, *America's Rasputin: Walt Rostow and the Vietnam War* (New York: Farrar, Straus and Giroux, 2008).

27. McNamara with VanDeMark, *In Retrospect*, p. 26.

28. Talbot, *Brothers*, p. 45.

29. Ibid.

30. Ibid., pp. 46–47.

31. Robert Dallek, *An Unfinished Life: John F. Kennedy, 1917–1963* (New York: Little, Brown, 2003), p. 364.

32. Bundy Fragment No. 91. See also Richard M. Bissell Jr. with Jonathan E. Lewis and Frances T. Pudlo, *Reflections of a Cold Warrior: From Yalta to the Bay of Pigs* (New Haven: Yale University Press, 1996), pp. 152–205. "To my great disappointment," Bissell wrote, "especially in light of the serious consequences of defeat, Kennedy would not allow the Navy to provide full air support" (ibid., p. 189).

33. Gordon Goldstein interview with McGeorge Bundy, November 28, 1995, p. 8.

34. Kenneth P. O'Donnell and David F. Powers with Joe McCarthy, *"Johnny, We Hardly Knew Ye": Memories of John Fitzgerald Kennedy* (New York: Pocket Books, 1972), p. 274, quoted in Talbot, *Brothers*, p. 47.

35. Talbot, *Brothers*, p. 47.
36. Bird, *Color of Truth*, p. 197.
37. Talbot, *Brothers*, p. 51.
38. Schlesinger, *Journals*, pp. 112–13.
39. Transcribed from handwritten duplicate copy from the 1961 Staff Memoranda series of the President's Office Files of the Presidential Papers of John F. Kennedy, February 7, 1974, John F. Kennedy Presidential Library, Boston, Mass.
40. McGeorge Bundy, "Some Preliminary Administrative Lessons of the Cuban Experience," April 24, 1961, courtesy of the National Security Archive, George Washington University. The author wishes to thank Professor James Blight for suggesting this citation. In another memo to the president following the Bay of Pigs, Bundy complained to Kennedy: "We can't get you to sit still. . . . The National Security Council . . . really cannot work for you unless you authorize work schedules that do not get upset from day to day." See Bundy memo to JFK, May 16, 1961, NSF Box 287-290, JFK Library, cited in Reeves, *President Kennedy*, pp. 113–14.
41. National Security Action Memorandum 55 ended exclusive CIA authority for the planning and execution of covert action operations. Presidential Directives on National Security from Truman to Clinton, NSDDINDEX Record no. 183, p. 1, cited in Richard H. Shultz Jr., *The Secret War Against Hanoi: Kennedy's and Johnson's Use of Spies, Saboteurs, and Covert Warriors in North Vietnam* (New York: HarperCollins, 1999), p. 358 n. 50.
42. Bundy Fragment No. 91.
43. Gordon Goldstein interview with McGeorge Bundy, January 17, 1996, p. 30.
44. Ibid.
45. Bundy Fragment No. 86.
46. Gordon Goldstein interview with McGeorge Bundy, January 17, 1996, p. 24.
47. Ibid., p. 31.
48. Neustadt-Bundy Oral History (1964), p. 88.
49. Schlesinger, *Journals*, p. 111.
50. Neustadt-Bundy Oral History (1964), p. 27.
51. Bundy Fragment No. 86.
52. Clifford with Holbrooke, *Counsel to the President*, p. 343. A memorandum by Clifford summarizing the meeting is reprinted in *The Pentagon Papers: The Defense Department History of United States Decisionmaking on Vietnam*, Senator Gravel edition, vol. 2 (Boston: Beacon Press, 1971–72), pp. 635–37.
53. Neustadt-Bundy Oral History (1964), p. 136.
54. Walter Isaacson and Evan Thomas, *The Wise Men: Six Friends and the World They Made* (New York: Simon and Schuster, 1986), p. 618.
55. *Pentagon Papers*, vol. 2, p. 42.
56. Telegram from the Department of State to Secretary of State Rusk, April 27, 1961, in *Foreign Relations of the United States, 1961–1963*, vol. 24, *Laos Crisis* (Washington: U.S. Government Printing Office, 1994), p. 147.

57. Bundy Fragment No. 94.

58. Arthur M. Schlesinger Jr., *A Thousand Days: John F. Kennedy in the White House* (Boston: Houghton Mifflin, 1965), p. 337.

59. Sorensen, *Kennedy*, pp. 644–45. See also notes on the 481st National Security Council Meeting, May 1, 1961, 4:10–6 p.m., in *FRUS 1961–63*, vol. 24, *Laos Crisis*, pp. 162–64.

60. Schlesinger, *Thousand Days*, p. 339. Sorensen reports that the president expressed the same view to him in September 1961. See Sorensen, *Kennedy*, p. 644. In a memorandum for the record dictated on June 1, 1961, the president's brother, Attorney General Robert Kennedy, observed: "I don't think there is any question that if it hadn't been for Cuba, we would have sent troops to Laos. We probably would have had them destroyed. Jack has said so himself." Robert F. Kennedy, memorandum dictated June 1, 1961, 3, Robert F. Kennedy Papers, cited in Arthur M. Schlesinger Jr., *Robert Kennedy and His Times* (Boston: Houghton Mifflin, 1978), p. 702 n. 7, and p. 999.

61. Bundy Fragment No. 94.

62. Neustadt-Bundy Oral History (1964), p. 136.

63. Herring, *America's Longest War*, p. 4.

64. Ibid., p. 25 and pp. 2–46. See also John P. Burke and Fred I. Greenstein, with the collaboration of Larry Berman and Richard Immerman, *How Presidents Test Reality: Decisions on Vietnam, 1954 and 1965* (New York: Russell Sage Foundation, 1989), p. 29.

65. Peter MacDonald, *Giap: The Victor in Vietnam* (New York: W. W. Norton, 1993), p. 80.

66. Ibid., p. 82.

67. Memorandum of Discussion of the 179th Meeting of the National Security Council, January 8, 1954, *Foreign Relations of the United States, 1952–1954*, vol. 13, *Indochina, Part 1*, pp. 947–55, cited in Burke and Greenstein, *How Presidents Test Reality*, pp. 31–32.

68. George Lardner Jr., "Tapes Show Eisenhower Resisted Vietnam Buildup," *International Herald Tribune*, June 17, 1997.

69. MacDonald, *Giap*, p. 134.

70. Cited in A. J. Langguth, *Our Vietnam: The War, 1954–1975* (New York: Simon and Schuster, 2000), p. 96.

71. Reeves, *President Kennedy*, p. 254.

72. *Congressional Record*, January 8, 1952, p. HR-5879, cited in Reeves, *President Kennedy*, pp. 254, 700.

73. Langguth, *Our Vietnam*, pp. 99–100. See also Brian VanDeMark, *Into the Quagmire: Lyndon Johnson and the Escalation of the Vietnam War* (New York: Oxford University Press, 1991), pp. 4–7.

74. See Lansdale's U.S. Air Force biography at http://www.af.mil/bios/bio.asp?bioID=6141.

75. Editorial Note, *Foreign Relations of the United States, 1961–1963*, vol. 1, *Vietnam 1961* (Washington: U.S. Government Printing Office, 1988), p. 12.

76. Paper Prepared by the Country Team Staff Committee, January 4, 1961, in *FRUS 1961–63*, vol. 1, *Vietnam 1961*, p. 6.

77. Summary Record of a Meeting, the White House, January 28, 1961, in *FRUS 1961–63*, vol. 1, *Vietnam 1961*, p. 14.

78. Memorandum from the President's Deputy Special Assistant for National Security Affairs to the President's Special Assistant for National Security Affairs, January 30, 1961, in *FRUS 1961–63*, vol. 1, *Vietnam 1961*, p. 17.

79. See Summary Record of a Meeting, the White House, January 28, 1961, in *FRUS 1961–63*, vol. 1, *Vietnam 1961*, p. 15 and National Security Action Memorandum no. 12, February 6, 1961, in ibid., p. 29. Despite the president's emphasis on making the South Vietnamese forces more effective, some of Kennedy's advisers, such as Walt Rostow, continued to push for a larger American role in countering the insurgency. See David Kaiser, *American Tragedy: Kennedy, Johnson, and the Origins of the Vietnam War* (Cambridge, Mass.: Harvard University Press, 2000), pp. 69–71.

80. Bundy Fragment No. 94.

81. Editorial Note, *FRUS 1961–63*, vol. 1, *Vietnam 1961*, p. 74.

82. "A Program of Action to Prevent Communist Domination of South Vietnam," in *FRUS 1961–63*, vol. 1, *Vietnam 1961*, pp. 93, 97.

83. Bundy Fragment No. 28.

84. *Pentagon Papers*, vol. 2, p. 2. In response to the Gilpatric report, McGeorge Bundy joined in a memo drafted by Theodore C. Sorensen, the president's special counsel, and also representing the views of David E. Bell, the director of the Bureau of the Budget. The three officials urged President Kennedy to be cautious. "We need a more *realistic* look," they warned. ". . . There is no clearer example of a country that cannot be saved unless it saves itself." See Memorandum from the President's Special Counsel to the President, April 28, 1961, in *FRUS 1961–63*, vol. 1, *Vietnam 1961*, p. 84.

85. *Pentagon Papers*, vol. 2, p. 2. A subsequent draft of the Gilpatric report, dated May 3, 1961, "blurred, without wholly eliminating, the Defense-drafted recommendations for sending U.S. combat units to Vietnam and for public U.S. commitments to save South Vietnam from Communism" (ibid., p. 2).

86. The Joint Chiefs offered a generous list of purposes that would be served by dispatching combat forces to the region, including the creation of a "nucleus" of forces for "additional U.S. or SEATO military operations in Southeast Asia." See *Pentagon Papers*, vol. 2, pp. 48–49.

87. See *Pentagon Papers*, vol. 2, p. 49. See also National Security Action Memorandum no. 52, May 11, 1961, in *FRUS 1961–63*, vol. 1, *Vietnam 1961*, pp. 132–34.

88. *Pentagon Papers*, vol. 2, pp. 65–66.

89. Ibid., p. 66.

90. *FRUS 1961–63*, vol. 24, *Laos Crisis*, p. 134, cited in Kaiser, *American Tragedy*, p. 81 and n. 69. It appears that McNamara did not pass the memorandum on to President Kennedy.

91. Walt Rostow for Dean Rusk, July 13, 1961, JFK, NSF, VN, General, 7/5–7/13/61,

Box 193; and *FRUS 1961–63*, vol. 24, *Laos Crisis*, p. 134; cited in Kaiser, *American Tragedy*, p. 80.

92. Paper Prepared by the President's Military Representative, July 15, 1961, in *FRUS 1961–63*, vol. 1, *Vietnam 1961*, p. 224.

93. *FRUS 1961–63*, vol. 1, *Vietnam 1961*, p. 248.

94. Ibid., p. 254.

95. Ironically, in May 1961 Lyndon Johnson argued against the deployment of combat troops. "If the Vietnamese government backed by a three-year liberal aid program cannot do this job, then we had better remember the experience of the French who wound up with several hundred thousand men in Vietnam and were still unable to do it." Report by the Vice President, undated, in *FRUS 1961–63*, vol. 1, *Vietnam 1961*, p. 156.

96. *FRUS 1961–63*, vol. 1, *Vietnam 1961*, p. 254.

97. Memorandum for the Record by the Deputy Secretary of Defense, October 11, 1961, in *FRUS 1961–63*, vol. 1, *Vietnam 1961*, pp. 343–44.

98. *Pentagon Papers*, vol. 2, p. 81.

99. The editors of the *Pentagon Papers* determined that a press report so authoritative in its conclusions could only come from one source. "It is just about inconceivable that this story could have been given out except at the direction of the President, or by him personally." *Pentagon Papers*, vol. 2, p. 82.

100. Telegram from the Embassy in Vietnam to the Department of State, October 16, 1961, in *FRUS 1961–63*, vol. 1, *Vietnam 1961*, p. 383.

101. *Pentagon Papers*, vol. 2, p. 84.

102. Telegram from the Embassy in Vietnam to the Department of State, October 20, 1961, in *FRUS 1961–63*, vol. 1, *Vietnam 1961*, p. 406.

103. Telegram from the President's Military Representative to the Department of State, October 25, 1961, in *FRUS 1961–63*, vol. 1, *Vietnam 1961*, p. 430.

104. Telegram from the President's Special Assistant for National Security Affairs to the President's Military Representative, October 28, 1961, in *FRUS 1961–63*, vol. 1, *Vietnam 1961*, p. 443.

105. Telegram from the Embassy in Vietnam to the Department of State, October 31, 1961, in *FRUS 1961–63*, vol. 1, *Vietnam 1961*, p. 456.

106. Memorandum from Senator Mansfield to the President, in *FRUS 1961–63*, vol. 1, *Vietnam 1961*, p. 467.

107. Paper Prepared by the President's Military Representative, in *FRUS 1961–63*, vol. 1, *Vietnam 1961*, p. 481. See also Letter from the President's Military Representative to the President, November 3, 1961, in ibid., p. 478.

108. Paper Prepared by the President's Military Representative, in *FRUS 1961–63*, vol. 1, *Vietnam 1961*, p. 501.

109. Memorandum for the Record, November 6, 1961, in *FRUS 1961–63*, vol. 1, *Vietnam 1961*, p. 533. The editors of *Foreign Relations of the United States* speculate that although the meeting was held November 4, the notes of it were not composed until two days later.

110. *Pentagon Papers*, vol. 2, p. 102.

111. Draft Memorandum from the Secretary of Defense to the President, November 5, 1961, in *FRUS 1961–1963*, vol. 1, *Vietnam 1961*, p. 539.

112. Ibid., p. 538.

113. Notes by the Secretary of Defense, November 6, 1961, in *FRUS 1961–63*, vol. 1., *Vietnam 1961*, p. 543.

114. Draft Memorandum from the Secretary of State to the President, November 7, 1961, in *FRUS 1961–63*, vol. 1, *Vietnam 1961*, pp. 550–52.

115. Draft Memorandum for the President, November 8, 1961, in *FRUS 1961–63*, vol. 1, *Vietnam 1961*, p. 561.

116. Richard Parker, *John Kenneth Galbraith: His Life, His Politics, His Economics* (New York: Farrar, Straus and Giroux, 2005), pp. 364–65.

117. John Kenneth Galbraith, *Ambassador's Journal: A Personal Account of the Kennedy Years* (Boston: Houghton Mifflin, 1969), p. 243, cited in Preston, *War Council*, p. 94.

118. John Kenneth Galbraith to John F. Kennedy, October 9, 1961, cited in Parker, *John Kenneth Galbraith*, p. 370.

119. Ball, *Past Has Another Pattern*, p. 366.

120. Ibid., p. 367.

121. Bundy Fragment No. 28.

122. Memorandum from the President's Special Assistant for National Security Affairs to the President, November 15, 1961, in *FRUS 1961–63*, vol. 1., *Vietnam 1961*, pp. 605–7.

123. Schlesinger, *Thousand Days*, p. 547.

124. There were a few midlevel advisers who did not join the consensus among the administration's top officials. See Preston, *War Council*, p. 95 and p. 271 notes 58 and 59.

125. Gelb and Betts, *Irony of Vietnam*, pp. 76–77. See also Preston, *War Council*, p. 96; and Rusk, *As I Saw It*, pp. 432–33. George Ball suggested that the secretary of state was predisposed to join with McNamara in revising their joint recommendation. "Dean Rusk, I knew, had serious reservations about the commitment of American combat forces. . . . But he did not want to get crosswise with McNamara." See Ball, *Past Has Another Pattern*, p. 368.

126. McNamara with VanDeMark, *In Retrospect*, pp. 38–39. Secretary of State Rusk's recollection of this period is sketchy. See Rusk, *As I Saw It*, p. 433.

127. See Robert L. Gallucci, *Neither Peace Nor Honor: The Politics of American Military Policy in Viet-Nam* (Baltimore: Johns Hopkins University Press, 1975), p. 24. See also Ball, *Past Has Another Pattern*, p. 368.

128. Gordon Goldstein interview with McGeorge Bundy, November 30, 1995, p. 34.

129. Neustadt-Bundy Oral History (1964), p. 56.

130. See Draft Memorandum for the President, November 8, 1961, in *FRUS 1961–63*, vol. 1, *Vietnam 1961*, p. 561.

131. Memorandum from the President's Deputy Special Assistant for National Security Affairs to the President, November 11, 1961, in *FRUS 1961–63*, vol. 1, *Vietnam 1961*, p. 575.

132. Notes of a Meeting, the White House, November 11, 1961, in *FRUS 1961–63*, vol. 1, *Vietnam 1961*, p. 577.

133. Lawrence Freedman, *Kennedy's Wars: Berlin, Cuba, Laos, and Vietnam* (New York: Oxford University Press, 2000), pp. 332–33.

134. Notes on the National Security Council Meeting, Washington, November 15, 1961, in *FRUS 1961–63*, vol. 1, *Vietnam 1961*, p. 608. The official culmination of the administration's deliberations was National Security Action Memorandum 111, drafted by Bundy and issued on November 22, 1961.

135. Talbot, *Brothers*, pp. 79–80.

136. Bundy Fragment No. 87.

137. Bundy Fragment No. 50.

138. Bundy Fragment No. 85.

139. James Blight, Vietnam Project File Memo, Watson Institute for International Studies, Brown University, August 28, 1996.

140. Ibid.

141. Gelb and Betts, *Irony of Vietnam*, p. 70.

142. Gordon Goldstein interview with McGeorge Bundy, November 28, 1995, p. 12.

143. See, for example, the description of "Operation Farm-Gate," in which American officers in civilian clothes would fly reconnaissance and attack missions over the jungle with South Vietnamese troops. Reeves, *President Kennedy*, p. 241.

144. Bundy Fragment No. 86.

LESSON TWO: **NEVER TRUST THE BUREAUCRACY TO GET IT RIGHT**

1. Bundy Fragment No. 66.

2. Memorandum for the Record of a Meeting with the President, Palm Beach, Florida, January 3, 1962, in *Foreign Relations of the United States, 1961–1963*, vol. 2, *Vietnam 1962* (Washington, D.C.: U.S. Government Printing Office, 1990), pp. 3–4.

3. The "strategic hamlet" program was originally developed by the British guerrilla war expert Sir Robert Thompson, as part of the successful counterinsurgency strategy tested in Malaya and the Philippines. For its application to South Vietnam see Roger Hilsman, *To Move a Nation* (Garden City, N.Y.: Doubleday, 1967), p. 432.

4. Herring, *America's Longest War*, p. 95.

5. Sheehan, *Bright Shining Lie*, pp. 262–64.

6. Langguth, *Our Vietnam*, pp. 201–2, and Kaiser, *American Tragedy*, pp. 180–84.

7. Ellen J. Hammer, *A Death in November: America in Vietnam, 1963* (New York: E. P. Dutton, 1987), p. 121.

8. Bird, *Color of Truth*, p. 227.

9. Ibid., p. 230.

10. Ibid., p. 232.

11. Ibid.

12. Ibid., p. 233.

13. Ibid., p. 234.

14. Gordon Goldstein interview with McGeorge Bundy, November 28, 1995, p. 18.

15. McNamara with VanDeMark, *In Retrospect*, p. 341.

16. Langguth, *Our Vietnam*, p. 211.

17. Malcolm Browne, *Muddy Boots and Red Socks: A War Reporter's Life* (New York: Times Books, 1994), pp. 9–11.

18. Clarence R. Wyatt, *Paper Soldiers: The American Press and the Vietnam War* (New York: W. W. Norton, 1993), p. 112.

19. McGeorge Bundy, Memorandum for the Record, October 20, 1963.

20. Langguth, *Our Vietnam*, pp. 205–6.

21. Bundy, Memorandum for the Record, October 20, 1963.

22. State Department Telegram 243, Ball to Lodge, August 24, 1963, in *Foreign Relations of the United States, 1961–1963*, vol. 3, *Vietnam, January–August 1963* (Washington, D.C.: U.S. Government Printing Office, 1991), pp. 628–29.

23. Gordon Goldstein interview with McGeorge Bundy, November 16, 1995, pp. 11–12.

24. Bundy, Memorandum for the Record, October 20, 1963.

25. CIA Saigon Station to Agency, August 26, 1963, in *FRUS 1961–63*, vol. 3, *Vietnam, January–August 1963*, p. 642.

26. Memorandum from the Director of the Bureau of Intelligence and Research to the Secretary of State, in *Foreign Relations of the United States, 1961–1963*, vol. 4, *Vietnam, August–December 1963* (Washington, D.C.: U.S. Government Printing Office, 1991), pp. 212–15.

27. Telegram from the White House to the Embassy in Vietnam, in *FRUS 1961–63*, vol. 4, *Vietnam, August–December 1963*, pp. 252–54.

28. Memorandum from the President to the Secretary of Defense, September 21, 1963, in *FRUS 1961–63*, vol. 4, *Vietnam, August–December 1963*, pp. 278–79.

29. Gordon Goldstein interview with McGeorge Bundy, December 5, 1995, p. 7.

30. McGeorge Bundy, Memorandum for the Record, dictated January 30, 1963.

31. Memorandum from the Chairman of the Joint Chiefs of Staff and the Secretary of Defense to the President, October 2, 1963, in *FRUS 1961–63*, vol. 4, *Vietnam, August–December 1963*, pp. 336–46. The quoted passages are on p. 338. For a discussion of the document's drafting, see William Conrad Gibbons, "Lyndon Johnson and the Legacy of Vietnam," in Lloyd C. Gardner and Ted Gittinger, eds., *Vietnam: The Early Decisions* (Austin: University of Texas Press, 1997), pp. 135–36.

32. For a recording and transcript of the October 2, 1963, White House morning meeting, see http://www.whitehousetapes.org/clips/1963_1002_vietnam_pm/index.htm.

33. According to the published transcript and audiotape, "we'll get a new date" is the unclear but likely way Kennedy completed his sentence.

34. Kennedy would be careful to avoid making the withdrawal a personal commitment of his own. According to the statement, "Secretary McNamara and General Taylor reported their judgment that the major part of the U.S. military task can be completed by the end of 1965, although there may be a continuing requirement for a

limited number of U.S. training personnel." Record of Action No. 2472, Taken at the 519th Meeting of the National Security Council, Washington, October 2, 1963, in *FRUS 1961–63*, vol. 4, *Vietnam, August–December 1963*, p. 353. As Secretary McNamara left the White House to meet the media, the president called after him, "And tell them that means all the helicopter pilots too." See O'Donnell and Powers with McCarthy, *"Johnny, We Hardly Knew Ye,"* p. 17.

35. McGeorge Bundy to William C. Gibbons, January 30, 1992, p. 1.

36. Transcript of John Newman interview with McGeorge Bundy, July 16, 1991, p. 9. See also John Newman, "The Kennedy-Johnson Transition: The Case for Policy Reversal," in Gardner and Gittinger, *Vietnam: The Early Decisions*, p. 165.

37. Deborah Shapley, *Promise and Power: The Life and Times of Robert McNamara* (New York: Little, Brown, 1993), p. 263. For a somewhat different view from Maxwell Taylor, then the chairman of the Joint Chiefs of Staff, see the Taylor interview with William Conrad Gibbons and Patricia McAdams cited in William Conrad Gibbons, "Lyndon Johnson and the Legacy of Vietnam," in Gardner and Gittinger, *Vietnam: The Early Decisions*, p. 153 n. 50.

38. National Security Action Memorandum No. 263, October 11, 1963, in *FRUS 1961–63*, vol. 4, *Vietnam, August–December 1963*, pp. 395–96.

39. Memorandum of a White House Staff Meeting, Washington, October 7, 1963, 8 a.m., in *FRUS 1961–63*, vol. 4, *Vietnam, August–December 1963* p. 387. The withdrawal provisions remain a subject of historical debate. For a skeptical analysis of Kennedy's decision, see Larry Berman, "NSAM 263 and NSAM 273: Manipulating History," in Gardner and Gittinger, *Vietnam: The Early Decisions*, pp. 177–200. For interpretations that observe the first steps of an extrication strategy, see Newman, "Kennedy-Johnson Transition," pp. 158–76.

40. Telegram from the President's Special Assistant for National Security Affairs to the Ambassador in Vietnam, in *FRUS 1961–63*, vol. 4, *Vietnam, August–December 1963*, p. 379.

41. McGeorge Bundy, Memorandum for the Record, October 24, 1963, 8:15 p.m.

42. McGeorge Bundy, Memorandum for the Record, dictated October 25, 1963, 7:25 p.m.

43. McGeorge Bundy, Memorandum for the Record, October 18, 1963.

44. Telegram from the President's Special Assistant for National Security Affairs to the Ambassador in Vietnam, October 29, 1963, 7:22 p.m., in *FRUS 1961–63*, vol. 4, *Vietnam, August–December 1963*, pp. 473–75.

45. Memorandum of Conference with the President, October 29, 1963, 4:20 p.m., JFKP: National Security File, Meetings and Memoranda Series, Box 317, Meetings on Vietnam, October 29, 1963, JFK Library. For a transcript of the meeting as well as an audio CD recording of it, see John Prados, *The White House Tapes: Eavesdropping on the President* (New York: Free Press, 2003).

46. Telegram from the Commander, Military Assistance Command, Vietnam to the Director of the National Security Agency, November 1, 1963, 2:24 p.m., in *FRUS 1961–63*, vol. 4, *Vietnam, August–December 1963*, p. 505.

47. Telegram from the Central Intelligence Agency Station in Saigon to the Director of the National Security Agency, November 1, 1963, 2:34 p.m., in *FRUS 1961–63*, vol. 4, *Vietnam, August–December 1963*, pp. 505–6.

48. Telegram from the Embassy in Vietnam to the Department of State, November 1, 1963, 3 p.m., in *FRUS 1961–63*, vol. 4, *Vietnam, August–December 1963*, pp. 506–7.

49. Telegram from the Embassy in Vietnam to the Department of State, November 1, 1963, 4 p.m., in *FRUS 1961–63*, vol. 4, *Vietnam, August–December 1963*, p. 510.

50. Telegram from the Central Intelligence Agency Station in Saigon to the Director of the National Security Agency, November 1, 1963, 5 p.m., in *FRUS 1961–63*, vol. 4, *Vietnam, August–December 1963*, p. 512.

51. Telegram from the Embassy in Vietnam to the Department of State, November 1, 1963, 6 p.m., in *FRUS 1961–63*, vol. 4, *Vietnam, August–December 1963*, p. 513.

52. Stephen Kinzer, *Overthrow: America's Century of Regime Change from Hawaii to Iraq* (New York: Times Books, 2006), p. 169.

53. Memorandum for the Record of Discussion at the Daily White House Staff Meeting, November 4, 1963, in *FRUS 1961–63*, vol. 4, *Vietnam, August–December 1963*, p. 556.

54. Kinzer, *Overthrow*, p. 169.

55. Kaiser, *American Tragedy*, pp. 276–77 and n. 86.

56. McGeorge Bundy, Memorandum for the Record, November 4, 1963, 8:10 a.m.

57. Ibid.

58. Ibid.

59. McGeorge Bundy, Memorandum for the Record, November 4, 1963, 7:20 p.m.

60. Ibid.

61. Ibid.

62. Neustadt-Bundy Oral History (1964), pp. 6–7.

63. NSF, NSAM File, NSAM 273, South Vietnam, Box 2, London Baines Johnson Library, Austin, Tex. Reproduced in Gibbons, "Lyndon Johnson and the Legacy of Vietnam," pp. 141–43, and p. 155 n. 67. According to the editors of the official State Department record, Bundy's draft National Security Action Memorandum "was almost identical to the final paper," which was issued on November 26, 1963. National Security Action Memorandum No. 273, November 26, 1963, in *FRUS 1961–63*, vol. 4, *Vietnam, August–December 1963*, p. 637 n. 1.

64. Memorandum for the Record of Discussion at the Daily White House Staff Meeting, November 22, 1963, in *FRUS 1961–63*, vol. 4, *Vietnam, August–December 1963*, pp. 625–26.

65. McGeorge Bundy, Memorandum for the Record, November 14, 1963, 7:30 p.m.

66. Robert Manning, "Development of a Vietnam Policy, 1952–1965," in Harrison Salisbury, ed., *Vietnam Reconsidered* (New York: Harper and Row, 1984), p. 43.

67. Bundy Fragment No. 73.

68. Ibid.

69. William J. Rust, *Kennedy in Vietnam* (New York: Da Capo Press and U.S News and World Report, Inc., 1985), p. 119; and Bird, *Color of Truth*, p. 254.

70. Gordon Goldstein interview with McGeorge Bundy, November 28, 1995, p. 25.

71. Gordon Goldstein interview with McGeorge Bundy, November 16, 1995, pp. 14–15.

72. Ibid., p. 15.

73. "American involvement in Vietnam," argues Lloyd C. Gardner, "was sealed by a decision in 1963 to intervene—against Ngo Dinh Diem, whose government had proven incapable of waging America's war in Vietnam." Gardner, *Pay Any Price*, p. 542.

74. Gordon Goldstein interview with McGeorge Bundy, December 5, 1995, p. 3.

75. *Public Papers of the Presidents of the United States: John F. Kennedy, 1963* (Washington, D.C.: U.S. Government Printing Office, 1964), pp. 846–48.

LESSON THREE: POLITICS IS THE ENEMY OF STRATEGY

1. Bundy Fragment No. 6.

2. Bundy Fragment No. 53.

3. Ibid.

4. Telephone conversation between Lyndon Johnson and McGeorge Bundy, March 4, 1964, 7:26 p.m., in Michael Beschloss, ed., *Taking Charge: The Johnson White House Tapes, 1963–1964* (New York: Simon and Schuster, 1997), pp. 266–67.

5. Gordon Goldstein interview with McGeorge Bundy, September 22, 1995, p. 30.

6. Bundy Fragment No. 71.

7. Gordon Goldstein interview with McGeorge Bundy, December 12, 1995, p. 14.

8. Bundy Fragment No. 53.

9. Moss-Bundy Oral History, January 12, 1972, pp. 24–25.

10. Bundy Fragment No. 71.

11. Ibid.

12. Ibid.

13. Gordon Goldstein interview with McGeorge Bundy, September 22, 1995, pp. 19–20.

14. McGeorge Bundy, Memorandum for the Record, December 16, 1963.

15. McGeorge Bundy, Memorandum for the Record, December 4, 1963.

16. McGeorge Bundy, Memorandum for the Record, December 5, 1963, 7:45 p.m. Johnson's remarks were drafted by Bundy, Bill Moyers, and Bromley Smith and were based on earlier remarks the president had delivered at a meeting of the National Security Council.

17. James Chace, *Acheson: The Secretary of State Who Created the American World* (New York: Simon and Schuster, 1998), p. 411.

18. McGeorge Bundy, Memorandum for the Record, December 7, 1963.

19. Telegram from the Department of State to the Embassy in Vietnam, December 6, 1963, in *FRUS 1961–63,* vol. 4, *Vietnam, August–December 1963,* p. 685.

20. See Memorandum for the Record of a Meeting, Executive Office Building, Washington, November 24, 1963, in *FRUS 1961–63*, vol. 4, *Vietnam, August–December 1963*, pp. 635–37.

21. Memorandum from Michael V. Forrestal of the National Security Council Staff to the President, Washington, December 11, 1963, in *FRUS 1961–63*, vol. 4, *Vietnam, August–December 1963*, p. 698.

22. Memorandum of a Telephone Conversation Between the Secretary of State and the Secretary of Defense, Washington, December 7, 1963, 12:40 p.m., in *FRUS 1961–63*, vol. 4, *Vietnam, August–December 1963*, p. 690.

23. McGeorge Bundy, Memorandum for the Record, December 21, 1963, 6:20 p.m.

24. Ibid.

25. Ibid.

26. Memorandum from the Secretary of Defense to the President, December 21, 1963, *FRUS 1961–63*, vol. 4, *Vietnam, August–December 1963*, pp. 732–33.

27. "It is abundantly clear," McCone informed Johnson, "that statistics received over the past year or more from the GVN officials and reported by the U.S. mission on which we gauged the trend of the war were grossly in error." See Letter from the Director of Central Intelligence to the President, December 23, 1963, in *FRUS 1961–63*, vol. 4, *Vietnam, August–December 1963*, p. 737.

28. See Editorial Note in *Foreign Relations of the United States, 1964–1968*, vol. 1, *Vietnam 1964* (Washington, D.C.: U.S. Government Printing Office, 1992), p. 35. See also *Pentagon Papers*, vol. 3, pp. 496–99.

29. Fredrik Logevall, *Choosing War: The Lost Chance for Peace and the Escalation of War in Vietnam* (Berkeley: University of California Press, 1999), p. 111.

30. David Nes to Henry Cabot Lodge, February 17, 1964, Box 1, Papers of David G. Nes, LBJ Library, cited in Logevall, *Choosing War*, p. 112.

31. Memorandum from the Joint Chiefs of Staff to the Secretary of Defense, March 2, 1964, in *FRUS 1964–68*, vol. 1, *Vietnam 1964*, pp. 112–18.

32. Telephone conversation between Lyndon Johnson and McGeorge Bundy, March 4, 1964, 7:26 p.m., in Beschloss, *Taking Charge*, pp. 266–67.

33. Walter Lippmann, *Washington Post*, February 4, 1964.

34. Logevall, *Choosing War*, pp. 84–85.

35. McGeorge Bundy to Lyndon Johnson, January 6, 1964, Box 1, National Security File, Memos to the President, LBJ Library; and McGeorge Bundy to Lyndon Johnson, January 9, 1964, Box 1, National Security File, Vietnam, LBJ Library.

36. Telephone conversation between Lyndon Johnson and McGeorge Bundy, February 6, 1964, 12:52 p.m., in Beschloss, *Taking Charge*, p. 226.

37. Logevall, *Choosing War*, pp. 130–31.

38. Ronald Steel, *Walter Lippmann and the American Century* (Boston: Little, Brown, 1980), pp. 549–50.

39. Walter Lippmann, *Washington Post*, May 21, 1964.

40. Telephone conversation between Lyndon Johnson and Richard Russell, May 27, 1964, in Beschloss, *Taking Charge*, pp. 363–70.

41. Telephone conversation between Lyndon Johnson and McGeorge Bundy, May 27, 1964, in Beschloss, *Taking Charge*, pp. 370–73.

42. Draft Memorandum from the President's Special Assistant for National Security Affairs to the President, May 25, 1964, in *FRUS 1964–68*, vol. 1, *Vietnam 1964*, pp. 374–77.

43. Telephone conversation between Lyndon Johnson and McGeorge Bundy, May 27, 1964, in Beschloss, *Taking Charge*, pp. 370–73.

44. Logevall, *Choosing War*, p. 143.

45. Draft Memorandum by the President's Special Assistant for National Security Affairs, June 10, 1964, in *FRUS 1964–68*, vol. 1, *Vietnam 1964*, pp. 493–96. The Bundy memorandum was discussed that day at a White House meeting. See Summary Record of a Meeting, White House, June 10, 1964, in ibid., pp. 487–93.

46. See Robert Dallek, *Flawed Giant: Lyndon Johnson and His Times, 1961–1973* (New York: Oxford University Press, 1998), p. 143. Dallek identifies the memo's author as William Bundy but according to *FRUS 1964–68*, vol. 1, *Vietnam 1964*, its author was McGeorge Bundy. See note 45 above.

47. Memorandum from the President's Special Assistant for National Security Affairs to the President, June 6, 1964 in *FRUS 1964–68*, vol. 1, *Vietnam 1964*, pp. 472–73.

48. McGeorge Bundy, Memorandum for the Record, December 16, 1963.

49. Gordon Goldstein interview with McGeorge Bundy, November 28, 1995, p. 2.

50. McGeorge Bundy, Memorandum for the Record, December 16, 1963.

51. Dallek, *Flawed Giant*, pp. 135–39.

52. Moss-Bundy Oral History, January 12, 1972, pp. 27–28.

53. McGeorge Bundy, "Notes on First Reading," memorandum to Lyndon Johnson, March 22, 1970, p. 10. Bundy wrote this memorandum for the benefit of Johnson and his collaborators assisting with the preparation of his memoir, *The Vantage Point*.

54. Moss-Bundy Oral History, January 12, 1972, p. 28.

55. See Jeff Shesol, *Mutual Contempt: Lyndon Johnson, Robert Kennedy, and the Feud That Defined a Decade* (New York: W.W. Norton, 1997).

56. Moss-Bundy Oral History, January 12, 1972, pp. 28–29.

57. Shesol, *Mutual Contempt*, pp. 202–3.

58. Ibid., p. 202.

59. Ibid., pp. 204–5, 207.

60. Moss-Bundy Oral History, January 12, 1972, pp. 26–27.

61. Shesol, *Mutual Contempt*, p. 207.

62. McNamara with VanDeMark, *In Retrospect*, pp. 130–31.

63. See Logevall, *Choosing War*, p. 197.

64. Editorial Note, *FRUS 1964–68*, vol. 1, *Vietnam 1964*, p. 589. The attack occurred about ten miles off of the coast of North Vietnam. Assuming a three-mile territorial limit, such as the French had observed during the colonial period, the American ships were in international waters.

65. McNamara with VanDeMark, *In Retrospect*, p. 131.

66. Hughes presented his notes of the meeting at a conference of Vietnam War historians and former senior U.S. government officials. See "Kennedy, Johnson and Vietnam: The Impact of the Presidential Transition on the Course of the War and Lessons for U.S. Foreign and Defense Policy," conference transcript, Watson Institute for International Studies and Arca Foundation Musgrove Conference Center, St. Simon's Island, Ga., April 8–10, 2005, p. 60.

67. Ibid., pp. 60–61. See also the book drawing further on themes of the Musgrove conference, James G. Blight, Janet M. Lang, and David A. Welch, *Virtual JFK: Vietnam, If Kennedy Had Lived* (Lanham, Md.: Rowman & Littlefield, forthcoming, January 2009).

68. President Johnson met with, among others, Rusk, Ball, Vance, and Wheeler. See Frank E. Vandiver, *Shadows of Vietnam: Lyndon Johnson's Wars* (College Station: Texas A&M University Press, 1997), p. 22.

69. Editorial Note, *FRUS 1964–68*, vol. 1, *Vietnam 1964*, p. 590. See also William Conrad Gibbons, *The U.S. Government and the Vietnam War: Executive and Legislative Roles and Relationships*, part 3, *January–July 1965* (Princeton: Princeton University Press, 1989), p. 10.

70. Johnson, *Vantage Point*, p. 113.

71. Memorandum by the Chairman of the Vietnam Coordinating Committee, *FRUS 1964–68*, vol. 1, *Vietnam 1964*, pp. 598–600.

72. Bird, *Color of Truth*, p. 288.

73. Editorial Note, *FRUS 1964–68*, vol. 1, *Vietnam 1964*, pp. 604–5. See also McNamara with VanDeMark, *In Retrospect*, p. 132.

74. Bundy Fragment No. 71.

75. See the President's Daily Diary, August 4, 1964, LBJ Library.

76. Bundy Fragment No. 71.

77. Gordon Goldstein interview with McGeorge Bundy, November 28, 1995, p. 19.

78. Bundy Fragment No. 71.

79. Telephone conversation between Lyndon Johnson and Robert McNamara, August 4, 1964, 9:43 a.m., in Beschloss, *Taking Charge*, pp. 496–97.

80. Editorial Note, *FRUS 1964–68*, vol. 1, *Vietnam 1964*, p. 608.

81. Ibid., p. 609.

82. See Summary Notes of the 538th Meeting of the National Security Council, August 4, 1964, in *FRUS 1964–68*, vol. 1, *Vietnam 1964*, pp. 611–12. See also McNamara with VanDeMark, *In Retrospect*, p. 135.

83. McNamara with VanDeMark, *In Retrospect*, p. 131.

84. Scott Shane, "Vietnam Study, Casting Doubts, Remains Secret," *New York Times*, October 31, 2005.

85. Ted Gittinger, ed., *The Johnson Years: A Vietnam Roundtable* (Austin, Tex.: Lyndon Baines Johnson Library, 1993), p. 35.

86. See Notes of the Leadership Meeting, August 4, 1964, in *FRUS 1964–68*, vol. 1, *Vietnam 1964*, pp. 615–21.

87. Bundy Fragment No. 71. A similar conclusion has been drawn by Nicholas Katzenbach, deputy attorney general at the time of the Gulf of Tonkin incident

and undersecretary of state from 1966 to 1969. See Gittinger, *Johnson Years*, p. 38.

88. Bird, *Color of Truth*, p. 287.

89. Memorandum from the President's Special Assistant for National Security Affairs to the President, August 31, 1964, in *FRUS 1964–68*, vol. 1, *Vietnam 1964*, pp. 723–24.

90. Remarks in Oklahoma at the Dedication of the Eufala Dam, September 25, 1964, in *Public Papers of the Presidents of the United States: Lyndon B. Johnson, 1963–64*, vol. 2 (Washington, D.C.: U.S. Government Printing Office, 1965), pp. 1126–27.

91. Remarks in Manchester to the Members of the New Hampshire Weekly Newspaper Editors Association, September 28, 1964, in *Public Papers: LBJ 1963–64*, vol. 2 pp. 1164–65.

92. Bird, *Color of Truth*, p. 290. Johnson reiterated his limitation on combat troop deployments in an October 21, 1964, speech at Akron University. See Remarks in Memorial Hall, Akron University, October 21, 1964, *Public Papers: LBJ 1963–64*, vol. 2, p. 1391.

93. Gittinger, *Johnson Years*, p. 40.

94. Portions of the memo are reprinted in George W. Ball, "Top Secret: The Prophecy the President Rejected," *Atlantic Monthly*, July 1972, pp. 35–49.

95. Ball, *Past Has Another Pattern*, p. 383. The memo was first circulated on October 5, 1964. See McNamara with VanDeMark, *In Retrospect*, p. 156, and Editorial Note in *FRUS 1964–68*, vol. 1, *Vietnam 1964*, p. 812.

96. As McNamara recounts, "Dean, Mac and I . . . agreed that advocating a political solution with no means to achieve it was tantamount to advocating unconditional withdrawal." See McNamara with VanDeMark, *In Retrospect*, p. 157.

97. Logevall, *Choosing War*, pp. 250–51.

98. George McT. Kahin, for example, asserts that "although McGeorge Bundy, McNamara, and Rusk all read Ball's brief, none (sic) chose to send it on to Johnson. . . . (It was only with the help of William Moyers of the White House staff that the memorandum finally reached the President, more than a month later.)" George McT. Kahin, *Intervention: How America Became Involved in Vietnam* (New York: Alfred A. Knopf, 1986), p. 243. Quote from Gordon Goldstein interview with McGeorge Bundy, September 22, 1995, pp. 24–25.

99. Bundy Fragment No. 71.

100. Transcript, McGeorge Bundy Oral History Interview 2, February 17, 1969, by Paige E. Mulhollan, p. 10, LBJ Library. Online: http://www.lbjlib.utexas.edu/johnson/archives.hom/oralhistory.hom/McGeorgeB/McGeorge.asp.

101. Logevall, *Choosing War*, p. 122.

102. Bundy Fragment No. 71.

103. For an explanation of President Johnson's decision not to retaliate to the first attack on August 2, 1964, see Johnson, *Vantage Point*, p. 113.

104. Bundy Fragment No. 71.

105. Bundy, "Notes on First Reading," p. 23.

106. Bundy Fragment No. 11.

107. Gordon Goldstein interview with McGeorge Bundy, pp 2–3. This interview transcription was not originally dated but appears to have been conducted on December 7, 1995.

108. Gordon Goldstein interview with McGeorge Bundy, November 9, 1995, pp. 26–27.

109. Gordon Goldstein interview with McGeorge Bundy, November 28, 1995, p. 17.

110. Gordon Goldstein interview with McGeorge Bundy, December 19, 1995, p. 15.

111. Gordon Goldstein interview with McGeorge Bundy, November 8, 1995, pp. 13–14.

112. Mulhollan-Bundy Oral History Interview 2, p. 7.

113. Gittinger, ed., *Johnson Years*, pp. 24–25.

114. Telephone conversation between Lyndon Johnson and McGeorge Bundy, May 27, 1964, in Beschloss, *Taking Charge*, pp. 370–73.

115. Bundy Fragment No. 4.

116. Notes on the National Security Council Meeting, November 15, 1961, *FRUS 1961–63*, vol. 1, *Vietnam 1961*, pp. 607–8.

117. Gordon Goldstein interview with McGeorge Bundy, November 21, 1995, p. 24.

118. Gordon Goldstein interview with McGeorge Bundy, December 12, 1995, p. 13.

119. Gordon Goldstein interview with McGeorge Bundy, September 19, 1995, pp. 3–4.

120. President's News Conference, April 7, 1954, *Public Papers of the Presidents of the United States: Dwight D. Eisenhower, 1954* (Washington, D.C.: U.S. Government Printing Office, 1960), p. 383.

121. Bundy Fragment No. 51.

122. Bundy Fragment No. 39.

123. Gordon Goldstein interview with McGeorge Bundy, November 9, 1995, p. 15.

124. Gordon Goldstein interview with McGeorge Bundy, December 7, 1995, p. 20.

125. Gordon Goldstein interview with McGeorge Bundy, September 19, 1995, pp. 3–4.

126. Gordon Goldstein interview with McGeorge Bundy, November 14, 1995, p. 9.

127. "You will recall," John McCone reminded Bundy, "the President made inquiry concerning this subject last Saturday." Memorandum from the Board of National Estimates to the Director of Central Intelligence, June 9, 1964, *FRUS 1964–68*, vol. 1, *Vietnam 1964*, p. 484 n. 1.

128. The Board of National Estimates (Sherman Kent) to Director John McCone, June 9, 1964, in *FRUS 1964–68*, vol. 1, *Vietnam 1964*, p. 485.

129. Bird, *Color of Truth*, p. 285.

130. Logevall, *Choosing War*, p. 123.

131. Harold P. Ford, *CIA and the Vietnam Policymakers: Three Episodes 1962–1968* (Washington, D.C.: History Staff, Center for the Study of Intelligence, Central Intelligence Agency, 1998), p. 57.

132. Ibid., p. 58 and n. 119, citing Ball's letter to Rusk in *FRUS 1964–68*, vol. 1, *Vietnam 1964*, p. 404.

133. H. R. McMaster, *Dereliction of Duty: Lyndon Johnson, Robert McNamara, the Joint Chiefs of Staff, and the Lies That Led to Vietnam* (New York: HarperPerennial, 1997), pp. 155–58.

134. See also Courses of Action for South Vietnam, September 8, 1964, *FRUS 1964–68*, vol. 1, *Vietnam 1964*, p. 748. The memorandum was drafted by William Bundy.

135. Bird, *Color of Truth*, pp. 296–97.
136. Preston, *War Council*, p. 180.
137. Mulhollan-Bundy Oral History Interview 2, p. 7.

LESSON FOUR: **CONVICTION WITHOUT RIGOR IS A STRATEGY FOR DISASTER**

1. David Halberstam, *The Best and the Brightest: Twentieth Anniversary Edition* (New York: Ballantine Books, 1992), p. x.
2. Ibid., p. xi.
3. Ibid., p. xx.
4. Private memorandum to the author from a guest at the dinner.
5. "What *about* withdrawal?" asked Halberstam in 1965. "Few Americans who have served in Vietnam can stomach this idea. It means that those Vietnamese who committed themselves fully to the United States will suffer the most under a Communist government. . . . It means a drab, lifeless, and controlled society for a people who deserve better. Withdrawal also means that the United States' prestige will be lowered throughout the world, and it means that the pressure of Communism on the rest of Southeast Asia will intensify." David Halberstam, *The Making of a Quagmire* (New York: Random House, 1965), p. 315.
6. Halberstam, *Best and the Brightest*, Bundy's notes on p. 178.
7. Ibid., pp. 178–79.
8. Ibid., p. 209.
9. Bundy Fragment No. 36.
10. Blight, Vietnam Project File Memo, August 28, 1996.
11. Bundy Fragment No. 51.
12. Herring, *America's Longest War*, p. 141.
13. Paper Prepared by the President's Special Assistant for National Security Affairs, December 28, 1964, in *FRUS 1964–68*, vol. 1, *Vietnam 1964*, pp. 1051–52.
14. Telegram from the President to the Ambassador in Vietnam, December 30, 1964, in *FRUS 1964–68*, vol. 1, *Vietnam 1964*, pp. 1057–59.
15. Document 29a from National Security File, Vietnam Country File, Box 195, Folder: "President/Taylor NODIS CLORES," LBJ Library.
16. McGeorge Bundy to Larry Berman, December 7, 1981, p. 3.
17. Telegram from the Embassy in Vietnam to the Department of State, January 6, 1965, in *Foreign Relations of the United States, 1964–1968*, vol. 2, *Vietnam, January–June 1965* (Washington, D.C.: U.S. Government Printing Office, 1996), p. 21.
18. Embtel 2052-2058 (Saigon), Maxwell Taylor to President Johnson, January 6, 1965, Deployment of Major U.S. Forces to Vietnam, July 1965, vol. 1, tabs 1–10, National Security Council History, Box 40, NSF, LBJ Library, cited in McNamara with VanDeMark, *In Retrospect*, pp. 165–66.
19. Memorandum from the President's Special Assistant for National Security Affairs to President Johnson, January 27, 1965, in *FRUS 1964–68*, vol. 2, *Vietnam, January–June 1965*, pp. 95–97.

20. Gordon Goldstein interview with McGeorge Bundy, November 30, 1995, p. 9.

21. Gittinger, *Johnson Years*, p. 47.

22. Ibid., p. 48.

23. Telegram from the Department of State to the Embassy in Vietnam, January 27, 1965, in *FRUS 1964–68*, vol. 2, *Vietnam, January–June 1965*, pp. 98–99.

24. Telegram from the President's Special Assistant for National Security Affairs to Director of Central Intelligence McCone, February 4, 1965, in *FRUS 1964–68*, vol. 2, *Vietnam, January–June 1965*, pp. 140–41.

25. Telegram from the Embassy in Vietnam to the Department of State, February 6, 1965, in *FRUS 1964–68*, vol. 2, *Vietnam, January–June 1965*, p. 154.

26. In addition to the casualties suffered, sixteen helicopters and six fixed-wing aircraft were damaged or destroyed. See Phillip B. Davidson, *Vietnam at War: The History, 1946–1975* (New York: Oxford University Press, 1988 and 1991), pp. 335–36.

27. Gordon Goldstein interview with Senior Lieutenant General Dang Vu Hiep, Hanoi, June 1997.

28. See, for example, Halberstam, *Best and the Brightest*, p. 520.

29. Westmoreland, *A Soldier Reports*, pp. 138–39.

30. Bundy Fragment No. 22.

31. Preston, *War Council*, p. 176.

32. Memorandum for the Record, Washington, February 6, 1965, in *FRUS 1964–68*, vol. 2, *Vietnam, January–June 1965*, pp. 159–60.

33. Karnow, *Vietnam*, pp. 429–30.

34. Preston, *War Council*, p. 180.

35. Among the most influential works of the period was by Thomas Schelling, a Harvard professor of economics and a former trade negotiator. See Thomas Schelling, *The Strategy of Conflict* (Cambridge, Mass.: Harvard University Press, 1960).

36. McMaster, *Dereliction of Duty*, pp. 18–19.

37. Bruce Kuklick, *Blind Oracles: Intellectuals and War from Kennan to Kissinger* (Princeton: Princeton University Press, 2006), pp. 143–44.

38. See Memorandum from the President's Special Assistant for National Security Affairs to President Johnson, February 7, 1965, in *FRUS 1964–68*, vol. 2, *Vietnam, January–June 1965*, pp. 174–81.

39. Annex A: Paper Prepared by Members of the Bundy Mission, A Policy of Sustained Reprisal, in *FRUS 1964–68*, vol. 2, *Vietnam January–June 1965*, pp. 181–85.

40. According to *Foreign Relations of the United States*, "Bundy met with the President from 10:48 to 11:25 p.m. on February 7." See *FRUS 1964–65*, vol. 2, *Vietnam January–July 1965*, p. 174 n. 1.

41. Mulhollan-Bundy Oral History Interview 2, p. 11.

42. Bundy, "Notes on First Reading," p. 23.

43. Bundy Fragment No. 12.

44. Bundy Fragment, Unnumbered.

45. Gittinger, *Johnson Years*, p. 60.

46. Gordon Goldstein interview with McGeorge Bundy, September 2, 1995, p. 18.

47. Memorandum from Senator Mike Mansfield to President Johnson, February 8, 1965, in *FRUS 1964–68*, vol. 2, *Vietnam, January–June 1965*, p. 205.

48. Letter from the President's Special Assistant for National Security Affairs to Senator Mike Mansfield, February 9, 1965, in *FRUS 1964–68*, vol. 2, *Vietnam, January–June 1965*, p. 210.

49. Memorandum from Acting Secretary of State Ball to President Johnson, Washington, February 13, 1965, in *FRUS 1964–68*, vol. 2, *Vietnam, January–June 1965*, pp. 252–61.

50. Ball, *Past Has Another Pattern*, pp. 504–5 n. 8.

51. Memorandum of a Meeting with President Johnson, February 17, 1965, in *FRUS 1964–68*, vol. 2, *Vietnam, January–June, 1965*, pp. 298–308. See also McGeorge Bundy, *Danger and Survival: Choices About the Bomb in the First Fifty Years* (New York: Vintage Books, 1990), p. 240.

52. Memorandum of a Meeting with President Johnson, February 17, 1965, in *FRUS 1964–68*, vol. 2, *Vietnam, January–June, 1965*, p. 305.

53. Bundy Fragment, Unnumbered.

54. According to McNamara, President Johnson's decision to "begin regular strikes against the North" was made on February 19, 1965. See McNamara with VanDeMark, *In Retrospect*, p. 173. Another interpretation is that Johnson approved the "Rolling Thunder" bombing campaign in a cable to General Taylor on February 13. See Preston, *War Council*, p. 180.

55. Memorandum from the President's Special Assistant for National Security Affairs to President Johnson, February 19, 1965, in *FRUS 1964–68*, vol. 2, *Vietnam, January–June 1965*, p. 331. That same day Bundy submitted to the president an equivocal national intelligence estimate that acknowledged the possibility that "sustained air attack" might encourage North Vietnam "to intensify the struggle, accepting the destructive consequences in the North." See *FRUS 1964–68*, vol. 2, *Vietnam, January–June 1965*, p. 322, and Bundy's cover memo for Johnson, February 19, 1965, in National Security Files, Memos to the President, McGeorge Bundy, Box 2, Folder 1/1–2/28/65, vol. 8, LBJ Library.

56. Memorandum from Vice President Humphrey to President Johnson, February 17, 1965, in *FRUS 1964–68*, vol. 2, *Vietnam, January–June 1965*, p. 311.

57. See Preston, *War Council*, p. 181; and Dallek, *Flawed Giant*, p. 253.

58. See *FRUS 1964–68*, vol. 2, *Vietnam, January–June 1965*, p. 349 n. 3. See also p. 351, in which General Westmoreland cables CINCPAC and notes: "In view of the great importance of the Da nang air base to current U.S. strategy, augmentation of U.S. security forces is desirable soonest."

59. Telegram from the Embassy in Vietnam to the Joint Chiefs of Staff, February 22, 1965, in *FRUS 1964–68*, vol. 2, *Vietnam, January–June 1965*, p. 347.

60. Ibid., pp. 347–49. Ambassador Taylor ultimately agreed to the deployment of a marine battalion landing team to protect the air base in Da Nang. In a memorandum for the record, Bill Bundy reported on March 15, 1965, that both Taylor and his deputy, U. Alexis Johnson, had approved of the deployment despite their stated

reservations. Memorandum for the Record, March 15, 1965, in *FRUS 1964–68*, vol. 2, *Vietnam, January–June 1965*, p. 444.

61. Telegram from the Department of State to the Embassy in Vietnam, February 26, 1965, in *FRUS 1964–68*, vol. 2, *Vietnam, January–June 1965*, p. 376.

62. VanDeMark, *Into the Quagmire*, p. 94.

63. Memorandum from the President's Special Assistant for National Security Affairs to President Johnson, March 6, 1965, in *FRUS 1964–68*, vol. 2, *Vietnam, January–June 1965*, pp. 403–4.

64. McNamara with VanDeMark, *In Retrospect*, p. 177.

65. Memorandum from Chester L. Cooper of the National Security Council Staff to the President's Special Assistant for National Security Affairs, March 10, 1965, in *FRUS 1964–68*, vol. 2, *Vietnam, January–June 1965*, pp. 433–34.

66. The first luncheon was held on February 4, 1964, and twenty more followed in the spring and summer. The luncheons continued into 1965 and became a principal vehicle for Johnson to confer privately with his most senior advisers. Bundy, Rusk, and McNamara formed the nucleus of the weekly gatherings. See McMaster, *Dereliction of Duty*, pp. 88–89. See also Henry F. Graff, *The Tuesday Cabinet: Deliberation and Decision on Peace and War Under Lyndon B. Johnson* (New York: Prentice Hall, 1970).

67. Memorandum by the President's Special Assistant for National Security Affairs, March 16, 1965, in *FRUS 1964–68*, vol. 2, *Vietnam, January–June 1965*, pp. 448–49.

68. Bundy's White House notes from March 21, 1965, are among the holdings of the LBJ Library and are quoted throughout the Vietnam historical literature. See, for example, Gibbons, *U.S. Government and the Vietnam War*, part 3, pp. 161–9 and 179–80; VanDeMark, *Into the Quagmire*, pp. 97–98; and Dallek, *Flawed Giant*, p. 255.

69. For a historical explication of the assumptions that governed China's policy toward the Vietnam conflict in the spring of 1965, see Chen Jian, "China's Involvement in the Vietnam War, 1964–1969," *China Quarterly* 143 (June 1995), p. 366. See also Zhai Qiang, "Beijing and the Vietnam Conflict, 1964–1965: New Chinese Evidence," *Cold War International History Project Bulletin* 6–7 (Winter 1995/1996).

70. John McNaughton, Proposed Course of Action Re Vietnam, in *Pentagon Papers*, vol. 3, pp. 694–95. The blunt character of this particular memorandum has made it a subject of perennial historical interest. See John Lewis Gaddis, *Strategies of Containment: A Critical Appraisal of Postwar American National Security Policy* (New York: Oxford University Press, 1982), p. 241. See also Gittinger, *Johnson Years*, p. 96.

71. Memorandum by the President's Special Assistant for National Security Affairs, April 1, 1965, in *FRUS 1964–68*, vol. 2, *Vietnam, January–June 1965*, p. 508.

72. McGeorge Bundy to Larry Berman, December 7, 1981, p. 4.

73. Personal Notes of a Meeting with President Johnson, April 1, 1965, in *FRUS 1964–68*, vol. 2, *Vietnam, January–June 1965*, p. 511.

74. McNamara with VanDeMark, *In Retrospect*, p. 179. See also National Security Action Memorandum No. 328, April 6, 1965, in *FRUS 1964–68*, vol. 2, *Vietnam, January–June 1965*, p. 538. The marines were given approval to expand progres-

sively the area they patrolled—first to ten miles, then to thirty miles, and on June 1, 1965, to fifty miles. See Gibbons, *U.S. Government and the Vietnam War,* part 3, chap. 3, cited in Burke and Greenstein, *How Presidents Test Reality,* p. 162.

75. National Security Action Memorandum No. 328, April 6, 1965, in *FRUS 1964–68,* vol. 2, *Vietnam, January–June 1965,* p. 539.

76. Address at Johns Hopkins University: "Peace without Conquest," April 7, 1965, in *Public Papers of the Presidents of the United States: Lyndon B. Johnson, 1965,* vol. 1 (Washington, D.C.: U.S. Government Printing Office, 1966), pp. 395–96.

77. The day after President Johnson sketched his vision for peace in Southeast Asia—including his proposal for a "billion dollar American investment" in regional development—North Vietnamese premier Pham Van Dong spoke in Hanoi. In an address on April 8, 1965, before the United National Assembly, the premier defined his government's four-point agenda to end the conflict in South Vietnam. See Editorial Note, *FRUS 1964–68,* vol. 2, *Vietnam, January–June 1965,* pp. 544–45. The timing of Pham Van Dong's speech is certainly curious. But one of Hanoi's leading historians of the Vietnam War claims that the presentation of the four points was not a response to the Johns Hopkins speech but rather a statement of North Vietnam's negotiating position developed prior to Lyndon Johnson's Baltimore address. According to Luu Doan Huynh, a former official in the Foreign Ministry of North Vietnam, "The drafting was completed around the end of March. Thereafter, Prime Minister Pham Van Dong included the Four Points in his report to the National Assembly on April 8, 1965. It was not a reply to President Johnson's Baltimore speech of April 7." See Robert S. McNamara, James Blight, Robert Brigham, Thomas Biersteker, and Herbert Schandler, *Argument Without End: In Search of Answers to the Vietnam Tragedy* (New York: PublicAffairs, 1999), pp. 223–24 and p. 231.

78. Bundy, "Notes on First Reading," p. 24.

79. Frederik Logevall interview with McGeorge Bundy, March 15, 1994, p. 13.

80. Editorial Note, in *FRUS 1964–68,* vol. 2, *Vietnam, January–June 1965,* p. 553.

81. Maxwell Taylor to Department of State, April 14, 1965, cited in Burke and Greenstein, *How Presidents Test Reality,* p. 163. See also Editorial Note, in *FRUS 1964–68,* vol. 2, *Vietnam, January–June 1965,* p. 553.

82. Telegram from the Embassy in Vietnam to the Department of State, April 14, 1965, in *FRUS 1964–68,* vol. 2, *Vietnam, January–June 1965,* pp. 554–55.

83. Memorandum from the President's Special Assistant for National Security Affairs to President Johnson, April 14, 1965, in *FRUS 1964–68,* vol. 2, *Vietnam, January–June 1965,* p. 556.

84. Telegram from the Department of Defense to the Embassy in Vietnam, April 15, 1965, in *FRUS 1964–68,* vol. 2, *Vietnam, January–June 1965,* pp. 561–63.

85. Telegram from the Embassy in Vietnam to the Department of State, in *FRUS 1964–68,* vol. 2, *Vietnam, January–June 1965,* p. 564.

86. Memorandum from Secretary of Defense McNamara to President Johnson, April 21, 1965, in *FRUS 1964–68,* vol. 2, *Vietnam, January–June 1965,* pp. 574–76.

87. See Andrew F. Krepinevich Jr., *The Army and Vietnam* (Baltimore: Johns Hopkins University Press, 1986), p. 150. The quote is drawn from Krepinevich's interview with Ambassador Taylor on June 17, 1982. See p. 297 n. 69.

88. Memorandum for the Record, April 21, 1965, in *FRUS 1964–68*, vol. 2, *Vietnam, January–June 1965*, p. 579.

89. VanDeMark, *Into the Quagmire*, p. 127.

90. Ball, *Past Has Another Pattern*, p. 393.

91. Ibid.

92. Ibid., p. 394.

93. Intelligence Memorandum, April 21, 1965, in *FRUS 1964–68*, vol. 2, *Vietnam, January–June 1965*, pp. 594–95.

94. "For your wholly private information, and subject to private Congressional consultation," Rusk explained, "the President is inclined to favor McNamara's recommendations." Telegram from the Department of State to the Embassy in Vietnam, April 22, 1965, in *FRUS 1964–68*, vol. 2, *Vietnam, January–June 1965*, p. 602. President Johnson had authorized American troop deployments totaling 72,000, including thirteen U.S. combat battalions. Counting the four combat battalions committed by other countries, 82,000 men were slated to be under General Westmoreland's command. See Burke and Greenstein, *How Presidents Test Reality*, p. 198.

95. VanDeMark, *Into the Quagmire*, p. 131.

96. Herring, *America's Longest War*, pp. 150–51.

97. McNamara with VanDeMark, *In Retrospect*, p. 185.

98. Telegram from the Department of State to the Embassy in the Soviet Union, May 11, 1965, in *FRUS 1964–68*, vol. 2, *Vietnam, January–June 1965*, pp. 637–38. See also *Pentagon Papers*, vol. 3, p. 369.

99. Memorandum from the President's Special Assistant for National Security Affairs to President Johnson, May 13, 1965, in *FRUS 1964–68*, vol. 2, *Vietnam, January–June 1965*, pp. 651–52. On May 15 Secretary of State Rusk spoke informally with Soviet foreign minister Andrei Gromyko. According to a cable by Rusk dispatched from Vienna, Gromyko "said the temporary suspension of bombing was 'insulting.'" See Telegram from Secretary of State Rusk to the Department of State, in ibid., p. 644.

100. Notes of a Meeting, May 16, 1965, in *FRUS 1964–68*, vol. 2, *Vietnam, January–June 1965*, p. 666.

101. McNamara et al., *Argument Without End*, p. 263. In a 1997 conference, senior members of the Hanoi leadership dismissed the bombing pause, known as "Mayflower," characterizing it as simply a means for the United States to expand the war. "We thought it was a smoke screen to divert attention from the troop buildup that was under way," said Luu Doan Huynh, one of North Vietnam's leading experts on American affairs. "Mayflower was a way to force us to stop our assistance to the South. This would be the trade-off you required from us for stopping the bombing." See ibid., pp. 264, 265.

102. Bundy Fragment No. 24.

103. Ibid. For events in the Dominican Republic see also Burke and Greenstein, *How Presidents Test Reality*, p. 197.

104. Telegram from the Embassy in Vietnam to the Department of State, June 3, 1965, in *FRUS 1964–68*, vol. 2, *Vietnam, January–June 1965*, p. 710.

105. Telegram from the Embassy in Vietnam to the Department of State, June 5, 1965, in *FRUS 1964–68*, vol. 2, *Vietnam, January–June 1965*, p. 723.

106. Attending along with McGeorge Bundy were Rusk, McNamara, Llewellyn Thompson, George Ball, and William Bundy. See Burke and Greenstein, *How Presidents Test Reality*, p. 197.

107. William Bundy, unpublished manuscript, chap. 26, pp. 5–6, quoted in Burke and Greenstein, *How Presidents Test Reality*, pp. 197–98.

108. McNamara with VanDeMark, *In Retrospect*, p. 187.

109. Ibid., p. 188; VanDeMark, *Into the Quagmire*, pp. 153, 256; and *Foreign Relations of the United States, 1964–1968*, vol. 3, *Vietnam, June–December 1965* (Washington, D.C.: U.S. Government Printing Office, 1996), pp. 70, 98.

110. Telegram from the Commander, Military Assistance Command, Vietnam to the Joint Chiefs of Staff, June 7, 1965, in *FRUS 1964–68*, vol. 2, *Vietnam, January–June 1965*, p. 735.

111. Personal Notes of a Meeting with President Johnson, June 10, 1965, in *FRUS 1964–68*, vol. 2, *Vietnam, January–June 1965*, p. 746.

112. See ibid, p. 746 n. 2, which quotes from William Bundy's unpublished manuscript. See also VanDeMark, *Into the Quagmire*, p. 158.

113. Burke and Greenstein, *How Presidents Test Reality*, p. 200.

114. McNamara with VanDeMark, *In Retrospect*, pp. 188–89.

115. Bundy Fragment No. 54.

116. Bundy Fragment No. 22.

117. Bundy Fragment, January 12, 1996.

118. Bundy Fragment No. 19.

119. Bundy Note in *FRUS 1964–68*, vol. 2, *Vietnam, January–June 1965*, pp. 448–49.

120. Bundy Fragment No. 56.

121. See McNamara et al., *Argument Without End*, pp. 228–29 and pp. 259–61.

122. See ibid., p. 255.

123. Bundy Fragment No. 41.

124. Bundy Fragment, Unnumbered.

125. Bundy Fragment No. 51.

126. Bundy Fragment No. 41.

127. Bundy Fragment No. 54.

128. McGeorge Bundy to Larry Berman, December 7, 1981.

129. Mulhollan-Bundy Oral History Interview 2, p. 4.

130. Bundy Fragment No. 54.

131. Bundy Fragment No. 2.

LESSON FIVE: **NEVER DEPLOY MILITARY MEANS IN PURSUIT OF INDETERMINATE ENDS**

1. Bundy Fragment No. 34.
2. Ibid.
3. Bundy Fragment No. 3. "The Army," notes the military historian Andrew Krepinevich, "being denied the opportunity to win a decisive battle of annihilation by invading North Vietnam, found the attrition strategy best fit the kind of war it had prepared to fight." See Krepinevich, *Army and Vietnam*, p. 164.
4. Bundy Fragment No. 61.
5. Westmoreland, *A Soldier Reports*, p. 156.
6. Bundy Fragment No. 2.
7. Bundy Fragment No. 19.
8. Bundy Fragment No. 34.
9. Ibid.
10. Gordon Goldstein interview with McGeorge Bundy, November 28, 1995, p. 18.
11. *Pentagon Papers*, vol. 3, p. 392, cited in Burke and Greenstein, *How Presidents Test Reality*, p. 202.
12. Andrew Goodpaster to Lyndon Johnson, June 16, 1965, cited in Barrett, *Uncertain Warriors*, pp. 40–41.
13. The President's News Conference, June 17, 1965, in *Public Papers: LBJ, 1965*, vol. 2, p. 680.
14. Memorandum from the Under Secretary of State to President Johnson, June 18, 1965, in *FRUS 1964–68*, vol. 3, *Vietnam, June–December 1965*, pp. 18–19.
15. On June 19, 1965, McGeorge Bundy submitted a memorandum to the president weighing the competing arguments for and against a bombing pause. See Memorandum from the President's Special Assistant for National Security Affairs to President Johnson, June 19, 1965, in *FRUS 1964–68*, vol. 3, *Vietnam, June–December 1965*, pp. 21–22. The notion of a bombing pause was deferred, not to be revisited again until the end of 1965. The first bombing pause of 1965 lasted from May 10 to May 18. The second bombing pause began on Christmas Day, 1965, and was followed by an elaborate diplomatic offensive that proved futile. Bombing resumed on January 31, 1966. See George C. Herring, *LBJ and Vietnam: A Different Kind of War*, (Austin: University of Texas Press, 1994), pp. 100–101. See also Gardner, *Pay Any Price*, chap. 13, "The Pause That Failed," pp. 269–93.
16. William P. Bundy, unpublished manuscript, chap. 26, pp. 22–23, cited in Editorial Note, *FRUS 1964–1968*, vol. 3, *Vietnam, June–December 1965*, pp. 40–41.
17. Telegram from the Commander, Military Assistance Command, Vietnam to the Chairman of the Joint Chiefs of Staff, June 24, 1965, in *FRUS 1964–68*, vol. 3, *Vietnam, June–December 1965*, p. 42. Bundy comments in text.
18. Ibid.

19. McNamara's recommendation was drafted by McNaughton on June 26, 1965, and revised on July 1. Memorandum from the Secretary of Defense to President Johnson, July 1, 1965, in *FRUS 1964–68*, vol. 3, *Vietnam, June–December 1965*, pp. 97–104.

20. Telegram from the Chairman of the Joint Chiefs of Staff to the Commander, Military Assistance Command, Vietnam, June 28, 1965, in *FRUS 1964–68*, vol. 3, *Vietnam, June–December 1965*, pp. 69–70.

21. Telegram from the Commander, Military Assistance Command, Vietnam to the Chairman of the Joint Chiefs, June 30, 1965, in *FRUS 1964–68*, vol. 3, *Vietnam, June–December 1965*, p. 76.

22. See Memorandum Prepared in the Central Intelligence Agency, June 30, 1965, in *FRUS 1964–68*, vol. 3, *Vietnam, June–December 1965*, pp. 86–87.

23. Paper Prepared by the Under Secretary of State, in *FRUS 1964–68*, vol. 3, *Vietnam, June–December 1965*, pp. 62–66.

24. Mulhollan-Bundy Oral History Interview 2, p. 20.

25. Ibid.

26. Transcript, CBS News Special Report, "Vietnam Dialogue: Mr. Bundy and the Professors," June 21, 1965, pp. 2–3.

27. See John J. Mearsheimer, "Hans Morgenthau and the Iraq War: Realism versus Neoconservatism," Lecture given October 28–30, 2004, in Munich, adapted at openDemocracy, http://www.opendemocracy.net/democracy-americanpower/morgenthau_2522.jsp.

28. Langguth, *Our Vietnam*, p. 368.

29. Transcript, CBS News, "Vietnam Dialogue."

30. See Langguth, *Our Vietnam*, pp. 366–69. See also Bird, *Color of Truth*, pp. 321–22.

31. Gordon Goldstein interview with McGeorge Bundy, September 22, 1995, pp. 26–27.

32. Gordon Goldstein interview with McGeorge Bundy, September 19, 1995, pp. 17–18.

33. Bundy Fragment No. 48.

34. Ibid.

35. Bundy Fragment No. 22.

36. Gordon Goldstein interview with McGeorge Bundy, November 9, 1995, p. 3.

37. Gordon Goldstein interview with McGeorge Bundy, December 19, 1995, p. 25.

38. Gordon Goldstein interview with McGeorge Bundy, November 9, 1995, pp. 3–4.

39. Gordon Goldstein interview with McGeorge Bundy, December 19, 1995, p. 25.

40. Gordon Goldstein interview with McGeorge Bundy, December 12, 1995, p. 12.

41. Gordon Goldstein interview with McGeorge Bundy, September 19, 1995, p. 18.

42. Bundy Fragment No. 29 and Bundy Fragment No. 22.

43. McGeorge Bundy Memorandum to Lyndon Johnson, February 2, 1965, cited in Bird, *Color of Truth*, pp. 301–2.

44. Memorandum from the President's Special Assistant for National Security Affairs to President Johnson, June 27, 1965, in *FRUS 1964–68*, vol. 3, *Vietnam, June–December 1965*, p. 54.

45. Memorandum from the President's Special Assistant for National Security Affairs to President Johnson, June 30, 1965, in *FRUS 1964–68*, vol. 3, *Vietnam, June–December 1965*, pp. 79–85.

46. Emphasis in original. McGeorge Bundy, personal notes, June 30, 1965.

47. Memorandum from the President's Special Assistant for National Security Affairs to Secretary of Defense McNamara, June 30, 1965, in *FRUS 1964–68*, vol. 3, *Vietnam, June–December 1965*, pp. 90–91.

48. McGeorge Bundy to Larry Berman, December 7, 1981, p. 6.

49. Memorandum from the President's Special Assistant for National Security Affairs to Secretary of Defense McNamara, June 30, 1965, in *FRUS 1964–68*, vol. 3, *Vietnam, June–December 1965*, pp. 90–91.

50. In 1995, McNamara wrote, "Except for Mac's reference to nuclear weapons, and the implication that we should consider threatening their use, I shared all his views and concerns." McNamara with VanDeMark, *In Retrospect*, p. 194.

51. Bundy Fragment No. 82.

52. Memorandum by the Assistant Secretary of State for Far Eastern Affairs, July 1, 1965, in *FRUS 1964–68*, vol. 3, *Vietnam, June–December 1965*, pp. 113–15.

53. Memorandum from the President's Special Assistant for National Security Affairs to President Johnson, July 1, 1965, in *FRUS 1964–68*, vol. 3, *Vietnam, June–December 1965*, pp. 117–18.

54. VanDeMark, *Into the Quagmire*, p. 171.

55. Gordon Goldstein interview with McGeorge Bundy, November 16, 1995, p. 9.

56. Bundy to Johnson, January 21, 1965, National Security Files, Memos for the President, McGeorge Bundy, Box 2, LBJ Library.

57. Gordon Goldstein interview with McGeorge Bundy, November 16, 1995, p. 9.

58. Pres. Johnson 1965 (2), Post-Pres.; Gettysburg-Indo, Box 2, Eisenhower Library, cited in David M. Barrett, ed., *Lyndon B. Johnson's Vietnam Papers: A Documentary Collection* (College Station: Texas A&M University Press, 1997), pp. 201–2.

59. William P. Bundy, unpublished manuscript, chap. 27, p. 13, cited in Editorial Note, *FRUS 1964–68*, vol. 3, *Vietnam, June–December 1965*, p. 119. For a discussion of a White House meeting with a group of outside advisers known as "the wise men," see William Bundy, unpublished manuscript, chap. 27, p. 21, cited in Burke and Greenstein, *How Presidents Test Reality*, pp. 212–13.

60. Bundy Fragment No. 45.

61. Remarks to the National Rural Electric Cooperative Association, July 14, 1965, in *Public Papers: LBJ, 1965*, vol. 2, pp. 751–52.

62. McGeorge Bundy to Larry Berman, December 7, 1981.

63. Gordon Goldstein interview with McGeorge Bundy, November 28, 1995, p. 19.

64. McGeorge Bundy to Clark Clifford, May 22, 1991.

65. Gordon Goldstein interview with McGeorge Bundy, September 22, 1995, pp. 16–17. Although the Vance cable is not reprinted in the *Pentagon Papers*, it is summarized there, as described in *Pentagon Papers*, vol. 3, p. 475.

66. According to the *Pentagon Papers* account: "When McNamara left Washington, the

44 battalion debate remained unresolved. While he was in Saigon, he received a cable from Deputy Secretary of Defense Vance informing him that the President had decided to go ahead with the plan to deploy all 34 of the U.S. battalions. The debate was over." See *Pentagon Papers*, vol. 3, p. 475.

67. Telegram from Acting Secretary of Defense Vance to Secretary of Defense McNamara, in Vietnam, July 17, 1965, 3:42 p.m., in *FRUS 1964–68*, vol. 3, *Vietnam, June–December 1965*, p. 162. The cable was designated "Top Secret; Literally Eyes Only." According to the accompanying footnote: "Sent to MACV headquarters in Saigon with an instruction to the Duty Officer to deliver it personally to McNamara only. The source text has a stamped indication that Secretary McNamara saw it." The cable notes approval of a thirty-four-battalion deployment of U.S. forces, which was to be supplemented by ten battalions of allied troops.

68. Gordon Goldstein interview with McGeorge Bundy, November 9, 1995, p. 23. Vance himself was equivocal in his interpretation of the July 17, 1965, cable. See Burke and Greenstein, *How Presidents Test Reality*, p. 215 n. 30.

69. Memorandum from Secretary of Defense McNamara to President Johnson, July 20, 1965, in *FRUS 1964–68*, vol. 3, *Vietnam, June–December 1965*, pp. 171–75.

70. Ibid.

71. Notes of Meeting, July 21, 1965 (10:40 a.m.), in *FRUS 1964–68*, vol. 3, *Vietnam, June–December 1965*, pp. 190–91.

72. President Johnson arrived at 11:30 a.m, forty minutes after the start of the meeting. Notes of Meeting, July 21, 1965 (10:40 a.m.), in *FRUS 1964–68*, vol. 3, *Vietnam, June–December 1965*, p. 189. The notes were prepared by Jack Valenti and can also be found in Valenti, *A Very Human President* (New York: W. W. Norton, 1975), pp. 319–40.

73. According to Taylor, his return from Saigon in the summer of 1965 was a condition he negotiated before accepting the post. Taylor, *Swords and Plowshares*, p. 348.

74. Notes of Meeting, July 21, 1965, 10:40 a.m., in *FRUS 1964–68*, vol. 3, *Vietnam, June–December 1965*, pp. 192–93.

75. Ibid., p. 194.

76. Ibid.

77. Ibid., p. 195.

78. Ibid., p. 196.

79. A second set of notes from the meeting was composed by Chet Cooper, Bundy's NSC staff specialist for Vietnam. See Memorandum for the Record (Afternoon Session, 2:30 p.m.) in *FRUS 1964–68*, vol. 3, *Vietnam, June–December 1965*, p. 203.

80. See ibid., pp. 202–4.

81. Gordon Goldstein interview with McGeorge Bundy, November 9, 1995, pp. 5–6.

82. Gordon Goldstein interview with McGeorge Bundy, November 14, 1995, p. 22.

83. Transcript, McGeorge Bundy Oral History Interview 1, January 30, 1969, by Paige E. Mulhollan, p. 28, LBJ Library. Online: http://www.lbjlib.utexas.edu/johnson/archives.hom/oralhistory.hom/McGeorgeB/McGeorge.asp.

84. Gordon Goldstein interview with McGeorge Bundy, November 14, 1995, p. 7.

85. McGeorge Bundy to Larry Berman, December 7, 1981, p. 6. This view was shared by William Bundy, who concluded that the late July meetings appeared to be "a bit of a set piece . . . you felt it had been scripted to a degree." See William Bundy Oral History, p. 42, LBJ Library, cited in Barrett, *Uncertain Warriors*, p. 214 n. 105.

86. Gordon Goldstein interview with McGeorge Bundy, September 2, 1995, pp. 18–19.

87. Gordon Goldstein interview with McGeorge Bundy, December 12, 1995, p. 18.

88. Bundy Fragment, January 12, 1996.

89. Minutes of the meeting are drawn from the notes of Valenti, *Very Human President*, pp. 340–52. This quote is drawn from the original minutes reprinted in Notes of a Meeting, July 22, 1965, in *FRUS 1964–68*, vol. 3, *Vietnam, June–December 1965*, pp. 215–16. Valenti's second version omits Johnson's remark "I haven't taken a position."

90. Valenti, *Very Human President*, p. 351.

91. Ibid., p. 352.

92. Bundy Fragment No. 48.

93. W. W. Rostow, "The Case for War," *Times Literary Supplement*, June 9, 1995.

94. Bundy Fragment No. 48.

95. Bundy Fragment No. 100.

96. Bundy Fragment, Unnumbered.

97. Bundy Fragment No. 51.

98. Bundy Fragment No. 100.

99. Bundy Fragment No. 12.

100. McGeorge Bundy to Harry Middleton, October 14, 1994.

101. Memorandum from the President's Special Assistant for National Security Affairs to the President, November 15, 1961, in *FRUS 1961–63*, vol. 1, *Vietnam 1961*, pp. 605–7.

102. Draft Memorandum from the President's Special Assistant for National Security Affairs to the President, May 25, 1964, in *FRUS 1964–1968*, vol. 1, *Vietnam 1964*, pp. 374–77.

103. William C. Gibbons, *The United States and the Vietnam War: Executive and Legislative Roles and Relationships*, vol. 2 (Princeton: Princeton University Press, 1986), pp. 349–50.

104. Ball, *Past Has Another Pattern*, pp. 504–5 n. 8.

105. Annex A: Paper Prepared by Members of the Bundy Mission, A Policy of Sustained Reprisal, in *FRUS 1964–68*, vol. 2, *Vietnam, January–June 1965*, pp. 181–85.

106. Bundy Papers, March 21, 1965, LBJ Library.

107. Bundy Fragment No. 53.

108. On Indonesia and the events of 1965, see Bird, *Color of Truth*, pp. 351–53.

109. Bundy Fragment No. 74. Bundy noted that his figures were drawn from McNamara with VanDeMark, *In Retrospect*.

110. Bundy Fragment No. 56.

111. Ibid.

112. See Harry G. Summers Jr., *On Strategy: The Vietnam War in Context* (Carlisle Barracks, Pa.: U.S. Army War College, 1981), p. 65.

113. See Westmoreland, *A Soldier Reports*, p. 153.

114. Bundy Fragment No. 3.

115. See Westmoreland, *A Soldier Reports*, p. 156.

116. Bundy Fragment No. 34.

117. McNamara et al., *Argument Without End*, p. 311.

118. Bundy Fragment No. 3.

119. Bundy Fragment No. 1.

120. Young, *Vietnam Wars*, pp. 161–62.

121. Gordon Goldstein interview with McGeorge Bundy, November 14, 1995, p. 6.

122. Gordon Goldstein interview with McGeorge Bundy, November 28, 1995, p. 18.

123. See Bruce Palmer Jr., *The 25-Year War: America's Military Role in Vietnam* (New York: Simon and Schuster, 1984), pp. 45–46.

124. Cited in Larry Berman, *Lyndon Johnson's War*, p. 3.

125. Bundy Fragment No. 56.

126. Bundy Fragment No. 99, First Draft Introduction.

LESSON SIX: INTERVENTION IS A PRESIDENTIAL CHOICE, NOT AN INEVITABILITY

1. McGeorge Bundy, "The History-Maker," Proceedings of the Massachusetts Historical Society (1978), p. 84.

2. McGeorge Bundy, "John F. Kennedy and the 'Rewarding Job of President,'" Remarks at Hofstra University, March 28, 1985.

3. Richard Neustadt was a consultant to the Kennedy administration and the author of an influential analysis of the presidency that John Kennedy had studied and praised. See Richard Neustadt, *Presidential Power: The Politics of Leadership* (New York: John Wiley, 1960). See also Kuklick, *Blind Oracles*, pp. 89–94.

4. Neustadt-Bundy Oral History (1964), pp. 140–41. It is true that Kennedy did not publicly question the domino theory. "No, I believe it," Kennedy said of the domino theory in an interview with Chet Huntley and David Brinkley on September 9, 1963. *Public Papers: JFK, 1963*, p. 659.

5. Neustadt-Bundy Oral History (1964), pp. 137–38.

6. McMaster, *Dereliction of Duty*, p. 202.

7. Gordon Goldstein interview with McGeorge Bundy, September 22, 1995, p. 29.

8. Blight, Vietnam Project File Memo, August 28, 1996.

9. Bundy Fragment No. 99, First Draft Introduction.

10. Bundy Fragment No. 98.

11. Bundy Fragment No. 99, First Draft Introduction.

12. Bundy Fragment No. 87.

13. Bundy Fragment No. 18.

14. Bundy Fragment No. 39.

15. Bundy Fragment No. 40.

16. James K. Galbraith, "Exit Strategy," *Boston Review* (October/November 2003). A

comprehensive effort to demonstrate the existence of a Kennedy withdrawal plan has been made by John Newman in *JFK and Vietnam: Deception, Intrigue, and the Struggle for Power* (New York: Warner Books, 1992). Another significant study of Kennedy's extrication plans and tactics is Howard Jones, *Death of a Generation: How the Assassinations of Diem and JFK Prolonged the Vietnam War* (New York: Oxford University Press, 2003).

17. Gordon Goldstein interview with McGeorge Bundy, November 16, 1995, p. 7.
18. Neustadt-Bundy Oral History (1964), p. 137.
19. See the Congressional Record, January 8, 1952, p. HR-5879, cited in Reeves, *President Kennedy*, pp. 254, 700. See also Fredrik Logevall, "Kennedy, Vietnam, and the Question of What Might Have Been," in Mark J. White, ed., *Kennedy: The New Frontier Revisited* (New York: Palgrave Macmillan, 1998), p. 40.
20. Robert F. Kennedy, Memorandum Dictated August 1, 1961, p. 1, RFK Papers, cited in Schlesinger, *Robert Kennedy and His Times*, pp. 703–4, and p. 1000 n. 13.
21. O'Donnell and Powers with McCarthy, *"Johnny, We Hardly Knew Ye,"* p. 13.
22. William Brubeck interview with Alexis Johnson (1964), pp. 33–34, JFK Oral History Program, cited in Schlesinger, *Robert Kennedy and His Times*, p. 704, and p. 1000 n. 14.
23. L. J. Hackman interview with Maxwell Taylor, November 13, 1969, p. 47, cited in Schlesinger, *Robert Kennedy and His Times*, p. 704, and p. 1000 n. 15.
24. Arthur Krock, *Memoirs: Sixty Years on the Firing Line* (New York: Funk & Wagnalls, 1968), pp. 332–33, cited in Richard Reeves, *President Kennedy*, p. 244, and p. 499 n. 244. Schlesinger paraphrases Krock, in a different account, as recalling that Kennedy "was stalling the military, he said, by sending Maxwell Taylor and Walt Rostow to look at South Vietnam." Arthur Krock, *In the Nation: 1932–1966* (New York: McGraw-Hill, 1966), pp. 324–25, p. 447, cited in Schlesinger, *Robert Kennedy and His Times*, p. 704, and p. 1000 n. 16.
25. Memorandum from the Ambassador to India to the President, April 4, 1962, in *FRUS 1961–63*, vol. 2, *Vietnam 1962*, pp. 297–98.
26. Memorandum of a Conversation Between the President and the Assistant Secretary of State for Far Eastern Affairs, April 6, 1962, in *FRUS 1961–63*, vol. 2, *Vietnam 1962*, pp. 309–10.
27. Hilsman, *To Move a Nation*, p. 439.
28. O'Donnell and Powers with McCarthy, *"Johnny, We Hardly Knew Ye,"* p. 16.
29. Mansfield explained to the historian Francis Winters: "President Kennedy did inform me in early 1963 that he did plan to begin the withdrawal of some troops from Vietnam following the next election." Letter from Senator Mike Mansfield to Francis X. Winters, October 24, 1989, cited in Francis Winters, *The Year of the Hare* (Athens: University of Georgia Press, 1997), pp. 21, 232.
30. See O'Donnell and Powers with McCarthy, *"Johnny, We Hardly Knew Ye,"* p. 16.
31. Langguth, *Our Vietnam*, p. 208.
32. See the President's News Conference of May 22, 1963, *Public Papers: JFK, 1963*, p. 421.

33. O'Donnell and Powers with McCarthy, *"Johnny, We Hardly Knew Ye,"* p. 18.

34. Roswell Gilpatric quoted in O'Brien interview, August 12, 1970, p. 1, cited in Schlesinger, *Robert Kennedy and His Times*, pp. 709–10.

35. Bird, *Color of Truth*, p. 259, and p. 442 n. 26.

36. James M. Gavin, "We Can Get Out of Vietnam," *Saturday Evening Post*, February 24, 1968, cited in Schlesinger, *Robert Kennedy and His Times*, pp. 722–23, and p. 1002 n. 110.

37. Roger Hilsman, "McNamara's War," *Foreign Affairs* 74, no. 4 (July–August 1995), pp. 164–65.

38. Roger Hilsman, letter to the editor, *New York Times*, January 29, 1992.

39. Bird, *Color of Truth*, p. 260.

40. Henry Brandon, *Anatomy of Error* (London, 1970), p. 30, cited in Schlesinger, *Robert Kennedy and His Times*, p. 722 and p. 1002 n. 105.

41. Michael V. Forrestal interview transcript, CBS News, "Vietnam Special," December 21, 22, 1971, pp. 12–14, cited in Bird, *Color of Truth*, pp. 260–61, and p. 443 n. 33.

42. Logevall, "Kennedy, Vietnam, and the Question," pp. 41–42.

43. See Herring, *America's Longest War*, p. xi.

44. Gardner, *Pay Any Price*, p. 542.

45. Garry Wills, *The Kennedy Imprisonment: A Meditation on Power* (Boston: Little, Brown, 1981), p. 280.

46. Jonathan Schell, *The Time of Illusion* (New York: Alfred A. Knopf, 1976), pp. 9–10, cited in Logevall, "Kennedy, Vietnam, and the Question," pp. 38–39.

47. Draft Memorandum from the Secretary of Defense to the President, November 5, 1961, in *FRUS 1961–63*, vol. 1, *Vietnam 1961*, p. 538.

48. Bernard Brodie, *War and Politics* (New York: Macmillan, 1973), p. 132, cited in Logevall, "Kennedy, Vietnam, and the Question," p. 60 n. 60.

49. Memorandum from the President's Special Assistant for National Security Affairs to the President, November 15, 1961, in *FRUS 1961–63*, vol. 1, *Vietnam 1961*, p. 605.

50. See Logevall, "Kennedy, Vietnam, and the Question," p. 42. For President Kennedy's comment to Taylor in 1961, see Hammer, *Death in November*, pp. 35–36.

51. September 3, 1963, President Kennedy interview with Walter Cronkite, *Public Papers: JFK, 1963*, pp. 651–52.

52. Jones, *Death of a Generation*, pp. 10–11.

53. See McNamara with VanDeMark, *In Retrospect*, p. 96.

54. Bundy's comment is recorded in the margin of Schlesinger, *Robert Kennedy and His Times*, p. 708.

55. McGeorge Bundy to William Bundy, November 14, 1969, Criticism and Comments, Box 5, Additional William Bundy Papers, Mudd Library, Princeton University. Cited in Kuklick, *Blind Oracles*, p. 131.

56. Blight, Vietnam Project File Memo, August 28, 1996.

57. Gordon Goldstein interview with McGeorge Bundy, December 5, 1995, p. 1.

58. Press Conference of September 12, 1963, *Public Papers: JFK, 1963*, p. 673.

59. "My own recollection is that remembered conversation in the airplane," he said.

Gordon Goldstein interview with McGeorge Bundy, November 28, 1995, p. 26. For a similar reference to opening a relationship with communist China in a second Kennedy term, see Langguth, *Our Vietnam*, p. 209.

60. Blight, Vietnam Project File Memo, August 28, 1996.
61. Gordon Goldstein interview with McGeorge Bundy, December 19, 1995, p. 13.
62. Ibid., p. 15.
63. Robert Dallek interview with McGeorge Bundy, March 30, 1993, p. 14, Internet copy, LBJ Library.
64. Gordon Goldstein interview with McGeorge Bundy, December 19, 1995, p. 13.
65. Bundy Fragment No. 39.

ACKNOWLEDGMENTS

Any list of acknowledgments identifying individuals critical to this book must obviously begin with McGeorge Bundy. As I have attempted to convey in the preceding chapters, there was a great contrast in intellectual and personal temperament between the historical record of Bundy in power as national security adviser and my own experience with him decades later. The man I worked with was engaged in a probing, honest, and ultimately inconclusive examination of his own role in what he called "a great failure." That he embarked on this difficult journey at all merits acknowledgment and, I believe, respect for the enduring sense of responsibility he felt to confront the legacy of Vietnam, a challenge he had deflected for many years. He remained committed throughout to the obligation he defined for himself, to answer the question, "What can we learn from this episode that will help us do better in the world ahead?" I must also acknowledge the exquisite care Bundy exercised in our relationship.

He was unfailingly respectful, kind, and patient. I will always consider it a great privilege to have worked with McGeorge Bundy.

One of the principal advocates of Bundy's retrospective study of Vietnam was Dr. David Hamburg, the former president of the Carnegie Corporation of New York and himself a highly accomplished analyst of international security affairs. Dr. Hamburg strongly supported the completion and publication of the posthumous Yale University Press volume and was a champion of that work's independence and impartiality. I am very grateful for his support over the years. In addition, I would like to thank David Speedie and Georganne V. Brown, both of whom also supported my work associated with the Carnegie Corporation. John Ryden, the former director of Yale University Press, was an indispensable adviser, ally, and friend during my extended period of research.

In the course of my study of the Vietnam decisions of the Kennedy and Johnson administrations, various colleagues of McGeorge Bundy shared their views about the former national security adviser, the presidents he served, and the inflection points on the path to the Americanization of the war. While none of these individuals were consulted in the preparation of *Lessons in Disaster*—and like others identified here should not be presumed to concur with its conclusions—their generosity and prior help merits acknowledgment. Robert S. McNamara, the former secretary of defense, allowed me to participate in unique conferences in Vietnam and Italy that deepened my understanding of the war. The late, great historian Arthur M. Schlesinger Jr. offered encouragement, insights, and delightful periodic luncheons at the Century Association in Manhattan. The late Chester Cooper, a principal Vietnam expert on the staff of the National Security Council, had an encyclopedic knowledge of the conflict and a deep discernment about its key players. He was also a wonderful friend. Nicholas Katzenbach, formerly of the departments of justice and state, offered valuable assistance when it was needed. McNamara, Schlesinger, Cooper, and Katzenbach all shared a deep commitment to historical scholarship about the Vietnam War uncompromised by the ideological bias and political debate that still swirls around the subject.

Among the experts of the Vietnam era with whom I was fortunate enough to engage, a special expression of thanks must be reserved for A. J. Langguth, who served as the Saigon bureau chief for the *New York Times* in 1965 and is the author of one of the finest narrative histories of the Vietnam War. I have benefited significantly from Langguth's incomparable grasp of the period's grand themes and granular facts. He has been a cherished teacher, counselor, and friend. I owe a similar debt to James Blight and Janet Lang, both of the Watson Institute for International Studies at Brown University, a research center that allowed me to develop my analysis of the war further as a Wayland Fellow and guest lecturer. The critical oral history methodology pioneered by Blight and Lang has made an invaluable contribution to our understanding of the seminal crises of the Cold War, particularly the Vietnam War and the Cuban missile crisis. In addition, these gifted researchers and authors remain a source of magnanimous and unstinting support to the many scholars and students of history who are fortunate enough to be part of their circle. Fredrik Logevall, one of the world's preeminent scholars of the Vietnam War, has also had a significant influence on my work. Over the years he has repeatedly shared his expertise and provided inestimable support and advice for which he has my sincere thanks. Finally, I would like to acknowledge the historian Kai Bird, whose study of McGeorge and William Bundy, *The Color of Truth*, is a model of penetrating and balanced historical scholarship.

As described in this book's introduction, my goal has been to create an original and independent work about the Vietnam War that not only analyzes Bundy's performance as national security adviser but also distills the resonant lessons I believe are suggested by his conduct in power. This personal approach to my subject was conceived in partnership with

Paul Golob, the editorial director of Times Books. A superb editor and strategist, sophisticated historical analyst, and preternaturally efficient publishing executive, Paul brings together all of the variables into the equation of a book's conception and realization. I am indebted to him for his guidance, solidarity, and enormous talent. My agent, Esther Newberg, is a czarina of the publishing world. I am honored to be among her list of authors and thank her for the support she has shown this project, demonstrated in numerous and pivotal ways. Professor Richard N. Gardner, an admired mentor and dear friend from my years at Columbia University, has continued a legacy of generosity through different and essential acts of assistance. I am deeply grateful to the renowned diplomatic and presidential historian Michael Beschloss, who graciously agreed to read and comment on my manuscript although we shared no prior relationship. John Sterling and Dan Farley of Henry Holt and Company have been stalwart publishers for whom I am especially appreciative. Attorneys Alan U. Kaufman and Heather Florence, who provided me with thoughtful counsel, share in my deep thanks. Matt Tribbe of the University of Texas also has my thanks for providing archival research assistance at the LBJ Library.

A last word of acknowledgment and heartfelt appreciation is extended to my family. My father, Kenneth K. Goldstein, is a professor emeritus at Columbia University. When I was a boy he acknowledged my mother, my sister, and me in his books. Now it is my pleasure to do the same. His example has been an inspiration. As for my wife and children—Anne, Willa, and Avery—I am profoundly grateful for their love and support and hope this book proves a worthy testament to their shared sacrifice during the time I have devoted to grappling with the lessons of the Vietnam War.

INDEX

Minh, Guong Van "Big," 87–88, 106
Morgenthau, Hans, 194–96
Moyers, Bill, 196–97, 200, 217
Munich appeasement, 11
My Canh floating restaurant bombing, 190

N

National Guard, 209
nationalism, 51, 194
National Liberation Front (NLF), 150,
    155, 179, 186, 224
National Rural Electric Cooperation
    Association, 206–7
National Security Action Memoranda
    number 263, 84, 238
    number 328, 169
National Security Agency, 127
national security bureaucracy, 71–72, 92,
    94, 96, 101–2
National Security Council (NSC), 46–47,
    50, 54, 64–65, 77, 126–27, 142, 156
NATO, 106
naval blockade or quarantine
    Cuba and, 73–75
    Vietnam and, 108
Navarre, Henri, 49, 51
negotiated settlement, proposed, 130–31,
    152–54, 170, 173, 180, 223
Nes, David, 108
Neustadt, Richard, 43, 91, 230–31, 234
neutralization, proposed, 110–13, 115–16,
    132, 136, 140, 153
New Frontier, 31
Newman, John, 83–84
New Republic, 10
Newsweek, 14, 21, 121
New York Daily News, 37
New York Times, 3–6, 14, 17, 20, 37, 57,
    111, 146, 235
New York University, 19
New Zealand, 190
Nguyen Dinh Uoc, 127

Nhu, Madame (Tran Le Xuan), 76, 80
Nhu, Ngo Dinh, 72, 76, 78, 80, 87–88,
    90–91, 93
Nitze, Paul, 33–34, 156
Nixon, Richard M., 4, 25, 31–32, 109
Nolting, Frederick, 57–58
North Vietnam. *See also* Vietnam War
    attrition strategy and, 168, 173, 179–81,
        191, 209, 222, 224
    bombing of, 18, 45, 47, 108–9, 127,
        140–43, 152, 155–57, 174
    creation of, 50
    development program proposed for, by
        LBJ, 170
    JFK and, 55–56, 60–61, 65, 236
    LBJ assumption of presidency and,
        108–9, 114
    LBJ presidential campaign of 1964 and,
        129–30
    response to LBJ bombing and, 174
    Tonkin Gulf incident and, 18, 123–27
    use of nuclear weapons against, 203
North Vietnamese army, 174, 179,
    186, 225
Nosovan, Phoumi, 45
NSC-68 (1950), 34
nuclear weapons, 19, 47, 75, 108–9, 113,
    161, 203, 223

O

O'Donnell, Kenneth, 104, 235, 237–38
Okinawa, 47
On Active Service in Peace and War
    (Stimson and Bundy), 10
Ormsby-Gore, David, 61
Our Vietnam (Langguth), 146
Overlord, Operation, 10

P

Pacific Command, 45
Palmer, Bruce, Jr., 226
"paper tiger" concept, 167, 183, 212–13, 221

GORDON M. GOLDSTEIN is a scholar of international affairs who has served as an international security adviser to the Strategic Planning Unit of the Executive Office of the United Nations Secretary General and as a Wayland Fellow and guest lecturer at the Watson Institute for International Studies at Brown University. He received his BA, MIA, MPhil, and PhD degrees in political science and international relations from Columbia University, and his articles have appeared in *The New York Times*, *Newsweek*, and *The Washington Post*. He is a member of the Council on Foreign Relations and lives in Brooklyn, New York.